THE COMPLETE PORTUGUESE WATER DOG

The government of Portugal issued this stamp to commemorate the 50th Anniversary of the *Clube dos Caçadores Portugueses,* the governing body for the dog fancy in Portugal. The date was March 15, 1981.

Not too long ago the Portuguese Water Dog teetered on the brink of extinction. His traditional employment disappeared and many of his most loyal supporters in his native land died or went out of dogs. His comeback is an inspiring success story—a success that came about because enough determined dog fanciers cared about preserving a breed that is fascinating by itself and is also in the background of an amazing number of our favorite purebreds. What follows is the saga of the Portuguese Water Dog, his past, his present and a tantalyzing glimpse at his bright, promising future.   *Moments by Jane*

THE COMPLETE
Portuguese
Water Dog

*by Kathryn Braund
and Deyanne Farrell Miller*

First Edition—First Printing

1986

HOWELL BOOK HOUSE Inc.
230 Park Avenue
New York, N.Y. 10169

Library of Congress Cataloging-in-Publication Data

Braund, Kathryn.
    The complete Portuguese water dog.

    1. Portuguese water dog.   I. Miller, Deyanne Farrell.
II. Title.
SF429.P87B73   1986   636.7'52   86-7498
ISBN 0-87605-262-6

To the Portuguese Water Dog—the dogs who generated enthusiastic ownership;

To the owners and friends of the breed—the people who became boosters of the breed;

To the people in Portugal—the people who loved and furthered the breed;

To these, we dedicate our book.

Kathryn Braund
Deyanne Farrell Miller

Contents

About the Authors

Kathryn Braund

Kathryn Braund is a native of Redwood City, California, and was brought up in San Francisco. Following an early career in the theatre—stage, radio and vaudeville—she married. After raising her two sons, Patrick and Gary, she worked in advertising and public relations. She eventually became a writer and editor of technical publications for aerospace companies. When her sons were almost grown, she began writing professionally about the animals she has always loved—dogs.

Her previous books are *The Uncommon Dog Breeds* (Arco, 1975), *Dog Obedience Training Manual,* Volume I and *Dog Obedience Training Manual,* Volume II (Denlinger's Publishers, 1982 and 1983).

She has won eighteen awards from the Dog Writers' Association of America, including "Best Series About Dogs in a National Magazine," 1973 and 1975, and "Best Article About Dogs in an All-Breed Magazine," 1974 and 1975. Her award for "Best Article in a Canine Newspaper" in 1981 was about the Portuguese Water Dog. She has also won eleven Certificates of Merit for articles, feature stories, and columns which have appeared in newspapers and magazines devoted to dogs. Her *Obedience Training Manual,* Volume II, was nominated "Best Training Book" of 1983. She was Obedience Editor of the *Spotter,* the Dalmatian Club of America's quarterly magazine, for ten years.

Currently, she writes for *American Kennel Gazette, Canine Chronicle* and *Front & Finish.* Her article in *American Kennel Gazette* entitled "Fire in a Motor Home" won her a coveted Public Service Award (1983) from the Dog Writers' Association of America.

Another honor of which she is very proud is that she's been nominated twice for the Gaines Fido—the first time in 1975 and the second in 1983.

Kathryn has been a member of the Dog Writers' Association of America since 1971. She has served as its Secretary-Treasurer for three years, 1980 through 1983, and has been its Newsletter Editor since 1980.

The Dog Writers' Association of America recently honored Kathryn with its Outstanding Service Award for her newsletter contributions.

A breeder of both Dalmatians and Portuguese Water Dogs under the kennel name of Roughrider, Kathryn belongs to the Dalmatian Club of America, Chicagoland Dalmatian Club, Dalmatian Club of Canada, and the Portuguese Water Dog Club of America.

She and her husband, Cyril, retired in Great Falls, Montana. This is where she runs a dog obedience school and pursues hobbies such as fishing, hunting and gardening.

Kathryn has placed 19 obedience titles and 9 championship titles on her dogs. Ch. Farmion Geo, CDX (Diver), her first Portuguese Water Dog, purchased from Deyanne Miller in 1982, as part of her research effort on the Portuguese, was the second of the breed to win a Group and the first male to earn a Companion Dog Excellent (CDX) title.

Deyanne Farrell Miller

A British Canadian by birth, Deyanne O'Neil Farrell Miller was raised in Toronto and New York. She was educated at Rosemary Hall (Greenwich, Connecticut) and Finch College (New York City). She is married to Herbert H. Miller, Jr. They have four grown children and have lived in New Canaan, Connecticut, since the 1950s.

Mrs. Miller has enjoyed a lifelong interest in horses and dogs. She first exhibited at an American Kennel Club licensed show when she was ten years old.

As a hobby, Mrs. Miller exhibited Miniature and Standard Poodles in both obedience and breed. She registered her Farmion prefix with the American Kennel Club in 1952.

She and Mr. Miller became interested in Portuguese Water Dogs in 1965. She imported her first "Portie" in 1968. At the time the breed was nearly extinct. In 1972, she was a founding member of the Portuguese Water Dog Club of America. Her husband served as founding president for three years. Mrs. Miller served as president in 1980 and was elected president for 1985. In 1981, Mrs. Miller was one of the founding members of the Fairfield County Portuguese Water Dog Club and serves as president.

Mrs. Miller has judged Portuguese Water Dogs at Estoril and Lisbon International shows. With her husband she has traveled to Canada, England, Italy and extensively in Portugal gathering information about the breed and locating Portuguese Water Dogs. A voting member of the Clube Portugues de Canicultura, she is also FCI approved to judge the breed. Mrs. Miller is a member of the Canadian Kennel Club and an associate member of The Kennel Club, England. She imported the breed's first AKC Champion and Best-in-Show winner, Ch. Charlie de Alvalade.

Acknowledgments

THERE are numerous people who have been boosters of the breed—helping it along the way to its recognition. If they have not been in our direct story line, their names are not in the book. We'd like to give acknowledgment to them here. Without their aid, this wonderful breed couldn't have made such great strides in so short a time.

Thank you - - - -

Special Acknowledgments

THANK YOU, Bert Lindler, for your review of the manuscript and your suggestions for improvement. Thank you, Wayne Arnst, for your how-to-do-it photos. And thank you, Stuart White, for making many faded snapshots come alive again.

1

Origin and History
of the Portuguese
Water Dog

IN THIS CHAPTER we will attempt to detail all the history of the origin and development of the modern Portuguese Water Dog.

On our layman's tour, we'll untangle fiction from fact through a portion of very fascinating ancient history. The Portuguese Water Dog's story kindles the imagination and challenges the memory of any scholar of canine history.

Without the Portuguese Water Dog in their ancestries, there would be no modern Poodle, no Irish Water Spaniel, no Kerry Blue Terrier, no Labrador Retriever, no Curly Coated Retriever and no Newfoundland... perhaps no Puli. The fisherman's dog left his mark on all these breeds in various ways. Each is linked with each other, however subtly.

So that we may enjoy these links and fully appreciate the canine genetic camaraderie, we'll trace the background from which the modern Portuguese Water Dog evolved.

Ancient Influences

Picture Asia, the one continent which was in immediate contact with every ocean and with every other continent. Picture the wild central Asian steppes (the Kirghiz area of Russia). Here, near the Chinese border were vast, grassy, treeless tracts, with scattered mountains, valleys, lakes and rivers relieving the Spartan landscape. The region is characterized by extreme temperatures. The Tien Shien Highlands, the Pamir Mountains, the Karagiye Depression, the Ural Sea and Lake Balkhash lie here. These are terrains and waters guaranteed to nourish ruggedness.

The early people who lived here were hunters in the Old Stone Age (Mesolithic). They were gatherers in the New Stone Age (Neolithic). They lived from the land, eating its grains. Eventually, they began raising grain of their own and made their clothing from sheep's wool. Sheep were raised strictly for wool and cattle were raised for food. Depending upon the territory in which they lived, they also raised camels or horses.

Archeological findings indicate they reared herding dogs. Isolated from the rest of the world, full of courage and ferocity, the herding dogs were highly interbred within each ancestral clan. Some of these dogs developed into a definite type like the Portuguese Water Dog.

The perpetual tugs of wars resulted in frequent migration. The conquered, not waiting to count on miracles from the gods, took their animals and fled the steppes for the far corners of the world. The victors of the conflicts—Cimmerians (700-600 B.C.), Cimbri (100 B.C.), Goths (100-200 A.D.)—carried away herding dogs as well as other animals and people, as spoils of war. They spread these in all directions as they pillaged along the early roadways of the world. Before the captives finally settled in their new cultures, some had made incredible migrations.

Some Interesting Theories of Ancestry

One theory is that some of the rugged Asian herding dogs were captured by the fierce Berbers. The Berbers spread slowly across North Africa to Morocco. Their descendants, the Moors, arrived in Portugal in the eighth century A.D., bringing dogs with them.

Another theory suggests that some of the dogs left the Asian steppes with the Goths, a confederation of Germanic tribes. The Goths divided. Those that went west were the Ostrogoths and their dogs became the German pudel or pudelin. The Goths that traveled south to fight the Romans were the Visigoths and their dogs developed into the Lion Dog. In 400 A.D., when the Visigoths invaded Spain and Portugal (then known only as Iberia), the dogs found their homeland.

These theories vividly explain how the Poodle and even the Puli developed from the rugged herding dog. At one time the Poodle was a shaggy-coated dog, as is one variety of the Portuguese Water Dog. The Portuguese Water Dog and the Puli share a common heritage, although the latter is smaller and has a double rather than single coat.

There's another possibility. Some of the long-coated race of water dogs could have grown up with the prehistoric civilizations of shellfish eaters in Spain and Portugal. These people were known as Iberians. They migrated from lands which now belong to southwestern Germany. Swarming over the Pyrenees, circulating over the whole of western Europe, they established bases in Iberia (Portugal), as well as in Ireland, Wales and Brittany. The Irish Water Spaniel is believed to be a descendant of the Portuguese Water Dog.

Certainly, in past times the breed existed in fishing villages everywhere along the coast of Portugal. In a technique passed down by the ancient Romans, he was taught to herd fish into a net. He retrieved lost tackle, broken nets, and acted as courier from boat to boat and from boat to shore. He rode in the bobbing trawlers as fishermen worked their way to the cold fishing waters off the coasts of Iceland and Newfoundland, standing in the bow barking during periods of fog, thereby alerting other boats of the position of his boat.

In the sacred books of the Zend-Avesta (seventh century), the water dog was said to be the most valued of all dogs, including even the shepherd dog. The great god, Ahura-Mazda, gave him the qualities of a saint for his exceptional abilities.

Legend tells us that Zoroaster, the famed Persian prophet of the sixth century B.C., punished those who harmed a water dog.

In 1297, a monk reportedly described the Portuguese Water Dog that rescued a dying sailor from the sea: "The dog was of black coat, the hair long and rough, cut to the first rib and with a tail tuft. This tuft was white as were the feet and nose."

Water Dogs and the Armada

There's also a popular theory that numbers of the dogs sailed with the Spanish Armada in 1588, serving as messenger dogs between ships. Some of the ships of the Armada were in fact Portuguese since Portugal was ruled by Spain at the time. About 4,000 of the fleet's more than 28,000 men were Portuguese. When their masters were defeated and some of the ships in the fleet were left to flounder, dogs supposedly swam ashore. This theory suggests that the Portuguese Water Dogs bequeathed some of their character and looks to such breeds as the Kerry Blue Terrier, Curly-Coated Retriever and Irish Water Spaniel.

Clifford Hubbard, who wrote *Working Dogs of the World* (1947), told a Portuguese author, Margarida Ribeiro, that the water dog was taken from Portugal to Spain during its occupation of Portugal (1580-1640). "As the dogs filtered into Spain," wrote Margarida Ribeiro in a story about the Portuguese Water Dog, "they went to the streets where their robustness was immediately recognized. They were put at the service of the different ships in the invincible Spanish fleet, especially trained as life-saving dogs."

13

Josephine Z. Rine in *The World of Dogs* (1965) picks this theory up in her history of the Poodle. "The Poodle is descended from one of the water spaniels developed in 16th century Spain, where he was known as the Water Dog, the Rough-haired Water Dog and the Rough-haired Water Spaniel."

King Phillip II of Spain had lists drawn up of every statistic of his ill-fated Armada. According to these lists, every one of the mainly unseaworthy 130 ships were crammed full of men and supplies. The average ship carried a complement of sailors—average was 100—plus convicts and slaves for oarsmen, plus a minimum of 300 soldiers, plus officers and their servants, gunners, priests, etc. Listed among the detailed inventories were horses and mules. These were aboard to later support the Spanish "conquerors" over the conquered English soil. But when the battle had been lost and the remnants of the Armada turned tail to sail home, the Spaniards when hard at sea, "to save water, which was the worst worry of all . . . threw overboard the horses and mules they had brought for the land artillery. . . . A merchant ship that crossed the armada's track reported the sea full of animals, still swimming." Author David Howarth, who wrote *The Voyage of the Armada,* in which this text appears, conducted the bulk of his research at the castle of Simancas, Spain, where King Phillip established his archives. In all of these surviving documents, there is no suggestion of Cães de Áqua (Portuguese Water Dogs) being carried on the Armada. Looking at the matter logically, it is inconceivable that dogs, who require both care and food, would be allowed to take up space and time on these crowded ships. The hardships for humans aboard were unbearable. And the fleet did little cleaning up after themselves. Death from uneatable food and undrinkable water, from filth and infectious disease was rampant. Who would want to take care of and clean up after dogs on this disastrous undertaking? Oddly enough, listed in the fleet's statistics were four small Portuguese galleys, oared. So the theory is possible! Still, most of the wild Irish, Scottish and English tribes living along the shorelines who first rescued and then often killed many of the scattered survivors, seldom had food enough for themselves. It's unlikely they would have allowed dogs that landed on their shores to remain alive. They would have eaten them.

The Cosmopolitan Water Dog

Portuguese Water Dogs may have landed on the British Isles as a result of trade. Long before the Armada sailed, Galway, Ireland and Bristol, England were ports of call for Portuguese ships carrying goods to Iceland. Prince Henry of Portugal sent an African lion to Galway in 1429! Lisbon, throughout the fifteenth century, was one of the busiest ports in all of Europe. The Portuguese story of glorious seamanship had its roots in its deep sea fishermen's exploration of the cold, windy sea routes to Iceland.

A treaty in 1353 between the Holder of the Port of Lisbon and the King of England permitted the "Portuguese fisherman to be able to fish in the ports of the kingdom and Britain and other ports of congenial places, paying merely the customary taxes."

The Portuguese fishermen of the middle ages sailed almost all of the seven seas. Labrador was named by Portuguese sailors for a Portuguese sea captain with the nickname *labrador* (farmer). This was before 1490.

In 1497-1499 several ships under the command of Paulo da De Gama sailed from Portugal around the Cape of Good Hope. Part of the voyage was described by one of his men, called Old Alvaro. He kept a daily log. He described the Hottentots, the people who lived near the Bay of St. Helens in southeast Africa. "All they eat is the flesh of seal, whales and gazelles and the roots of herbs. They are dressed in skins . . ." his log reads. "Near the bay are gulls, doves and other birds. The Hottentots' dogs look like Portuguese dogs and bark like them," wrote Old Alvaro. Now, the Portuguese Water Dog has a unique bark that climbs up and down the octave. The Hottentots are descendants of the Berbers and Berbers carried herding dogs away from their ancient Asian homeland! Truly, the possibilities are intriguing.

The water dog's fame spread in the middle centuries, especially with the English. "The Water dogge is a creature of . . . general use," wrote Gervase Markham in 1621 in *The Arte of Fowling by Water and Land*. He described the Portuguese Water Dog as if he had viewed it today.

Topsell's *History of the Foure-Footed Beaste of 1607* pictures the breed.

The Museum of Animal Nature (1708) tells us that "the Rough Water Dog is a most intelligent animal, is robustly made, and covered in deep, curly hair; it exceeds the Water Spaniel in size and strength; but has the same aquatic habits and docility; it is much used as a retriever by the shooters of water fowl."

William Taplin, in *The Sportsman's Cabinet* (1803), states that the dog, "jet-black with white feet" stands high in estimation. He lists the rough water dog as having "a head rather round," the nose short, the ears, long, broad and pendulous, the neck thick and short, the shoulders broad. Coat, "natural elastic short curls, rather loose, which might be either long or shaggy," the long coats being considered to indicate strength of constitution, the shaggy coats bodily weakness.

In *Pictures in the Royal Collection* (1969), there is a painting of Frederica, Duchess of York, 1807. Frederica is described as ". . . surrounded by four dogs: a running dog, a gun dog, a Portuguese Water Dog and a Maltese."

Reinagle depicted the water dog in *The Sportsman's Repository* (1831). His painting is thought to have been completed in 1812. Freeman Lloyd in "Some Wonderful Dogs of a Century Ago" (*Pure-Bred Dogs— American Kennel Gazette,* February 28, 1926) says of the etching:

Mrs. Gibbs's Poodle, Ronto, appeared in Cassell's *Illustrated Book of the Dog.*

"Water Spaniel" is an oil on canvas by George Stubbs, A.R.A. (1724-1806), Yale Center for British Art, Paul Mellon Collection.

Reinagle's water dog, in appearance, will be a revelation to many of my younger readers, but some of us may have seen such dogs and, perhaps, heard them described as Russian retrievers or large Russian poodles. This particular dog was certainly a very sagacious animal, his poodle head, long ears, curly coat, big bone, compact large feet, and rudder tail, stamping this old breed of dog as very likely an "uncle" or some sort of other relation to the water spaniels—both English, Irish, French and Russian—and griffons of France, Germany and other countries. . . . Such a dog could not be allowed in a boat with only a couple of thwarts—no room for dogs. So his master calls to his four footed friend to come along—walking cane and all. This breed of water dog is practically extinct. Yet, as before remarked, we may be able to recognize his blood in some of our modern dogs, especially of the European sheepdog, cattle dog, poodle, spaniel and barbet kinds.

An oil by French artist Eugene Louis Bauden, titled "On the Beach at Trouville" (1866), shows five dogs. One is a Great Dane, one is a spaniel, and three resemble the Portuguese Water Dog.

Farley Mowat, author of *The Boat Who Wouldn't Float* (1969), lived on the remote southern coast of Newfoundland and grew to know the water dogs that lived there. His book contains one whole chapter about the feats of a water dog named Blanche. She didn't belong to him. She didn't belong to anyone else, either. She made her home in a shipyard and on her own picked up drifting wedges for the workers. She toiled so well as a retriever for the yard, they put her on the payroll!

Mowat was fascinated by her abilities. He wrote to Deyanne Miller in 1973: "Her performance so astounded me that I managed to get a male pup, named Albert. My interest in the species led to a lot of research."

Mowat learned that the dogs were in Nova Scotia and Newfoundland early in the 16th century in the possession of the Beothuk and MicMac Indians. Since he knew that Portuguese cod fishermen were fishing Newfoundland waters as early as the middle of the 15th century, he considered the possibility that the Newfoundland water dog might be derived from their dogs. The fact is, he tells Deyanne Miller, that the black water dog, both short and long haired versions, existed all along the Newfoundland, Labrador and Gaspe coasts from almost the beginning of colonial settlement.

Mowat also discovered that about 1720, one of the British Admirals commanding Newfoundland allowed members of his "suite" to take some of these dogs to England. There for a time they were bred pure to type, but some were eventually crossed with either the Great Pyrenees or Saint Bernard to produce what is now called the Newfoundland. Meanwhile, Yankee fishermen had been bringing the original fishing dogs back with them on voyages to the Labrador and Newfoundland fishing grounds.

Mowat told Deyanne Miller that "the web-footed, especially evolved water dog type probably only originated at one time and place, and I

"So his master calls to his four-footed friend to come along—walking cane and all." "The Water Dog" is by Reingale from *The Sportsman's Repository* (1803). This has been reproduced in many breed books as being ancestor to many breeds.

18

A freshly clipped young Portuguese Water Dog shows his resemblance to a Chesapeake Bay Dog, below. *Kathryn Braund*

A Chesapeake Bay Dog of Maryland, as depicted in *The Dog Book* by James Watson, 1906.

suspect that all true water dogs are offshoots of a single stock type. This would mean that the Portuguese Water Dogs are closely related to the Newfoundland, as historical evidence already suggests."

In his book, Mowat wrote:

> Grand Bruit (an island in Newfoundland) is famous for its black water dogs, which are not to be confused with either the kennel-bred Labrador or the giant Newfoundland breed. Both of these types were developed from the native dog which seems to have developed naturally in Newfoundland, or perhaps on St. Pierre, from a now-vanished European species brought over by Portuguese fishermen hundreds of years ago. These dogs, whose aquatic prowess is truly phenomenal were, until recently, carried on almost every fishing vessel. They had a dual task: to act as lifesavers if a man fell overboard and to retrieve codfish that escaped from the jigger as it was hauled to the surface.

Mowat's remarks tie in with a statement made by W.C.L. Martin in *History of the Dog*:

> It is now well proven that Newfoundland was discovered by the Vikings in the year 1000 . . . as early as 1500 the fisheries were operated by French, Portuguese, Basque, and other people. It is perhaps to the European settlers of the 16th and 17th centuries that the introduction of the original stock of the Newfoundland dog is owing . . .

There is a rock, a 40-ton sandstone boulder, called Dighton Rock, which sits on the Taunton River, upstream from Narragansett Bay in Massachusetts. The carvings on the rock, claimed to be Portuguese, include the date 1511. The late Dr. Edmund Delabarre, a psychology professor interested in Portuguese history, went to Lisbon and discovered through royal charters that Gaspar Corte Real sailed for North America in 1501 and that his brother, Miguel Corte Real, left Lisbon in 1502, presumably to find Gaspar. Although neither returned to Spain with their ships or were ever heard of again, it has been noted that Indians later found in the area (by Verrazano) were quite light in color. If the land under the grass around Dighton Rock holds any information about these adventurers in their seafaring caravelles it would be fascinating to know if they carried dogs with them. They were Portuguese fishermen!

Harry Glover in McGraw Hill's *A Standard Guide to Purebred Dogs* (1978) writes of the Portuguese Water Dog:

> His ancestry is obviously closely linked with the old Water Dog of other European countries, the dog that produced the modern Poodle and even the Irish Water Spaniel . . . the earliest known animal portrait in English art, that of Sir John Harington's dog Bungy, painted nearly 400 years ago, is undoubtedly a portrait of a Portuguese Water Dog.

Most people in the middle centuries were convinced the Poodle was the ancestor of the "common water-dogges." The reverse is probably true.

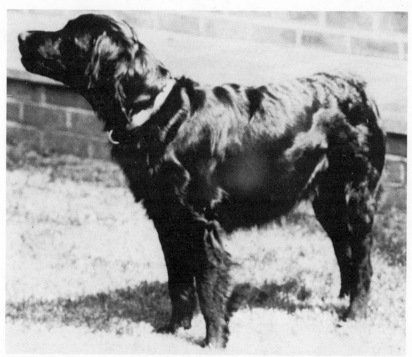

Notice the resemblance of this improperly coated Portuguese Water Dog to the old-fashioned Newfoundland dog, below.

Jardine in his *Naturalist's Library* alludes to the "water dog or Poodle." He says it was of German origin in its most perfect state, rising into favor first in Germany during the revolutionary wars and carried by troops into France, later becoming known in Spain, Britain and the Netherlands.

In his article in *Der Pudel Kraus und Pfeffig,* von Ulrich Maurach says:

> The Poodle looked quite different once and with this fact contributes to the dispute about his origin. The French and the Germans claim the creation of this curly dog for themselves . . . the Barbet and the Cão de Áqua belong to his ancestors. The first, a curly Shepherd Dog from North Africa, with a passion for swimming, came through the wars of the Moors to Portugal and Spain. There he crossbred with the Portuguese Water Dog of the local fishermen, the Cão. This dog is a water-loving hunting dog, spirited, obedient and feisty who looks more like his Poodle descendants than the Barbet. But the mustachioed African gave as his heritage his wooly coat as well as his alertness, trainability and loyalty to his descendants.
>
> The result of this cross—so it is said—was a dog with a wavy coat who, because of his use in water hunting, was shorn on parts of his body to make swimming easier. On other parts of his body the coat was left at full length to avoid problems with rheumatism. Science gave him the Latin name *Canis aquaticus* (water dog) without pinpointing the exact time of his existence.

A writer as late as 1954 confused the long-coated variety of the Portuguese Water Dog with the Poodle. Sacheverell Sitwell describes the curly-coated variety of the Portuguese Water Dog in his book *Portugal and Madeira.* "The other race," he writes, "still more restricted in number, is the Pelo Encara Colado, more like a Poodle."

While the Poodle is similar, all modern strains have conformed to refinement, a consequence of fame. The Portuguese Water Dog remained constant in his homeland. Cloistered along the remote cliffs along the coast of the southern part of Portugal, the barren Algarve region (Algarve in Arabic means "the west"), he acquired the name Cão de Áqua (pronounced Kown-d'-Ahgwa). Cão means dog; de Áqua means of the water. He was also called by the nicknames, "Diving Dog," and "Portuguese Fishing Dog." Spaniards called him the "Sea Dog." Whatever he was called, he retained much of his original skull shape and original conformation.

While much of the origin and history of the Portuguese Water Dog is circumstantial, it is quite clear the breed has an excellent historical background and has survived all of the rigors of the centuries to become the dog he is today.

2

The Portuguese Water Dog's Homeland

THE PORTUGUESE WATER DOG mirrors the daily life of his working ancestors.

It's instinctive for him to love to retrieve from water, to feast on fish, to herd whatever gathers together, to guard people and property, to be stoic when required yet be full of powerful exuberance, and to play tug of war as if the pulling contest engages his memory in a long-ago serious endeavor of pulling nets or people to safety.

Portugal is a long, narrow country bordering Spain on the north and east and the Atlantic Ocean on the south and west. It is the southwestern-most country in Europe.

It is 345 miles long and 140 miles wide and covers but 35,510 square miles. For a country only a little larger than the state of Maine, it has a tumultous, varied and extraordinary history.

The People

The Iberians were its first inhabitants; then a variety of conquerors moved in—Phoenicians and Carthaginians (800 B.C.), Romans (100 B.C.), Alans and Visigoths (499 A.D.), and Arabs or Moors (700 A.D.). Spanish Christians took over in 1000 A.D.

Each invader, in turn, exposed the people and their descendants to a variety of conversions and mixtures just as each invader assimilated habits

23

The Portuguese Water Dog mirrors the daily life of his background. Scene from Albufeira, Algarve.
George Jacobs

of their conquered. The Portuguese are, consequently, a varied race—originally Iberian or Basque, Celtic, Jewish, Arabic and African.

Dom Alfonso Henriques (Alfonso I) made Portugal an independent kingdom in 1143. He named it after Portus Calle (now the city of Oporto), whose harbors were the first seized by the kingdoms of Castile and Leon when they wrested the land from the Moors.

King Diniz (1279-1325), son of Alfonso II, became Portugal's champion of agriculture, navigation, commerce and learning. He encouraged farming, rabbit breeding and forestry. He earned two titles from his countrymen: Farmer and Father of Portugal.

King (Don) John, illegitimate brother of King Ferdinand, crowned Joao the Bastard, was well deserving of the title later given to him, Joao the Good. He furthered maritime adventures. Under John I, who was crowned king in 1385, Portuguese explorers sailed down the African coast. King John I also made a permanent political alliance with England in 1386. It's still in force and is the longest-kept alliance between any two countries in the world.

Explorers were challenged by John's son, Henry, Prince Henry the Navigator (1394-1460). This prince-scientist pioneered the Portuguese journeys of discovery which eventually made Portugal masters of the world.

Spain conquered Portugal in 1580. Portugal recovered only temporarily from the sixty years of Spanish rule when John, Duke of Braganza, incited a revolution and was subsequently crowned John IV.

Other catastrophies followed. In 1755, Lisbon was two thirds demolished by an earthquake. In 1807, Napoleon took the country's young men, forcing them to join his forces in the Napoleonic wars. In 1861, a devastating plague killed many Portuguese, including their king. In 1910, a republic was formed, but the country experienced 18 revolutions in the following 16 years.

Keeping its 600-year alliance with England, Portuguese fought against Germans in World War I. After the war, the country was impoverished.

In 1957, hoping to improve economic outlook, the government took charge of agriculture, fishing and canning, among other industries. Portugal began getting back on its feet. It was aided, in part, by an embryonic tourist industry. People over the world were discovering the full sweep of varied beauty of Portugal.

The Land

At first, Portugal, like many lands, was forest and marsh and barren land. The highest mountain range, Serra da Estrella, lies in the north and stretches up to 6,537 feet. There are other mountains, most of which are continuations of Spanish ranges. Portugal has a wealth of large rivers, streams and lakes. Here and there are valleys and plains, all remarkably fertile. Twenty-one harbors indent the land, but only a few are important. In the south, in the Algarve, rugged cliffs and reefs make some navigation dangerous. But also in the south are almond trees, fig trees, orange trees, lemon trees—all manner of succulent fruit trees. The Atlantic lies on both south and west edges, to the north lie mountains, while Spain and the sluggish Guadiana River stretch to the east.

Since Portugal borders the Atlantic, the climate is moderate, although the heights of the mountains make the winters a bit rigorous. But winters are always very short. Because of the southern latitude, some areas remain green year round. For this reason, most of the country enjoys two springs; two harvests. The first is in February. Everything remains lush until July. In that month and also in August the heat is often extreme. There is no rain. In late September the rains come. Another spring appears. Only in November does winter arrive. Snow falls and clings to the higher elevations; rain falls in deluges in the south. Winter lasts only two months. It is spring again!

The Working Water Dog

The Cão de Áqua's function through the centuries was similar to that of a hunting dog. In hunting, a dog is supposed to simplify the job. The dog finds and retrieves shot game for the hunter. The difference between the Cão de Áqua and the hunting dog is that the Portuguese Water Dog worked every day of the year, while the traditional hunting dog's work is seasonal.

The fisherman who went into the sea in his fragile boat, or Caique, had to have a dog who could assist him in everything. Plus, the dog had to have a good supply of courage. Life on a fishing boat wasn't easy.

Then too, the dog had to have the instinctive desire to chase and retrieve fish lost to the fisherman. This is why the Cão de Áqua usually sat in the bow of the boat so he could see everything that was going on in the water. If he saw a school of fish he barked so the fisherman could take advantage. If a fish got free from a net, he would immediately jump into the water to catch it. He didn't need to be told.

There was something else he had to have. He had to recognize danger. Many of the waters the fishermen worked in were shark-infested.

When the dog wouldn't jump in after escaping fish, if instead he left his seat in the bow and went, tail between his legs, to the bottom of the boat and hid under the tarps, fishermen didn't prod him to go overboard. They left him alone.

Some dogs they had forced into the water had been eaten by sharks. So the fishermen learned to take hangdog actions as a sign that sharks were nearby. After a while, the dog would get up again, resuming his place and work. This was a signal the sharks were gone.

The fisherman had to have a dog who could assist him in everything. Although almost unseen, there is a dog in this picture. He's carrying metal gear in his mouth.

Margaride Rebeiro

a fish got free from the net, he would immediately
mp into the water to catch it. The dog pictured
ere is Leao.   *Bensaude Archives*

The fishermen were as close to their dogs as they were to their human friends.   *Margaride Rebeiro*

How did the dogs know there were sharks in the water? We assume that he was able to detect his enemy in the water because of extremely good vision. This is also how he could tell when they were gone. There is no other way this could be possible, unless the sharks have a scent we don't know about which forewarned the dogs.

Dogs on shipboard, no matter how small the boat, learned to relieve themselves on ropes that hung over the side. They had to have enough seaworthiness not to fall overboard when standing on three legs wetting down a jib boom or when squatting.

It was the custom of the fishermen to grant the working Cão de Áqua a daily portion of fish, equal to 1/4 or 1/2 the stipend of each man on a fishing vessel. If a fisherman mistreated a dog, his fellow workers gave the dog to someone else to care for or else saw that the fisherman mended his ways. On a large vessel, the offending fisherman's salary would be forfeited for a time.

Sometimes, of course, there were dogs who didn't like the sea. A few had to be trained to go into it. Fishermen gave praise for going into the water and gentle but firm corrections if the dogs didn't.

The fishermen used older trained dogs as leader dogs and on board these taught the younger dogs.

If the dog still didn't like the sea, the fishermen took the recalcitrant dog by the scruff of his neck and threw him into the sea. This was done in deep water far from shore. Few Cães de Áqua needed to be thrown in more than once. When the dog was allowed back into the boat he was a good swimmer. Then, when the dog was accustomed to the water, he was trained in swimming and diving exercises. He was expected to retrieve.

The dogs were taught to put their heads under water as puppies. Tidbits of fish were held near the water line, then at the water line, then under water until the dogs immersed their heads eagerly. The exercise may have taken months to learn. Diving followed.

The dog was well repaid for his work. He dined well on fish. He had a place to sleep. The fishermen, with whom he lived, grew to love him deeply. He became an integral part of their crew. The fishermen were as close to their dogs as they were to their human friends.

There were other things the dogs had to do. They would haul the fishing nets as draft dogs. They would carry mail in waterproof pouches to fishermen on other boats. They would guard the catch when it was being unloaded.

When not out in the water with the fishermen, most dogs stayed on board and guarded the boats. While the fishermen mended the nets, the dogs were sent home to bring the lunch pails. If a fisherman was fairly well off he had two dogs, one for the house and one for the boat. The dog at home would stay and guard the house when the family was away.

Some of the fishermen didn't own a dog; they rented dogs. The dogs'

28

owners might be older men who had retired from fishing and wanted to make money. Many fishermen never retired the older dogs. They permitted them to go out with the fleet.

In 1712, the University of Coimbra (founded by King Diniz) lists the Cão de Áqua's aquatic feats as well as naming the two types of coats found in the breed—wavy and curly.

King Carlos I (1853-1908), who loved marine biology and studied oceanographic life at Sagres, became enamored with the breed when he saw one aboard a caique. He was "offered two beautiful examples of the breed" and they rendered him excellent service during his maritime studies on his yacht Donna Amalia. In 1897, King Carlos gave the royal charter for the *Clube dos Caçadores Portugueses,* the forerunner of the *Clube Portugues de Canicultura (CPC).*

After the Turn of the Century

In the early 20th century, as the requirement for the Cão de Áqua's canine expertise diminished, so did his numbers, until he was found only in the southern province of Algarve, along the shores of the *Mare Ibericum,* on which he supposedly landed over a thousand years ago.

In Olhao, in the Algarve, many bones of these dogs have been found. Oddly, on the same desolate, windracked shores which almost became the modern graveyard of the Portuguese Water Dog, Prince Henry's fifteenth century seagoing dreams became reality.

First Portuguese Dog Shows

So few of the breed were left that a writer for *Hutchinson's Popular Illustrated Dog Encyclopedia* didn't even know the breed existed after he had visited Portugal. This is what he wrote:

This writer is well acquainted with the dog fancy in Portugal, having judged, several years before the Great War (World War I), the very first dog show held in that country. It was organized by the then only sporting journal of Portugal, *A Caça,* or rather by its editor-proprietor, Dr. Anachorita, of Lisbon.

The fixture lasted a whole week; the judging took place from the catalogue, a thing unheard of in England.

The dog fancy in Portugal is still in its infancy, although the *Clube dos Caçadores Portugueses* (Club of the Portuguese Shooting Men) does much toward the popularization of different breeds of dogs in Portugal by organizing shows.

There are two breeds native to Portugal, the *Podengo Portuguese* and the *Serra da Estrela.* The latter may be dismissed with the remarks that it is a guard or watch dog, used as a sheep dog. Of more importance is the Podengo, called Podenco in Spain . . . it was formerly used for hunting boars, of which there are none left in Portugal. It is now employed for hunting rabbits.

During this period, certain hunting dog fanciers were awakening an interest in dogs in the Portuguese people.

The aforementioned *Clube dos Caçadores Portugueses,* a hunting magazine, and an association of hunters held a canine exhibition on July 20, 1902 in the Crystal Palace at Porto (now Oporto). It was a first for the country. At the three-day affair, 257 dogs were shown.

On May 31 and June 1, 1903, in the town of Evora, another association of hunters held a canine exhibition. Many of the 110 dogs taking part had been imported by affluent Portuguese.

Five years later, in 1908, a week-long exhibition of dogs was held in Lisbon. Canine exhibitions became a yearly affair.

Nevertheless, it wasn't until 1929 that international canine shows were held in Portugal. One was held in Lisbon and the other in Porto.

The dates, locales, number of dogs and the types of "canine exhibitions" held during the early part of the 20th century in Portugal are listed below:

Year	Locale	Number of Dogs Exhibited	Type of Show
1902	Porto	235	International
1903	Evora	110	International
1908	Lisbon	375	International
1912	Mantugas	?	Regional
1913	Mantugas	?	Regional
1914	Mantugas	?	Regional
1915	Mantugas	?	Regional
1929	Covelha	?	Regional
1929	Lisbon	102	International
1929	Porto	233	International
1930	Lisbon	142	International
1930	Porto	170	International
1931	Lisbon	138	International
1932	Lisbon	172	International
1933	Lisbon	219	International
1933	Porto	?	International
1934	Lisbon	207	International
1934	Estoril	105	International

However, nothing slowed the Cão de Aqua from dying out. If he was seen at any one of these shows, he was a curiosity only.

As new equipment for fishing and communications was developed, the fishermen no longer needed a dog for a shipmate. The fishermen went to work on larger boats for daily wages.

There was no reason for them to breed the young Cão de Água bitch anymore. Let her remain barren. Let her grow old and die. Let all the fishermen's dogs grow old and die! The working Cão de Água had outlived its time.

Vasco Bensaude

Then, something wonderful happened. A wealthy man, who owned shipping lines, heard about the breed. He was Vasco Bensaude, a versatile man of varied interests. He was an avid gardener, aviculturist, bee keeper, photographer and marine architect.

He was already raising dogs as well. At his house, Quinta dos Soeiros, in Benfica, he bred Irish Wolfhounds, Cocker Spaniels and Clumber Spaniels. He had kennels and employed a kennel master and trainers.

His interest in the Cão de Água began with friends born and raised in Sesimbra, a small town on the Algarve, where the Cão de Água still worked on boats. They were Sr. Renato Pinto Soares and medical veterinary professor Dr. Manuel Fernandes Marques. Dr. Marques, who later wrote the standard for the breed, told Vasco Bensaude about a magnificent dog who was owned by a retired fisherman.

There are two stories telling how Vasco Bensaude acquired Leao, the "magnificent working Cão de Água."

Vasco Bensaude and Senhor Daniel da Silva Lane and Dr. Marques went to Albuferia, where the fisherman lived with this brilliant Cão de Água. After Vasco Bensaude saw the dog work, he eagerly offered to buy him. The fisherman said, "No, definitely no. He does my work for me. I will never sell him for any price. I will sell him only on the day I leave the earth . . . in grand style." No matter how much money or what other enticements Vasco Bensaude offered, the fisherman refused to give up Leao. Bensaude returned to Lisbon deflated but not defeated. He did not give up hope that one day he would acquire Leao.

The day came sooner than expected. It was only weeks later that he received a letter from the son of the fisherman. The father had died. Vasco Bensaude could have Leao.

Story number two: Vasco Bensaude and Senhor Daniel Lane and Dr. Marques went to Albuferia, where the fisherman lived with this brilliant Cão de Água. After Vasco Bensaude saw the dog work, he eagerly offered to buy him. The fisherman said, "No, definitely no. He does my work for me. I will never sell him." Finally, weary of Vasco Bensaude's counter offers, the fisherman smiled and said, "All right, I'll sell him—but only if and when I win the lottery."

Several weeks later, Vasco Bensaude received a note from the fisherman's son. It said his father had won the lottery and Leao was his.

Whichever story is true, when Vasco Bensaude acquired Leao, the renaissance of the Portuguese Water Dog began!

Senhor Fausto Pereira dos Santos, Bensaude's kennel master, went to get the dog. He took him to Lisbon to Dr. Marques for a thorough examination. Dr. Marques pronounced him an excellent canine specimen.

Leao adapted to his new home. He enjoyed riding in cars, just like the

Leao, the magnificent working Cão de Áqua.   *Bensaude Archives*

children of the house did. And he allowed himself to be trained by Fausto.

Still, every now and then during the first few years, Leao ran away. Each time they found him at the house of his former master.

Vasco Bensaude took Leao with him to many places and the dog became famous. He was noted for his intelligence, his affection and his temperamental, almost moody nature. S̈ome people who knew him said he should have been born a human. They said the only problem was that he had four legs and couldn't talk.

He could break ice with his teeth. He would dive even in the winter.

He dove for bricks. His favorite water toy, however, was a hard rubber ball which floated when Fausto attached it to a cane.

Fausto, who oversaw all the training for Vasco Bensaude's kennels, and personally trained all the Portuguese Water Dogs, told Deyanne Miller he was sorry he had not clipped Leao for the now famous pictures of him (see Chapter 7). In those particular pictures, he said, Leao had too much hair over his eyes and head; this would have been bad when the dog got wet. "You have to trim an inch or two inches above the eye so the dog can see." But they're not doing that today—in Portugal, anyway.

Leao and a Cocker Spaniel lived together in Vasco Bensaude's home in Lisbon. If the door to a bathroom was left open, Leao would walk in, open the water faucet in the tub and lie in the water!

Leao lived in the kennels too, particularly when Vasco Bensaude was travelling. Then Fausto, who believed in daily conditioning and loved Leao as if he were his own dog, would let him out of the kennels. Leao would go bounding down to the big pool with the water lilies in it and take a broad jump, vaulting the back wall and the stone wall before diving into the pool.

Some of Vasco Bensaude's dogs, like Nero, Venesa and Cigana, were located by Bensaude's fishing captains on the Algarve. They always had orders to buy Cães de Áqua when they saw them—with the trade of a boat, oar, or fishing gear, if necessary. Others were descendants of Leao. These were cross bred with Nero and Venesa.

Bensaude named his kennels "Algarbiorum" but did not sell his dogs. He retained them in order to see how type and intelligence proved itself. Every once in a while he let go of some of the dogs—usually those with characteristics he didn't want to preserve. Presumably, that was how several found their way to England in 1954.

Leao is the dog upon which the standard was based. He was born in 1931 and died in 1942. He had the title of C.B.-Dual (Working-Trial-Show Champion) Leao. He was buried under a magnolia tree, in Soeiros.

Vasco Bensaude was a member of the hunting dog club (Clube dos Caçadores Portugueses) and when it became the Clube Portugues de Canicultura (CPC), he was its Secretary General for many years. He encouraged his friends, Dr. Marques and Capitao Frederico M. Pinto Soares, to study the breed and write the standard.

Fausto personally trained all the Portuguese Water Dogs in the two pools at the Algarbiorum Kennels.   *Bensaude Archives*

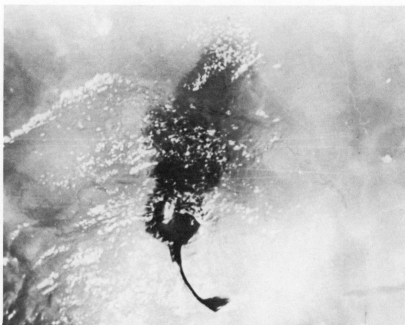

When Fausto would let Leao out of the kennels, Leao would go bounding down to the big pool with the water lilies in it and dive in.   *Bensaude Archives*

Leao, the dog upon which the standard is based, is shown here sitting protectively alongside a young Bensaude family member. *Bensaude Archives*

Leao and a Bensaude family member standing on the beautiful grounds of the Bensaude villa. *Bensaude Archives*

As Vasco Bensaude aged, he lost interest in most phases of his dog hobby. He retained several dozen excellent Cães de Áqua though, mostly so his employee, kennel master and head trainer, Fausto could continue training them. Those who didn't work out, he gave away. A Portuguese emigrant, presently living in New York State, worked for Vasco Bensaude in the shipping business before coming to America. He relates this anecdote. "One day Senhor Bensaude told me he would give me a Cão de Áqua and asked me to come to the house to choose the one I wanted. I was excited and went to see the dogs. The dogs offered were large dogs and very happy animals." He said that when he was leaving, "with my selection, several other gentlemen came to see the dogs. They had learned about them from an advertisement in the newspaper."

Fourteen days before his death on August 5, 1967, Vasco Bensaude wrote the following letter to a Mrs. Frances Grant of Philadelphia who was inquiring about the breed.

Dear Mrs. Grant:
Your letter of the 14th inst., addressed to the Algarbiorum Kennels, owned by me, has just come to hand, forwarded from my Lisbon home.

As far as I know no Portuguese Water Dogs can be found either in Canada or in Mexico. I rather think that, in Mexico, they would not do well owing to the heat.

The situation in the U.S. I am not so sure about. My daughter (she lived in Massachusetts) sent me a newspaper article, a few years ago, in which a gentleman—from New England, somewhere, as far as I can recollect— purported to be breeding them. However the illustrations accompanying the article showed *extremely atypical* animals and Heaven only knows where or how he got hold of them. If you wish to drop my daughter a line, maybe she can still remember details about the gentleman in question, his address and so forth. I cannot put my hands on the copy she sent me until next Fall, as I always spend the summer in my Ponto Delgada home.

As you are considering this breed—and propose keeping the dogs abroad, if I have understood you right—you would do well to limit your choice to fairly young animals (say between nine and 12 months old) so as to be able to train them yourself. At the present writing my kennels have no youngsters of around this age for sale. Price would depend on ascendency, naturally, but young males or females of Algarbiorum blood would run from $150.00 up.

I have no idea what shipping costs would be, but you should be able to get this information quite easily on your side. Any maritime-forwarding concern will be able to give you the names of the various shipping lines running between Lisbon and New York and, by dropping them a note or by contacting their New York agents, you should be able to get the tariff.

I am sending you, enclosed, a Standard of the Breed. The English translation starts on page 29. I had this second edition published in 1951, when I was still Secretary General of our Kennel Club of which I am a founder. The photographs—which I took—are all of Algarbiorum dogs. May be that Dr. A.

An Algarbiorum Portuguese Water Dog at a Lisbon Dog Show. Senhor Fausto is at the left. Note how far above the dog's eyes the hair is clipped.   *Bensaude Archives*

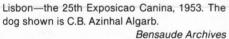

Lisbon—the 25th Exposicao Canina, 1953. The dog shown is C.B. Azinhal Algarb.
                    Bensaude Archives

Lisbon—the 26th Exposicao Canina, 1954. Algarbiorum dogs from left to right are Nodal, Narval, Nadao and C.B. Azinhal.   *Bensaude Archives*

Lisbon—Dog Show, May 1957. Dogs are Pacato Algarbiorum and Pera Algar. Note that the dogs are clipped to the third or fourth rib—the middle of the body.   *Bensaude Archives*

Cabral (who substituted me in our Kennel Club) told you that I saved the breed from extinction 35 years ago, and that now—owing to modified fishing systems—the breed can no longer be found, working, even on the Algarve coast of Portugal.

As a matter of interest, World War II is responsible for this breed not being properly established in the U.S. by now. When, in early 1939, Mrs. Kermit Roosevelt visited me, she decided to start breeding the Portuguese Water Dog on your side of the ocean but, at that moment, I had no suitable animals available so we put the matter off until I had . . . A great pity.

Please excuse the long-windedness of this letter. I hope that the information will prove of use to you.

Very sincerely,

signed, Vasco Bensaude

Enter Conchita Branco

On Vasco Bensaude's death, none of his family had the inclination to take over any of his hobbies. Senhora Bensaude remained grief-stricken for a long time.

In early 1968, after a great deal of consideration, she gave the 14 remaining dogs to Senhora Conchita Cintron Costello Branco, a former lady bullfighter, horsewoman and dog fancier of some note.

When Senhora Bensaude asked Senhora Branco to take over Algarbiorum Kennels in 1968, Senhora Branco was delighted. She bred and exhibited the *Perdigueiro Portugues,* kin to the old Spanish Pointer and a forerunner of many pointing breeds, until she met the Cão de Áqua through the dog shows.

Senhora Branco, who took the prefix do Al Gharb, didn't realize what a monumental, expensive task taking over the kennels would be. She thought of the enjoyment she would have by showing, breeding, and selling the dogs. The dogs were quartered in a large, fenced area on her property.

The bitches had large litters of six, eight and ten. Soon she had too many to care for. Worse, few answered her advertisements. There was little demand for these dogs. In Portugal, dogs had to be utility dogs—a guard dog, a hunting dog—and when there were no reasons to have one of these, there were no sales. Some of her dogs reverted to a wild state. In 1969, desperate, she put down a portion of her stock. At the time she was showing several and her dogs dominated the shows.

In May 1972, she put down more dogs, telling officials that personal tragedies had developed which made it impossible for her to keep the Algarbiorum-do Al Gharb line alive.

Dr. Antonio Cabral

Following Vasco Bensaude's footsteps in breeding the Cão de Áqua

Dr. Antonio Cabral, (third from left) former president of the CPC, shown at a Lisbon dog show in 1984 with his wife, Dra. Maria Eugenia (sitting to his left). Deyanne Miller is on the far left.

was Dr. Antonio Cabral. Dr. Cabral made significant contributions to the advancement of the breed.

Dr. Cabral began his breeding avocation with Smooth Fox Terriers and then expanded into breeding all Portuguese breeds, with the idea of preserving and developing those that were dying out. He was vitally concerned with keeping bloodlines different from those of Algarbiorum kennels. In June 1954, he registered the first Cão de Áqua of his de Alvalade line. The dog's name was Silves.

Although Dr. Cabral closed his de Alvalade kennels upon his retirement as CPC president in 1983, he contributed greatly to the importation of new bloodlines to America for use in redeveloping the breed. His daughter and her husband, M. and Mme. Jean-Pierre Naudin, carry on the de Alvalade suffix.

Carla Molinari

Another Portuguese lady, Senhorina Carla Molinari, also became an influential Portuguese Water Dog breeder. She bred Afghans and Salukis and her do Vale Negro champions are famous the world over. Senhorina

Carla Molinari, vice president of the CPC, has become an influential Portuguese Water Dog breeder. Pictured with her is Arriba de Alvalade at his first dog show at age ten months.

Molinari helped Dr. Cabral in raising Portuguese Water Dogs and sometimes co-owned dogs with him. She became secretary of the CPC, a post in which she also served on the Board of Directors and currently serves as Vice-President. She visited the United States several times and judged the PWDCA National Specialty Match in 1977.

The CPC is composed of members elected by the General Assembly. Seven members are elected for a period of three years to form a Head Committee. Under this committee are sub-committees: 1) Stud Book, 2) Shows, 3) Working Trials, 4) Judges, and 5) Scientific Matters.

Senhorina Molinari, Dr. Cabral, the CPC, and the dog fanciers of Portugal who desired the Cão de Áqua to prosper as a breed, breathed a deep sigh of relief and hope when Deyanne Miller had come onto the horizon in 1968.

They knew that, under the care of this vital and dynamic dog fancier, the future of the Cão de Áqua was in good hands.

3

The Portuguese
Water Dog
Comes to America

THE LEAD LINE in a story about the Portuguese Water
Dog by the late John Rendel which appeared in the *New York Times,* April
29, 1965 was this:

> The Portuguese Water Dog is a rarity in America . . . Breed First Brought
> Here in 1960 Now Numbers Only 19.

The Remarkable Influence of a Landmark Litter

In the story, Rendel gave the name of a fledgling dog club seeking
public recognition for the uncommon breed, told about a newly whelped
litter of the uncommon puppies, and described the background of the
breed.

Little did Rendel or anybody else dream his story about the
Portuguese Water Dog would start a tempest—not in a teapot but amongst
dog fanciers in the United States.

Several people who read his story set the tempest whirling.

Sonja and James Santos of Hampton Bays, Long Island, New York
answered a "For Sale" advertisement for the puppies (after reading
Rendel's story) and bought one as a pet. That was all they wanted at the

time—a pet for the children! She and her husband James—who traces his family background to the Portuguese in the Azores—became totally enamored of the extraordinary intelligence and unique habits of the female they purchased. Today they own one of the most prominent Portuguese Water Dog kennels in the United States.

Deyanne and Herbert H. Miller, Jr. of Farmion Kennels (AKC registered 1952), New Canaan, Connecticut, went to see the same puppies. The Millers raised Standard Poodles and Herb thought this rare breed might be kin to the Poodle. Unlike the Santos, they did not purchase a pup. Their main intention was to seek information on the breed when they visited Mr. and Mrs. Phillip Houghton of Bedford Hills, who owned the rare puppies.

They learned the pups were the offspring of two English-bred Portuguese Water Dogs shipped from Taunton, England by Mrs. R.J. Wood on March 22, 1960. The dogs were sent to Mr. and Mrs. Arthur Harrington of Rensselaer, New York. In exchange they sent her a pair of Affenpinschers. One dog, Berta of Tallwood (KC 126875/60), born in England, January 8, 1959, was black. The other, Amello of Tallwood (KC 53467/57), also whelped in England, was gray. Berta had been shipped as an emergency replacement because the dog Mrs. Wood originally intended to ship developed a skin condition and the English custom officers would not allow her off the islands.

Subsequently the dogs were bred, and two puppies from this mating were born on November 2, 1961. The male, Pedro Dom Emmons, was black with a white chest and the female, Topsy-Turvy, was gray with a white chest and legs. Topsy-Turvy was bred back to her father, Amello, and whelped seven puppies. Mr. Harrington had given Amello to Joseph and Betty Gratton of Albany, New York. In fact, Mr. Gratton had the records on the breed. He had also formed a Portuguese Water Dog Club. When it finally disbanded from lack of interest, the treasury had total monies of $32 and not a meeting had been held.

Three puppies from the Amello/Topsy-Turvy litter were gray—two of these had white markings. One was white, one was fawn, and two were black with white markings. One puppy went to California, one to Texas, one to New Jersey and the rest remained in New York. None, as far as is known, produced puppies (certainly not Portuguese Water Dog puppies!) when they reached adulthood. Accordingly, the strain eventually died out.

After Mr. and Mrs. Miller saw the Houghton's remaining two puppies (gray and white), they asked the Houghtons if they had a breed standard. They did. After the Millers read through the French and English translations of the CPC standard, they thanked the Houghtons for showing them the puppies. Mr. Houghton suggested that if the Millers were still interested in the breed, they contact the aforementioned Joseph Gratton. He had acquired all the information on Portuguese Water Dogs

The Miller family in 1962 with their Standard Poodles.

A Farmion Standard Poodle litter.   *Ozzie Sweet*

in the United States and could furnish more information.

On the way back to Connecticut, as Deyanne sat in the car mulling over what she had seen and heard and read at the Houghtons, she said to Herb: "If you like this breed, why don't we wait until we return to Portugal and at least get a specimen you like." The Millers were eager to revisit Portugal. They had spent a vacation there in 1962.

A second article on the breed appeared. This one was in the "This Week" feature section of the *Herald Tribune*. Deyanne Miller read it. It piqued Deyanne's curiosity about the breed.

She sent to the CPC for a copy of the Portuguese Water Dog standard.

She telephoned Mrs. Sherman R. Hoyt, a friend who bred Standard Poodles. Mrs. Hoyt had imported the first Poodles into America in the 1920s. She was an international dog judge, and one of the foremost authorities on the breed. At the time she was researching the Portuguese Water Dog history for a revision of her book *History of the Poodle*.

Deyanne told her about the dogs she had seen and Mrs. Hoyt urged Deyanne to seek more information on the breed.

Deyanne next wrote letters to dog fanciers in both England and Portugal. We reproduce two she received: one from C.H. Colpitts in Portugal and the other from Mrs. Wood in England.

July 20th

Dear Mrs. Miller:

Thank you for your letter of July 11th but I am afraid I am unable to help you very much. My only knowledge is that the only man in Portugal who was improving the breed has died and the current specimens are quite inferior to those in the past.

I am sorry that this is the best I can offer and hope you will find help elsewhere. With kindest regards I remain,

Yours sincerely,
C.H. Colpitts (for Don Luiz)

August 19, 1968

Dear Mrs. Miller,

Thank you for your letter received this morning.

I am very pleased to hear you are interested and working with the Portuguese Water Dog Club of the U.S.A. We do not have a club here.

At present I have no young stock for sale, but I have two bitches due in season anytime, although some are not easy to say when they are due in season, as they go from six to 11 months between seasons. One bitch is silver and silver-bred, this colour is very difficult to obtain. I was lucky enough to get a silver and white bitch in my first imports. A son of this bitch (Amello) was one of the first imports into the U.S.A., to Mr. A.L. Harrington of Albany, N.Y. Do you by any chance know if he is still alive, as I did not hear from him last Christmas, please let me know if you have any news of him.

You should have some silvers or steel greys among the Portuguese Water Dogs in the States, as in the imported bitch there was steel grey-and-white and black-and-white breeding; this is how silver turns up, but as there was silver on both the imported dog and bitch, it should still be there. To get that silver grey you must have some white on one or both parents, and also silver-grey in the grandparents. I have it here in my bloodlines.

If you are interested in importing a puppy of silver-grey, I will book you one from the next litter, but I cannot say if it will be a dog or a bitch. I usually get one or two in a litter of these bloodlines. If you have not imported new bloodlines from Portugal into the U.S.A., these puppies I shall have will be completely new to your bloodlines as far back as the great-great grandparents, there two ancestors are the same, so they would be an outcross.

Since Mrs. Harrington died, I have not received any news about the Porties in the U.S.A. How many are there now? Have any fresh bloodlines been imported? How are they taking on in the U.S.A.? I have not sold one here, gave two to friends, but one cannot get one out of me until I had these new bloodlines in. I have sent them all over the world, but would not sell here, until I had established the bloodlines here in my own kennels.

I am in touch with a Countess in Portugal who is the biggest breeder there and she will let me have new blood in exchange for some of my own breeding, that have different bloodlines, so I am alright for breeding.

Have the A.K.C. accepted the breed yet? Our K.C. have for Any Variety Unclassified registration.

Mr. Wood died five years ago, but I am still breeding and judging. I am judging at the Budapest International Show on September 14th and 15th. I hope one day to judge in the U.S.A., as I am passed for Allround judging under the F.C.I. ruling.

Looking forward to hearing from you soon.

Yours sincerely,
Muriel B. Wood

Deyanne Miller received the letter from Mrs. Wood after she, Herb, and two of their four children, Graham (13) and Deyanne (11) had returned from Portugal in July, 1968. Renting a car, they spent several days searching the Algarve fishing villages in vain for dogs of the breed. They drove back to Lisbon and met with Conchita Branco at dinner where they saw her Portuguese Champion (C.B.), Lis Algarbiorum. The next day they went to her home and saw some of her other dogs, including a one-day-old puppy bitch, sired by C.B. Lis Algarbiorum.

Renascenca do Al Gharb

Following the Millers' return home, Deyanne decided she wanted a Portuguese Water Dog and arranged to import a bitch puppy from Conchita Branco.

The cable received from Senhora Branco as she was preparing to send the puppy read:

PUPPY ARRIVING TUESDAY, SEPTEMBER 17, 1968, PAM. NAME MUST
BEGIN WITH THE LETTER "R."

Name the puppy with a name beginning with the letter "R?" Deyanne
looked in a Portuguese dictionary. She didn't need to ponder. There was
only one name for this pup: Renascenca—for the renaissance of the breed!

Before she could confirm the flight with PAM, she received a second
cable from Conchita Branco: "Held over at airport, now arriving Sept. 18,
1968."

Deyanne immediately called the airline and found out there might be a
problem if the flight arrived late. The immigration offices closed at 4 p.m.
daily, and the flight was due at 3:35 p.m. If the flight was delayed, the puppy
would be required to spend the night at the ASPCA facility at the airport.

I didn't want an eight-week-old puppy staying where all the zoo animals
from all over the world stayed. I didn't know about her inoculations or
protection for distemper, hepatitis or other diseases.

The gentleman from the immigration office was kindness personified, but
if the flight arrived after 4 p.m., then there was no way for the puppy to pass
customs that day.

Herb agreed to go with me to the airport but suggested I phone to make
sure the flight was on time.

I met Herb at his office and we drove out. When we arrived at JFK
Airport, not only was the flight already in earlier than had been expected but
the crate was sitting on the floor, just beyond the counter barrier. Having been
alerted, the cargo office men had looked at the pup, and reported to us that it
seemed fine.

We stood aside and the crate was put up on the counter. I opened the
door. I expected to see one tired pup who had been in transit since 11 a.m.
Tuesday.

Instead, she was standing—wriggling—and out she pranced, a saucy,
insouciant, self-assured black bundle of fur wagging her tail. She looked in top
form, full of kisses.

Herb held her while I looked on top of and finally inside the crate for any
instructions, any papers. All I found were some crumbs that looked like
zwieback but which I realized were Portuguese bread rolls and a blue rag rug.

We made haste to customs and the doctor passed her through,
commenting, "A Portuguese what?" I was to hear this question phrased
exactly the same way some thousand times over in the years ahead.

I had taken along a collar and lead and newspaper. She seemed to know
what the newspaper was for and took a lick of the bottled water I had also
brought along, hoping to avoid stomach upsets which occur when water is
changed.

During the trip home, she stationed herself on the front seat between us
. . . and literally and figuratively . . . that is where she stationed herself for the
rest of her life, dividing her attentions equally.

Renascenca seemed quite a moniker for this eight-week-old, born on July
12, 1968, so we wondered if she might give herself a name. The thing we

Renascenca, age eight weeks, with Deyanne Miller on Nantucket
Island.

Herb Miller with Renascenca.

Ruth Finch

noticed was her thumping tail. The children immediately began calling her *Thumperina*.

She quickly made herself at home, investigating every corner with curiosity. The tail never stopped wagging. She was also welcomed into the family by year-old Josie, a white Standard Poodle and by elderly Farmion Reveille of Ensarr. She gave her a wide berth.

She ate, seemed to drink worrisome quantities of water, but soon settled in. The four-foot-square pen I'd arranged in our dressing room she quickly informed me, was not where she planned to spend the night. Josie seemed to agree, though "Aunt" Reveille looked askance. So, after about 30 minutes, all my good intentions of not ever again having three dogs sleep on the bed went awry and my husband walked in cuddling her, claiming the poor thing "after such a long trip," etc. etc. "one night wouldn't hurt." Knowing better, as I've heard and used that refrain myself before, I acquiesced.

Resigning myself to Renascenca . . . that was to hold true for 15 years. I continually resigned myself to Renascenca. Soon I was to find that she had a knack of making me laugh even when I was annoyed with her—she would clown her way through anything—but get her way, she would. Part of it, in retrospect was that I was determined to be very open-ended and explore the adventure of getting to know this breed for itself . . . and thus found one of the most difficult things was to erase any thoughts of Poodles or other breeds, and just observe her.

For this same reason, I did not obedience train her. I consequently learned too late that this would be a major requirement with Portuguese Water Dogs . . . early training was a must . . . while the owner establishes leader dominance.

The die was cast. I was to rue the day from this decision as Renascenca ruled the roost, so to speak. Mind you, she did it so cleverly and so subtly that I didn't really realize it as it was happening.

I am not exactly uninitiated about animals, having owned my first dog since my fourth birthday, and been involved with my first love, horses, at an early age. I recall breaking an arm from a horse fall when I was five; so schooling horses, or training under Blanche Saunders in obedience and a general idea about being handy and how to train wasn't exactly foreign to me. But this Renascenca—Chenze—as she finally came to be called, was a dog with the authority and wisdom of a ten-year-old child.

Chenze died on September 1, 1983 at the age of 15 years.

Establishing the Portuguese Water Dog in America

In 1969, Herb Miller imported a Portuguese Water Dog male puppy eight weeks of age, Anzol. Hopefully, he was to be Chenze's future mate.

The No. 1 litter of ten puppies, seven of which survived—four females and three males—were sired by Anzol (Anzol do Al Gharb) with Chenze (Renascenca do Al Gharb) as dam. They were whelped on June 17, 1971 at the Miller's summer home on Siasconset, a small, former fishing village on

In 1969, Herb Miller imported Anzol do Al Gharb, age eight weeks.

The No. 1 litter of seven puppies shown with their dam, Renanscenca. Pups were four weeks old.
Folger

Nantucket Island, Massachusetts. It was the first litter of Portuguese Water Dogs of Portuguese breeding in America.

The next few years were difficult ones. Each pup whelped had to be placed in a home which would ensure breeding plus ensure survival. Females had to be placed very carefully so that owners would not spay them because they didn't like "heats." Every time Deyanne placed a pup she had to look 12 years down the line and *guestimate* what would happen to it during its lifetime. Pups had to be geographically distributed so the breed could be seen by dog fanciers who could later take on the breed as their own. Some pups would have to be returned to Portugal. Both sides of the ocean had to work together to cross rough bloodlines.

New blood had to be brought in constantly so as to ensure sound, interchangeable stock.

Deyanne and Herb made yearly trips to Portugal. Deyanne, for a time, had intermittent correspondence with Conchita Branco since it was from her that puppies were arriving. The Millers did not meet Vasco Bensaude's widow until 1972.

A letter from Conchita Branco, dated January 4th, 1970 arrived:

I trust that by now your puppy (Anzol do Al Gharb) has found himself at home. He has a marked personality. I would suppose more sensitive than "Renascenca" but easily adapted to movement and strangers. He was quite at home even at the airport. His teeth are fine. About his future, only time will tell.

Another letter from Conchita dated February 1970 was ominous in content:

... Now the Water Dog: Time has now run out and I cannot wait for official support any longer. Have reduced the Water Dogs to 18 adults and Juniors. Of these I am selling two champion females and one male. Keeping Juniors to take over.

This year I expect to have placed at least a dozen dogs—good ones—in the U.S. and this should be enough to keep the breed going over there. So I can and will reduce my kennel. Do you realize that I had 67 dogs?

Deyanne wrote back:

Please, for goodness sakes, the next time you want to reduce your kennel, telephone or telegraph me first. We'll get a rescue program going here . . . please.

Another letter from Conchita Branco arrived, dated February 16, 1970:

Have two champions of my kennel list for sale. Reducing (without diet) expenses to a more rational figure. Have now 17 Water Dogs. Good ones. All of them. The authorities have not replied and I have decided not to wait. Could end like Sisyphus and his proverbial rock.

April 5th, 1970:

Hello again! The name should begin with A. The names and prices of all dogs, at the moment, are annexed. I am expecting the visit of some American friends' friends, who apparently believe they may breed. For this reason even 11 times Best in Show (or near that figure) Espada Algarbiorum is on the list. So are Ch. Lis and Ch. Espia. This pair has passed a 100 percent good progeny test, producing several future champions. As you can imagine I am not particularly interested in selling the No. 1 animals on the list—but if the kennel is to go on, all animals must have a price. And moreover we are expecting a *huge* litter by Renascenca's parents, also excellent, fully approved, progeny-tested dogs.

Know any horse-fans? I have several fabulous Anglo-Arabian jumpers for sale. Young horses, good temper, olympic quality.

Ch. Espada Algarbiorum, U.S. Dollars	$3000
Ch. Enga Algarbiorum	$2000
Ch. Escuta	$2000
Ch. Espia	$6000
Ch. Lis	$6000
Ch. Lo	$2000
Young dogs	
Tarura	$1000
Tuzo	$1000
Ufana	$2000
Unica	$2000
All were shown as puppies and awarded cups, medals, etc.	
Xeai	$800
Sanube	$800
Sines	$800

All Al Gharb dogs of perfect teeth and conformation. Some more beautiful than others.

April 15, 1970:

Letter A. Give me the name please. . . . Now clipped, quite adult looking, the Water Dog group looks quite handsome. . . . Presently I have a new project on my hands, some trained . . . Jumpers (Olympic quality) Anglo-Arabians or pure Arabian for breeding between three and seven thousand dollars. Already sold 11 animals since August.

June 30, 1971:

Just a line to tell you that I have been obliged to rush back to Mexico. Dog papers are all in a confusion but will sort them out on my return (soon) to Lisbon.

December 11, 1971:

There is no more breeding at the Al Gharb Kennels unless orders for puppies are received. At the moment no female is in season but as there are so many one may turn up any day now. If you wish another male just let me know "formally" that this is the case. Lis and Espia are both in good shape and would be a change. Or Xeno is a very handsome animal that you do not know. He won best puppy in show at the age of one year.

The prices have not been altered for puppies (U.S. dollars 500.00) but as I am no longer keeping an overlarge kennel, I am willing to part with Lis (Champion several times) who is now between five and six years old, at a convenient price: one thousand dollars. It makes no difference if it is Lis or Lo only Lo is more difficult to handle. You may remember that Lis and Espia were the parents of the three pups that you liked very much, amongst them was Uivo that died.

One of the last letters was dated May 7, 1972:

I have just returned from Mexico and . . . as for dogs I have what will most likely be the last litter at home . . . if you are interested please let me know.

Deyanne did not purchase any of the adult dogs that were offered. In fact, the Millers did not purchase any more dogs until her trip in April 1972. Then they got one from Dr. Cabral's de Alvalade Kennels.

On Deyanne's and Herb's trip to Portugal in 1972, they had the first visit with Senhora Bensaude, Vasco's widow. They did not attempt to meet her in 1968 since Vasco Bensaude had died the year before. In Europe, people mourn two years. Deyanne didn't feel she should telephone and bother his widow to inquire about one of her late husband's hobbies.

When Deyanne and Herb visited Senhora Bensaude at her home, they learned that a Mrs. Kermit Roosevelt had been there from the United Shipping Lines before World War II and wanted to raise Portuguese Water Dogs but then World War II intervened before stock was available.

This startled us. The first litter of our dogs of Portuguese stock were born about three blocks away from the Roosevelt summer home in Nantucket.

At the end of the luncheon, in comes a Portuguese Water Dog, owned by the cook. They apologized that it was so fat but it loved to eat. It came up then that this breed does tend to corpulence. It's in the old standard.

While we were there, Patricia said to her mother, "The dogs have been shot." Her mother looked stunned. She had given the dogs out of good faith to the best person she could and she felt wronged. She had not been consulted on what had transpired. The moment must have been a very poignant moment for both mother and daughter.

We were told later by Conchita Branco's daughter, Anna Mafalda, that only three dogs remained, Lo, a brother of Lis and two bitches and that two or three years later, there were 35 dogs.

We didn't do much else except that we were shown into Vasco Bensaude's study. It was a lovely, big paneled room and it was left exactly as he left it. Around the wall there were medals of excellence, a lot of different mementos of Portuguese Water Dogs. I don't recall at the time seeing on his desk the Algarborium stamp. It now sits on my desk. It was given to me on a subsequent trip.

Deyanne Miller, Dr. Antonio Cabral and Carla Molinari in Portugal, 1974.

Senhora Bensaude and her daughter, Patricia, could not have been more gracious to Deyanne and Herb. They told them they were going to make every effort to get back all the different documentation and scrapbooks they had given with the dogs.

The Millers spent three weeks in Portugal that April. During that time, they met with the widow of Senhor Daniel de Silva Lane. He was the first president of the CPC. Senhora Maria Theresa de Silva Lane was instrumental in the Millers getting to know Dr. Antonio Cabral, president of the CPC. Dr. Cabral was the breeder of the de Alvalade Portuguese Water Dogs. From Dr. Cabral, they purchased Trovoada de Alvalade, 18 months old. Before the Millers returned home, they went to France and met with the president of the French Kennel Club. "There are no more of this breed in France," he told them.

They returned home, quite impressed with their visits with Senhora Bensaude and her daughter, Patricia. Senhora Bensaude died eight years after their initial visit. They remain good friends with her daughter, Patricia.

Deyanne returned from that visit determined to carry on with the Portuguese Water Dog.

4

The Portuguese
Water Dog Club
of America

THE NAMES of each American breeder of Portuguese Water Dogs listed in these pages should be written in a book of gold! Here is the story and names of those who loved the breed and aided greatly in its renaissance.

Establishment of the Club

On the afternoon of August 13, 1972, sixteen dedicated people gathered at the Farmion estate in New Canaan, Connecticut to organize the Portuguese Water Dog Club of America (PWDCA).

Not all the sixteen were owners of Portuguese Water Dogs. Between them, they owned 12 dogs. Whether they owned a dog or not, each was ardently attached to the endangered breed by interest. One was a Poodle authority.

It was a crucial moment for the Portuguese Water Dog breed. His mentors met determined to save the breed's life. They met determined to make the dog's presence felt throughout America.

At the moment of meeting, only these 12 Portuguese Water Dogs were known to live in the United States. Two private kennels in Portugal sheltered an additional dozen. These were the only known survivors of the breed. These were the only dogs that had not perished in the erosion of the old way of fishing life in Portugal.

Officers elected at the organization meeting were Herbert H. Miller, Jr. of Connecticut as president; Frank Parks of Illinois as vice president; James M. White of Georgia as recording secretary; Deyanne Miller of Connecticut as corresponding secretary, and Dora Badgett of Connecticut as treasurer. The other charter members were Mr. Joseph N. Gratton of New York, Miss Susan Hickert of Kansas, Mr. and Mrs. Sherman R. Hoyt of Connecticut, Mrs. Michael Krupa of New York, Mr. Joseph F. Orris, Jr. of Connecticut, Mrs. Frank L. Parks of Illinois, Mr. and Mrs. Antonio Pereira of New York, Mr. and Mrs. Peter W. Pierce of New York, and Miss Helen Roosevelt of Florida.

These 16 people initiated the steps to regenerate the breed. They did so with tremendous intensity, determination and energy.

From the initial nucleus of sixteen, membership swelled to 51 members on the first anniversary, 69 on the second, 92 on the third, 110 on the fourth. By the eighth anniversary in 1980, 339 dogs were geographically distributed in 32 states; there were 30 breeders of record.

The PWDCA celebrated AKC Miscellaneous Class approval in June 1981. Effective June 3, 1981, owners could exhibit their dogs in this rare breed class at all AKC all-breed dog shows. While the Miscellaneous Class exhibition offers no championship points, it serves as a showcase of rare breeds to dog fanciers and the public alike. As a Miscellaneous Class dog, the Portuguese Water Dog was also eligible to compete in all AKC-sponsored obedience trials and earn obedience titles.

Only two months and ten days after the breed entered the Miscellaneous Class, on the club's ninth anniversary, August 13, 1981, the PWDCA registrar counted a total of 226 members. 524 Portuguese Water Dogs lived in the United States. These were geographically distributed throughout 36 states. In addition, one Portuguese Water Dog lived in Canada. The PWDC of Canada had been founded on December 6, 1976. Several dogs had been shipped from the United States to Mexico, Bermuda, Norway and Ireland. One lived in Saudi Arabia!

At the organizational meeting in 1972, founders set annual meetings for February of each year in New York City. They wanted these to coincide with the activities held by the Westminster Kennel Club. The first meeting was held at the Yale Club, New York City on February 11, 1973.

The PWDCA retained the founding officers through 1974. Deyanne Miller held the post of corresponding secretary through 1976. Mrs. Jon R. (Pamela) Schneller became corresponding secretary in 1977. Named to the post in 1978 was Mrs. Philip A. Metcalf. She was replaced by Maryanne B. Murray in 1981. In 1983 Ms. Karen Miller took the post.

In 1975, when the breed was represented by approximately 130 members living in 30 states and Canada, Melvin M. Dichter of Connecticut became president. He was followed by Mrs. Anthony Ulcickas of New York in 1976; Mrs. Hermine H. Munro (Connecticut), a Kerry Blue Terrier breeder, was president for the year 1977. Mr. Thomas A. Barrows of New Jersey was president in both 1978 and 1979. Deyanne Miller served as president in 1980. For the years 1981 and 1982, Mrs. Pamela Schneller, New York, was president. Linwood A. Kulp, Jr., Pennsylvania, took office in 1983. He was reelected for the year 1984.

Communication is the lifeline of a national breed club. Deyanne Miller published the club's first newsletter. At the annual meeting in 1974, members began to establish a set format for the newsletter. Mrs. Noreen Lowery of New York became editor in 1977. The newsletter was formally named *The Courier* in 1980. In 1981, Noreen Lowery became *The Courier* publisher and Maryanne Murray, then corresponding secretary, became editor.

Club Registry

Registration of all dogs was handled by Deyanne Miller until 1977 when Bonnie Fischer assumed these duties followed by Mrs. David (Carolyn) Meisel of New York in 1980. Deyanne Miller retained the job of CPC registrar taking care of all foreign registration until full AKC recognition. (One of her duties as CPC registrar was to register American stock with the CPC. The CPC honored the PWDCA by according dual registration.)

In order for the AKC to even look at a rare breed club's dogs and activities, rare breed clubs must keep accurate stud book records and all imported foundation stock must be registered with the kennel club of their country of origin. The long-sighted and meticulous record-keeping of the founding members in maintaining accurate U.S. and foreign registration records is one of the reasons the breed advanced to AKC recognition so quickly.

Carolyn Meisel has written a text entitled *Establishing a Registry for a Dog Club,* which contains information that may be useful to other dog clubs dedicated to rare breeds. To obtain a copy, contact the Portuguese Water Dog Club of America, One Greeley Road, New Canaan, Connecticut 06840.

Carolyn Meisel was introduced to the PWDCA by Deyanne Miller. Carolyn was introduced to Deyanne Miller by the Secretary of the CPC, Carla Molinari, from whom she had purchased two Portuguese Water Dogs. Carolyn Meisel, whose kennel name is Canopus, is a para-legal (a lay attorney) in Geneseo, New York. Her work background helped her meet all challenges as PWDCA registrar in the months the PWDCA was opting for AKC registration and in the busy months before the PWDCA stud books were turned over to the AKC.

The job of registrar is of utmost importance for a rare breed club. The PWDCA was blessed with a smooth transition of duties whenever this position was transferred. How lucky the PWDCA was to have three able individuals handle this post, Deyanne Miller, Bonnie Fischer and Carolyn Meisel.

A Variety of Programs

The work accomplished by the early, growing membership is impressive. Here are some of the programs initiated during the 1970s:

a) Genetic Feedback
b) OFA Examination and Registration
c) Grooming Seminars
d) Fun Matches
e) Specialty Matches
f) Community Exhibitions
g) Fun Water Trials

Information about each of these programs may be obtained from the current PWDCA corresponding secretary.

Even before the organizational meeting in 1972, Deyanne Miller beseiged magazine and newspaper editors with breed information and many writers wrote stories about the Portuguese Water Dog. Some of the magazines and newspapers which featured breed articles and pictures were *Popular Dogs, Poodle Review, Dogs Magazine, The New York Times, Lost Angeles Times, Nantucket Inquirer, Mirror,* and the *New Canaan Advertiser.* These stories stimulated wide interest.

The book, *The Uncommon Dog Breeds,* by Kathryn Braund (Arco, 1975) also generated a great deal of interest in the breed.

Each year, coinciding with the annual meeting during the Westminster KC festivities, Portuguese Water Dogs were shown in New York City at affairs where the dog fanciers gathered.

Closer to Recognition

The first formal presentation of the breed to The AKC was made on April 17, 1980. On this committee were Deyanne Miller, President; Mrs. Phillip A. Metcalf, Corresponding Secretary; Mr. Thomas Scott Barrows, Treasurer; Mr. John J. Fisk, Board Member; and Mrs. Jon R. Schneller, Board Member.

The letter the PWDCA received from Mark T. Mooty, Secretary of the AKC, dated April 23, 1980, pleased the members. Recognition was getting closer.

A PWDCA standard committee immediately went to work. As described in Chapter 7, it was revised for AKC approval twice before acceptance.

At the next annual meeting in 1981, Deyanne Miller was appointed the club's AKC liaison. John Fisk, treasurer, was appointed Chairman of the AKC Presentations Committee.

When the AKC gave Miscellaneous Class status to the Portuguese Water Dog on June 1, 1981, Deyanne made the following statement:

> The breed is in the anteroom of fulfillment in the U.S.A. The Miscellaneous Class will be the proving ground for the Portuguese Water Dog.

She was grateful to dogs and people.

At Farmion, 18 litters were whelped in 13 years—from June 17, 1971 through June 30, 1983. The latter date was the first PWDCA Stud Book cut-off date given by the AKC in preparation for the breed to enter full registry. Renascenca whelped 17 pups in three litters, Trovoada whelped 50 pups in four litters, Delgadas whelped 39 pups in four litters, and Nazare whelped 41 pups in five litters.

A total of 106 litters were whelped during this period by American breeders.

Early Showing Activity

Most dogs born were black. There was one brown dog in litter No. 8, three in litter No. 21, two in litter No. 24, four in litter No. 26, one in litter No. 32 and one in litter No. 39, but the first all-brown litter was the 43rd litter, bred by Mr. and Mrs. Michael J. O'Neill of Manhasset, New York. When the O'Neills called Deyanne to confirm the news, she flew the Portuguese Water Dog flag that day. Deyanne often displayed colors at the Farmion 255-year old house in New Canaan. She flies the Canadian flag in honor of the country where she was born, and the Irish flag in honor of her heritage. When she flies the green and red flag of Portugal, something important has happened for the breed.

Getting back to our story, here is a list of PWDCA's first two Fun Matches and the Annual Specialty Matches held before the breed was accepted by the AKC as a fully recognized breed. The matches were always held with close attention paid to AKC's regulations and satisfaction. Listed along with dates and judges are the Best of Breed and Best of Opposite Sex winners.

Date/Location, Judge	Best of Breed and Best of Opposite Sex	Dog's Clip
Fun Match		
1 Sept. 14, 1974	BIM Anzol do Al Gharb	Working
New Canaan, Ct.	BOS Renascenca do Al Gharb	Working
Mrs. S. R. Hoyt		
Bernard Berman		

2	June 7, 1975	BIM Febo do Al Gharb	Working
	Greenwich, Ct.	BOS Trovoada de Alvalade	Working
	Bernard Berman		

Annual Specialty

1	Aug. 7, 1977	BOB Trezena Monte Clerico	Lion
	Roslyn, L.I., N.Y.	BOS Farmion Caravela	Working
	Carla Molinari		
2	Oct. 1, 1978	BOB Trezena Monte Clerico	Lion
	Princeton, N.J.	BOS Rainha do Mar	Lion
	Peggy Walton		
3	Sept. 16, 1979	BOB Bittersweet Hypolito	Working
	Stamford, Ct.	BOS Spindrift Genoa	Lion
	Peter Knoop		
4	Sept. 14, 1980	BOB Trezena Monte Clerico	Lion
	Stamford, Ct.	BOS Spindrift Genoa	Lion
	Donna Hausman		
5	Sept. 13, 1981	BOB Bittersweet Hypolito	Working
	Newtown, Pa.	BOS Trezena Konstelada	Lion
	Peter Thompson		
6	Sept. 19, 1982	BOB Spindrift Genoa	Lion
	North Hills, L.I., N.Y.	BOB Spindrift Galley	Lion
	Joseph J. Mellor		
7	Sept. 18, 1983	BOB Spindrift Galley, CD	Lion
	Bridgewater, N.J.	BOS Spindrift Genoa, CDX	Lion
	Barbara Amidon		

Leading the list of members who showed their Portuguese Water Dogs in the Miscellaneous Class in 1982 were Dr. and Mrs. Richard T. Woods of Gardena, California. They showed their dog, Shanesca Pico Alta (a Farmion dog) 31 times that year. Farmion Zimbreira, owned by Carla Doyle of Louisville, Kentucky, was shown 25 times in 1982. Ch. Charlie de Alvalade, owned by Deyanne Miller, was also shown 25 times in 1982. He was the first Miscellaneous Class winner. Canopus Galacia, owned by Mr. and Mrs. Rudy Pierce of Jonestown, Pennsylvania was shown 19 times. Trezena Konstelada, co-owned by Linwood Kulp and Maryanne Murray of Lansdale, Pennsylvania was shown ten times.

Ed and Barbara Whitney exhibited four dogs in both breed and obedience during 1982. Barbara gave the breed its first Utility dog only fifteen months after the breed entered the Miscellaneous Class. The dog was Spindrift Kedge. Kedge also earned the first Companion Dog (CD) title and the first Companion Dog Excellent (CDX) title for the breed. She won these on the following dates: CD on June 7, 1981, CDX on August 31, 1981 and UD on September 25, 1982.

Other PWDCA members who earned obedience titles on their dogs in

Second PWDCA Fun Match, June 7, 1975, Bernard Berman judging with Deyanne Miller handling Trovoada de Alvalade, BOS at the match, foreground.

Annual Specialty Match 2,
October 1, 1978: Judge
Margaret Walton, Sonja Santos,
Pamela Schneller, Tom Barrows.
Dog is Rainha do Mar, BOS.
Bernard W. Kernan

Exhibitors and friends at the Annual Specialty Match 2, October 1, 1978. *Left to right, back row:* M
Thomas S. Barrows, Mrs. Francis Grant (Felizardo), Mr. Thomas S. Barrows (Ninfeia), Miss A. Barrov
Mrs. Joanne Cakoyannis and children (Keel), Mrs. Bonnie R. Fischer (do Peixe), Mrs. Hermine Munro, M
and Mrs. Robert Hollander, Mrs. James E. Santos (do Mar), Mrs. Priscilla Pereira, Judge—Mrs. Marga
Walton, Dr. Malcolm Ekstrand (Greenwood), Mrs. Jon C. Schneller, Mr. and Mrs. H.E. Whitney (Spindr
Mrs. Herbert H. Miller, Jr. (Farmion), Mr. Earl Sandin (Warwickshire), Mr. James, Scott Bass. *Bottom ro*
Miss Katie Barrows, Mrs. Barrie Bell and children, Mrs. Joan Reynolds (Lusitania), Mrs. Adeline Regan, I
James Sweeney, Mr. Philip A. Metcalf, Mrs. Philip A. Metcalf and Jaime, Mr. and Mrs. Bernard Steine
Bernard W. Kerr

Annual Specialty Match 3, September 16, 1979: Judge, Peter Knoop; Miss Sherry Higgins with BOB Bittersweet Hypolito and H.E. Whitney with BOS Spindrift Genoa.

Keel Lobo, owned by Linda Powers, was Best Puppy in Sweepstakes at the PWDCA Spring Match, June 22, 1980.
Bernard W. Kernan

Annual Specialty Match 4, September 14, 1980: Deyanne F. Miller, Donna Hausman, Judge—Mrs. Raymond Boulanger, James Bass—Specialty Chairman, H.E. Whitney with Spindrift Genoa, BOS, and Pamela Schneller with Trezena Monte Clerico, BOB.

Annual Specialty Match 5, September 13, 1981: Judge—Joyce Reynaud with Pamela Schneller and Keel Beleza, CD, Best in Sweepstakes. *Bernard W. Kernan*

The best Junior Handler at two PWDCA Specialty Matches was Brad Grauer with Farmion Neptuno.

Annual Specialty Match 5, September 13, 1981: Judge—Peter B. Thompson, Maryanne Murray with Trezena Konstelada, BOS, and Show Chairman Linwood Kulp, Jr.

the Miscellaneous Class in 1981 and 1982 were Shanesca Pico Alta, CD (Dr. and Mrs. Richard T. Woods, California); Seacatch Xa, CD (Robert and Ruth Hollander, Bayport, L.I., N.Y.) who won a High in Trial (HIT) earning his title with a score of 198½; Keel Beleza, CD (Jon and Pamela Schneller, New York); Canopus Galaca, CD (Rudy C. and Eleanor Pierce, Pennsylvania); Farmion Oporta, CD (William D. and Mary Jackson, New York); Spindrift Genoa, CD (H. Edward and Barbara A. Whitney, New York.)

In 1983, the last year the Portuguese Water Dog was exhibited in the Miscellaneous Class, Clara C. Doyle (Kentucky) led the exhibitors by showing Farmion Zimbreira 24 times. P. E. and H. A. Philbrick (Washington) showed their dog Mareke Vencedor v. Baerbach ten times. Isadora do Mar, a bitch co-owned by B. F. Flohr (Arizona) and Sonja Santos (do Mar Kennels, New York) tied with R. O. Sylvia (Rhode Island) who showed her bitch, Cherna Praia Da Rocha, CD (Flor) eight times. Flor also earned her obedience title in 1983. Dr. Richard and Dawn Woods (California) showed Shanesca Pico Alta eight times also. Kathryn Braund showed Farmion Geo, CD (Diver) seven times in the show ring. Diver also earned his CD obedience title that year.

Edward and Barbara Whitney owned three dogs which earned obedience titles in 1983. Spindrift Galley earned her CD, Spindrift Genoa earned her CDX and Spindrift X-Hapi earned her CD. Both Galley and Genoa were each shown five times in the breed ring also. Maryanne Murray and L. A. Kulp, Jr. showed White Cap Bianca of Brinmar five times. Canopus Flagman, owned by C. H. Prangley was also shown five times.

Other dogs who earned obedience titles in 1983 were Peachtree Dalia, CD (bitch) and Peachtree Domingos Miguel, CD (dog), both owned by Penelope Joyce Hoffman. Madge Barton Sutter's bitch, Cherna Renewal, won her CD title also.

Dogs who were exhibited several times in the breed ring in 1983 by their owners were Keel Beleza (Jon and Pam Schneller), Umbrion Soberana (Mr. and Mrs. P. Hollander), Captree Lote (Noreen Lowery), Bittersweet Zelo (N. S. Hayes), Trezena Konstelada (M. B. Murray and L. A. Kulp, Jr.), Avalons Yestrala (Bobbe P. Kurtz), Farmion Neptuno (E. B. Grauer), Alfama Uberrimo of Regala (E. D. Pierce), Bittersweet Zleama (C. L. Petursson), Canopus Farina (C. B. Satherlie), Cherna Renewal (M.B. Sutter), Nativo do Mar (J. and J. Goodman), Varina Honroso (M. and J.E. Koestner), Rebento Cossart (B.M. Twiggs) and Farmion Oura (A.V. Wood).

The following dogs were also shown: Farmion Oura, Bittersweet Zizi, Firmanento Kalakua, Regala Arrebitado, Starviews Paolo, Farmion Fiberboard, Canopus Frangelica, Keel Tonel, Varina Honroso, Captree

Spindrift Kedge at Schooley's Mountain KC, August 31, 1981, earning her CDX title. Shown with Kedge are Judge Patricia Scully and Barbara Whitney. Kedge later won her Utility Dog (UD) title. She was the first in the breed to earn these obedience titles.

John L. Ashbey

Ch. Charlie de Alvalade, shown here with handler Ted Young, Judge—Elsworth Howell at the Longshore-Southport KC, June 1981. Charlie was the first Miscellaneous Class winner.

Gilbert

Judge E. Klinckhardt awards the Miscellaneous Class ribbon to Clara C. Doyle's Farmion Zimbreira.   *Dick and Diana Alverson*

Judge Anna Katherine Nicholas gives Charlie de Alvalade the Miscellaneous Class with C. Robert Cory and Farmion Olhao standing by. Ted Young is handling Charlie.   *John L. Ashbey*

Lote, Seamist Jade of Seawolf, Farmion Nautico, Nalate do Mar, and White Cap Belinha.

Some people were saying the Working Clip was put into the standard only to placate pet owners who wanted to show their dogs. This is not true. Although the original Portuguese standard lists only the Lion Clip for the show ring, the Portuguese fishermen—in their daily lives—kept the Portuguese Water Dog in a Working Clip. The dogs seldom appeared at shows in Portugal. They were working and needed the hair for insulation. This is why the full coat has been referred to as the Working Clip even though the Lion Clip described in earlier books was the show clip. This is why Portugal's postage stamp of the breed depicts the Working Clip.

On September 20, 1982 (a month after the 10th anniversary of the first organization meeting—August 13, 1972) there were 50 breeders of Portuguese Water Dogs, 90 litters had been born in the U.S. and a grand total of 650 dogs had been distributed. An additional six litters were expected by the end of the year. Dogs were dispersed in 41 states. These states had none: Arkansas, Hawaii, Indiana, Mississippi, Nebraska, Nevada, New Mexico, and North and South Dakota. The breed was soon to be accepted by the AKC as a registrable Working Dog.

A scant 13 years had passed since the Portuguese Water Dog was listed as an endangered breed with less than 25 known specimens remaining in the world.

What a triumph!

First PWDCA Stud Book Records

Following is the complete list of American breeders and litters they bred. Included in the summarization chart are the number of dogs and bitches whelped in each litter, sire and dam—each marked as import or number of litter in which the dog was whelped—and the dispersement by state of the members of each litter. In all cases, individuals were born black or black with white markings, unless identified as brown.

The litters are numbered 1 through 106, as recorded by the PWDCA just before its 11th anniversary and on the first stud book cut-off date by the AKC—June 30, 1983. Originally, litters were numbered A, B, C, etc. and then 1A, 1B, etc. We use the numbering system in our list.

Imports during this period are listed. They will be found at the end of the section.

The strict sequential records kept by the PWDCA beginning with the first litter whelped in the U.S. of Portuguese stock—on June 17, 1971 and ending with litter #106 bred by James and Sonja Santos on June 25, 1983—stand as a tribute to those who kept them.

68

PWDCA Litter No./Pups Whelped/Sire & Dam	Date Whelped/Breeder	Dispersement
1.　3 dogs, 4 bitches Anzol do Al Gharb (import) ex Renascenca do Al Gharb (import)	6-17-71 Deyanne F. Miller	Ca., Ct., Ma., Md., N.Y.
2.　4 dogs, 3 bitches Xino do Al Gharb (import) ex Farmion Areia (litter 1)	5-22-73 Judith K. Bartsch	Ca., Ct., Fl., N.Y., Pa.
3.　7 dogs, 2 bitches Anzol do Al Gharb (import) ex Trovoada de Alvalade (import)	9-20-73 Farmion Kennels	Ct., Fl., N.J., N.Y., Pa.
4.　5 dogs, 9 bitches Xelim de Alvalade (import) ex Trovoada de Alvalade (import)	4-10-74 Farmion Kennels	Ct., Md., Mi., N.J., N.Y., Pa., R.I., Va.
5.　2 bitches Xelim de Alvalade (import) ex Renascenca do Al Gharb (import)	5-2-74 Farmion Kennels	Ct., R.I.
6.　3 dogs, 4 bitches Ancora do Al Gharb (import) ex Farmion Alcantarilha (litter 1)	6-14-74 Rebecca S. Clover	Ca., N.Y.
7.　4 dogs, 4 bitches Farmion Azinhal (litter 1) ex Renascenca do Al Gharb (import)	11-23-74 Deyanne F. Miller	Ca., Ct., N.Y., R.I., Ireland

Deyanne Miller with puppies from the third litter. *Allan Mitchell*

Ancora do Al Gharb, sire of litters 6, 11, 12, 16, 17, 31, 33, 36, 37, 45 and 50.

8. 7 dogs, 2 bitches
1 dog BROWN
Xino do Al Gharb
(import) ex
Farmion Caravela
(litter 3)

9-13-75

Thomas S. Barrows

Az., Ct.,
N.J., N.Y.,
Pa., Tx.,
Wa.

9. 2 dogs, 7 bitches
Farmion Azinhal
(litter 1) ex
Farmion Endiabrada
(litter 5)

10-26-75
Dr. Malcolm Ekstrand

Ct., Ma.,
N.Y., Pa.,
R.I., Wa.,
Mexico

10. 2 dogs, 5 bitches
Febo do Al Gharb
(import) ex
Farmion Bordeira
(litter 2)

10-31-75
J. and L. Reynolds

Ct., Fl.,
Mi., Pa.

11. 1 dog, 2 bitches
Ancora do Al Gharb
(import) ex
Farmion Alfambra
(litter 1)

11-16-75
E. and B. Whitney

N.Y.

12. 3 dogs
Ancora do Al Gharb
(import) ex
Farmion Catarina
(litter 3)

12-29-75
J. C. Mandeville

N.Y., Pa.

13. 7 dogs, 3 bitches
Farmion Azinhal
(litter 1) ex
Farmion Defeza
(litter 4)

2-20-76
Jayne Kenyon

Fl., N.J.,
N.Y., Oh.,
Pa., Tx.

14. 12 dogs, 3 bitches
Farmion Azinhal
(litter 1) ex
Trovoada de Alvalade
(import)

6-22-76
Farmion Kennels

Az., Ca.,
Ct., Fl., Id.,
N.J., N.Y.,
Pa., Wa.

Farmion Endiabrada,
dam of litter 9.

A three-week-old
puppy from litter 11,
held by breeder,
Barbara Whitney.
Anthony Jerome

15. 2 dogs, 1 bitch
Febo do Al Gharb
(import) ex
Farmion Belixe
(litter 2)

11-30-76
Frances O. Grant

Fl., N.Y.,
Pa.

16. 6 dogs, 3 bitches
Ancora do Al Gharb
(import) ex
Farmion Esperanca
(litter 5)

4-16-77
Bonnie Fischer

Ct., Wash.
D.C., Mn.,
N.Y., Wi.,
Canada

17. 1 dog, 2 bitches
Ancora do Al Gharb
(import) ex
Lusitania Jaca
(litter 10)

5-12-77
Gerald Rorer

Ma., Pa.

18. 6 dogs, 4 bitches
Anzol do Al Gharb
(import) ex
Zingara de Alvalade
(import)

5-14-77
J. and S. Santos

N.H., N.Y.

19. 1 dog, 1 bitch
Farmion Cabo de Sta Maria
(import) ex
Greenwood Izeda
(litter 9)

6-22-77
C. and S. Zessos

Ct.

20. 4 dogs, 5 bitches
Febo do Al Gharb
(import) ex
Spindrift Keel
(litter 11)

6-27-77
Joanne Cakoyanis

Ct., N.J.,
N.Y., Pa.,
Wa.

21. 6 dogs, 3 bitches
2 dogs, 1 bitch BROWN
Farmion Cabo de Sta Maria
(litter 3) ex
Farmion Delgadas
(litter 4)

10-9-77

Deyanne F. Miller

Ak., Ct.,
N.C., N.Y.,
Ok., Or.

Farmion Esperanca,
dam of litter 16.

Rosmaninhal do Mar from litter 18 is the dam of
several champions.

Farmion Cabo de Sta Maria, sire of litters 19, 21,
24, 26, 28, 29 and 46. Cabo threw excellent
heads, eyes, temperament and water ability.

22. 3 dogs, 3 bitches Febo do Al Gharb (import) ex Greenwood Ilha da Faro (litter 9)	11-7-77 Dr. and Mrs. Saracino	Ma., N.Y.
23. 3 dogs, 6 bitches Trezena Marmelete (litter 13) ex Lusitania Joanica (litter 10)	12-2-77 Helen Ross	Fl., N.Y., Tx.
24. 6 dogs, 2 bitches 1 dog, 1 bitch BROWN Farmion Cabo de Sta Maria (litter 3) ex Farmion Dalva (litter 4)	12-22-77 Amanda Scola	Ct., N.Y., Saudi Arabia
25. 6 dogs, 3 bitches Anzol do Al Gharb (import) ex Greenwood Isna (litter 9)	1-14-78 E. and J. Rae Sandin	Ma., N.Y., R.I.
26. 3 dogs, 9 bitches 3 dogs, 1 bitch BROWN Farmion Cabo de Sta Maria (litter 3) ex Trovoada de Alvalade (import)	3-1-78 Deyanne F. Miller	Ct., N.J., N.Y.
27. 3 dogs, 3 bitches Trezena Monte Clerico (litter 13) ex Alvorada de Alvalade (import, BROWN)	3-10-78 Mr. and Mrs. James E. Santos	N.J., N.Y.
28. 1 bitch Farmion Cabo de Sta Maria (litter 3) ex Amorina de Alvalade (import)	6-18-78 Morgan Cole	Wa.

29. 1 dog, 2 bitches Farmion Cabo de Sta Maria (litter 3) ex Farmion Granja (litter 7)	7-13-78 Nancy W. Lutz	Ct., N.H.
30. 4 dogs, 1 bitch Trezena Marmelete (litter 13) ex Felizardo Odemira (litter 15)	10-1-78 Dr. Virginia M. Glover	Al.
31. 4 dogs, 4 bitches Ancora do Al Gharb (import) ex Trezena Manta Rota (litter 13)	11-2-78 Noreen J. Lowery	Ga., N.J., N.Y.
32. 4 dogs, 6 bitches 1 dog BROWN Limani Sagres (litter 19) ex Farmion Nazare (litter 14)	11-25-78 Deyanne F. Miller	Co., Ct., N.Y.
33. 2 dogs, 4 bitches Ancora do Al Gharb (import) ex Spindrift Kedge (litter 11)	12-1-78 H. E. and B. Whitney	Mi., N.Y., R.I.
34. 2 dogs, 5 bitches Farmion Azinhal (litter 1) ex Zinia de Alvalade (import)	1-12-78 Helen Roosevelt	Ct., Il., Ma., N.Y., R.I.
35. 5 dogs, 2 bitches Farmion Baia de Lagos (litter 2) ex Zaida (import)	11-6-78 Raymond Burr	Ca., Ok.
36. 1 dog Ancora do Al Gharb (import) ex Keel Tarouca (litter 20)	3-10-79 R. Adeline Regan	N.Y.

37. 2 dogs, 7 bitches Ancora do Al Gharb (import) ex Trezena Meia Praia (litter 13)	3-10-79 Jayne L. Kenyon	Ca., Ga., Il., Mi., Pa.
38. 6 dogs, 2 bitches Trezena Monte Clerico (litter 13) ex Spindrift Keel (litter 11)	3-18-79 Joanne Cakoyanis	Ca., Ct., N.J., N.Y., Wa.
39. 3 dogs, 4 bitches 1 bitch BROWN Adonis do Mar (litter 27) ex Rosmaninhal do Mar (litter 18)	10-14-79 Mrs. James E. Santos	Ca., N.J., N.Y., Pa.
40. 5 dogs, 4 bitches Real do Mar (litter 18) ex Alma do Mar (litter 27)	11-14-79 Mrs. J. E. Santos and Mrs. Salome Kaehny	Az., N.J., N.Y.
41. 4 dogs, 1 bitch Granja Cascais (litter 29) ex Limani Salema (litter 19)	12-10-79 Carole S. Boulanger	Ct., Tx., Va.
42. 4 dogs, 3 bitches Keel Tonel (litter 20) ex Peralva do Peixe (litter 16)	1-18-80 Shirley F. and Weston C. Elliot	Ca., Ct., N.J., N.Y.
43. 3 dogs, 4 bitches All BROWN Ninfeia Herculano (litter 8) ex Farmion Umbrias (litter 21)	1-23-80 Una Barrett O'Neill	Ct., Ma., N.Y.

Farmion Nazare,
dam of litters
32, 52, 67, 77
and 85.

Trezena Meia Praia,
shown at three
months of age,
is the dam of
litters 37 and 73.

Peralva do Peixe
is the dam of
litter 42.
Kathryn Braund

44. 7 dogs, 3 bitches Trezena Monte Clerico (litter 13) ex Rama do Mar (litter 18)	2-22-80 Ladd Carmen	Ca., Fl., N.H., N.Y., Pa., Tx.
45. 1 dog, 1 bitch Ancora do Al Gharb (import) ex Keel Tarouca (litter 20)	3-27-80 R. Adeline Regan	N.Y.
46. 5 dogs, 3 bitches Farmion Cabo de Sta Maria (litter 3) ex Farmion Delgadas (litter 4)	4-14-80 Deyanne F. Miller	Ct., Fl., Ma., N.Y., Tx.
47. 1 dog Farmion Azinhal (litter 1) ex Zinia de Alvalade (import)	6-24-80 Helen Roosevelt	Pa.
48. 5 dogs, 2 bitches Farmion Azinhal (litter 1) ex Lusitania Joanica (litter 10)	7-10-80 Andrew V. Christian, Jr.	Ct., N.Y.
49. 3 dogs, 1 bitch Charlie de Alvalade (import) ex Limani Salema (litter 19)	7-15-80 Carole S. Boulanger	Ct.
50. 1 bitch Ancora do Al Gharb (import) ex Spindrift Kedge (litter 11)	7-26-80 H. E. and B. Whitney	N.Y.
51. 4 dogs, 3 bitches Adonis do Mar (litter 27) ex Farmion Nelas (litter 14)	8-27-80 Philip A. Metcalf	Ct., La., N.Y., Pa., Ut., Wa.

52. 5 dogs, 7 bitches 3 dogs, 2 bitches BROWN Charlie De Alvalade (import) ex Farmion Nazare (litter 14)	8-31-80 Deyanne F. Miller	Ca., Ct., Id., Ky., Wa., Bermuda, Portugal
53. 4 dogs, 5 bitches 1 dog, 2 bitches BROWN Charlie de Alvalade (import) ex Granja Cherna (litter 29)	9-12-80 Barbara Brabson	Ca., Ct., N.C., N.Y., Oh.
54. 1 dog, 6 bitches Trezena Monte Clerico (litter 13) ex Keel Torreira (litter 20)	10-7-80 Joanne Cakoyanis	N.Y.
55. 3 dogs, 5 bitches Captree Estafeta (litter 31) ex Rainha do Mar (litter 55)	10-8-80 Mr. and Mrs. J. E. Santos	Ca., Il., N.Y.
56. 3 dogs, 6 bitches Portimao do Peixe (litter 16) ex Captree Esmeralda (litter 31)	10-27-80 Henry O. Muller, DVM	Ga., Ks., N.Y., Va.
57. 4 dogs, 2 bitches Real do Mar (litter 18) ex Captree Estrela (litter 31)	11-7-80 Lee Selinger	N.Y.
58. 7 dogs, 5 bitches Farmion V De Gama (litter 7) ex Farmion Delgadas (litter 4)	12-8-80 Deyanne F. Miller	Ca., Ct., Fl., Ma., Mi., N.J., N.Y., Or., Pa., Wash., D.C.

Morena do Mar, shown winning BOS at eight months of age at the 1980 Spring Specialty. She was the one brown bitch born in litter 39. Bred and handled here by Sonja Santos (do Mar).

Farmion V de Gama, shown here as a puppy in 1975, is the sire of litters 58, 67, 70, 77, 85, 95 and 97.

Michael McCall

59. 5 dogs, 2 bitches
2 dogs BROWN
Duke Jo Jamor
(import) ex
Alianca do Vale Negro
(import)

2-8-81

Grace M. Meisel

Il., Ky., Ma.,
N.Y., Oh.,
Pa., W.V.

60. 5 dogs, 3 bitches
Seadre Jarrow
(litter 36) ex
Bittersweet Herdade
(litter 34)

3-2-81
J. E. and G. McCarthy

N.Y.

61. 1 dog, 3 bitches
Ilha Intrepido
(litter 35) ex
Zaida
(import)

3-24-81
Raymond Burr

Ca.

62. 2 dogs, 5 bitches
Keel Tonel
(litter 20) ex
Amalia do Mar
(litter 27)

4-6-81
Jay and Janet Friedman

Ca., Me.,
Mi., N.Y.

63. 4 dogs, 2 bitches
1 dog, 1 bitch BROWN
Adonis do Mar
(litter 27) ex
Rosmaninhal do Mar
(litter 18)

5-2-81

Kathryn Bowlin Hovey

N.Y., Pa.,
R.I.

64. 7 dogs, 3 bitches
Adonis do Mar
(litter 27) ex
Captre Enfiada
(litter 31)

5-3-81
Noreen Lowery

Fl., N.Y.,
Pa.

65. 4 dogs, 3 bitches
Granja Cascais
(litter 29) ex
Farmion Ferrarias
(litter 32)

5-1-81
John J. Fisk

Az., Ct.,
N.Y., Wa.

66.   4 dogs, 6 bitches   7-11-81   Ct., Fl.,
3 dogs, 1 bitch BROWN   Me., N.Y.,
Charlie de Alvalade   Deyanne F. Miller   Oh.
(import) ex
Farmion Delgadas
(litter 4)

67.   2 dogs, 8 bitches   7-14-81   Az., Ct.
Farmion V de Gama   Deyanne F. Miller   Ma., N.Y.,
(litter 7) ex   Portugal
Farmion Nazare
(litter 14)

68.   4 dogs, 5 bitches   7-13-81   Fl., N.J.,
Redondo do Mar   Mr. and Mrs. J. E.   N.Y.
(litter 18) ex   Santos
Alvorada de Alvalade
(import)

69.   1 bitch   6-29-81   N.Y.
Farmion Baia de Lagos   Dean Long and M. Eloise
(litter 2) ex   Black
Trezena Konsocia
(litter 37)

70.   3 dogs, 6 bitches   7-19-81   Ca., Ct.,
Farmion V de Gama   Barbara Brabson   R.I., Wi.,
(litter 7) ex   Portugal
Granja Cherna
(litter 29)

71.   3 dogs, 2 bitches   8-14-81   Az., N.J.,
All BROWN   N.Y.
Charlie de Alvalade   Una Barrett O'Neill
(import) ex
Farmion Umbrias
(litter 21)

72.   2 dogs, 1 bitch   10-1-81   Ca.
Keel Lagos   Raymond Burr
(litter 38) ex
Zaida
(import)

73. 5 dogs, 4 bitches   12-21-81   Pa.,
Portimao do Peixe   Jayne L. Kenyon   Wash., D.C.,
(litter 16) ex   N.Y., W.V.
Trezena Meia Praia
(litter 13)

74. 5 dogs, 1 bitch   12-24-81   Wa.
Farmion Tafe   M. K. and M. T. Easter
(litter 46) ex
Baleeira
(litter 28)

75. 3 dogs, 1 bitch   1-9-82   Ct., R.I.
1 dog BROWN
Farmion Fiberboard   Deyanne F. Miller
(litter 58) ex
Fe
(import)

76. 2 dogs, 1 bitch   1-9-82   Az., Ky.
Farmion Baia de Lagos   Louis and Lillie B. White
(litter 2) ex
Ilha Iris
(litter 35)

77. 1 bitch   1-28-82   Ct.
Farmion V de Gama   Deyanne F. Miller
(litter 7) ex
Farmion Nazare
(litter 14)

78. 5 dogs, 3 bitches   2-23-82   Ct., Ma.,
1 dog BROWN   N.Y., Pa.
Victor's Venecedor   Helen Roosevelt
(litter 48) ex
Zinia de Alvalade
(import)

79. 3 dogs, 5 bitches   4-17-82   Ct., Il., Mo.,
Afilhado do Mar   Florence Recktenwald   N.Y.
(litter 40) ex   and Sonja Santos
Condessa do Mar
(litter 55)

84

Farmion Fiberboard, shown with Deyanne Miller, is the sire of litters 75, 98 and 101.   *Kathryn Braund*

Farmion Umbrias as a puppy, first brown bitch whelped in the U.S., was the dam of the first all-brown litter, number 43. She is also the dam of litters 71 and 89.

80. 3 dogs, 7 bitches Nativo do Mar (litter 40) ex Keel Beleza, CD (litter 54)	4-15-82 Pamela and Jon Schneller	N.J., N.Y., Pa.
81. 4 dogs, 3 bitches 2 dogs BROWN Cherna Agostos (litter 53) ex Farmion Urze (litter 21)	5-7-82 Betty M. Twiggs	Unknown
82. 4 dogs, 5 bitches Portimao do Peixe (litter 16) ex Trezena Konstelada (litter 37)	6-6-82 Maryanne B. Murray and Linwood A. Kulp, Jr.	Ca., De., Md., N.J., Pa., Wy.
83. 2 dogs, 7 bitches Afilhado do Mar (litter 27) ex Enchantress (litter 57)	6-14-82 Linda A. and John Powers	Fl., N.J., N.Y.
84. 3 dogs, 4 bitches All BROWN Charlie de Alvalade (import) ex Alianca do Vale Negro (BROWN import)	6-14-82 Grace M. Meisel	Ct., Mn., N.Y., Ok.,
85. 6 dogs, 1 bitch Farmion V de Gama (litter 7) ex Farmion Nazare (litter 14)	7-8-82 Deyanne F. Miller	Ca., Ct., Ks., Mt.
86. 1 dog, 3 bitches Farmion Talurdo (litter 46) ex Wharton do Colegio (litter 23)	8-4-82 Martha Sue and Ed Keegan	Tx.

87.   3 dogs, 6 bitches
C.B. Baluarte de Alvalade
(import) ex
Rainha do Mar
(litter 18)

7-14-82
J. E. and Sonja Sanos
Tx.

Az., Ca., Il.,
N.Y., Pa.,

88.   3 dogs, 2 bitches
Keel Tonel
(litter 20) ex
Keel Liberdade
(litter 38)

7-28-82
Joanne Cakoyanis

Ct., N.Y.

89.   3 dogs, 2 bitches
All BROWN
Charlie de Alvalade
(import) ex
Farmion Umbrias
(litter 21)

9-10-82

Una Barrett O'Neill

N.J., N.Y.
Pa.

90.   3 dogs, 5 bitches
4 BROWN
Farmion Tacoes
(litter 46) ex
Raia
(litter 44)

9-14-82

Jennifer Abbott

Ma., N.H.,
S.C., Vt.

91.   5 dogs, 3 bitches
Ilha Irmao
(litter 35) ex
Trezena Konsocia
(litter 37)

9-27-82
Dean Long and M. Eloise
   Brown

Az., Ca.

92.   3 dogs, 2 bitches
Trezena Monte Gordo
(litter 13) ex
Marquesa do Mar
(litter 39)

9-25-82
Mrs. K. Hurwitz

Pa., Va.

93.   8 dogs, 2 bitches
1 BROWN
Raio
(litter 44) ex
Cherna Abilheira
(litter 53)

10-13-82

Maureen Dahms

Ca., Ga.

94. 3 dogs, 1 bitch Avalon Yestrela (litter 51) ex Mareke Vitoria (litter 74)	11-14-82 Bobbe Kurtz	Ca., Wa.
95. 3 dogs, 5 bitches Farmion V de Gama (litter 7) ex Shanesca Passafrio (litter 42)	11-17-82 Lesley B. Stricker	Ct., N.Y.
96. 3 dogs, 3 bitches 2 BROWN Charlie de Alvalade (import) ex Farmion Zimbreira (litter 52)	11-19-82 Clara Corcoran Doyle	Ct., Ky.
97. 3 dogs, 2 bitches Farmion V de Gama (litter 7) ex Farmion Flagday (litter 58)	1-3-83 Mary Ellen Vernon	Ct., Mi.
98. 4 dogs, 5 bitches Farmion Fiberboard (litter 58) ex Farmion Onix (litter 67)	1-14-83 Michael F. Julian	Ct., Mt., N.Y., Pa., Known.
99. 3 dogs, 7 bitches Spindrift Galley (litter 33) ex Avalon Yvivo (litter 51)	1-23-84 Sharon A. Broadhead	Ct., N.C., N.J., Mi.
100. 5 dogs, 1 bitch Spindrift Galley (litter 33) ex Zinia de Alvalade (import)	3-12-83 Helen Roosevelt	Ct., Ma., Mi., N.Y.
101. 5 dogs, 1 bitch Farmion Fiberboard (litter 58) ex Cherna Renewal (litter 70)	3-13-83 Madge Barton Sutter	Mi., N.Y., Pa., Va.

Afilhado do Mar is the sire of litters 79 and 83.

Puppies from litter 101.   *Kathryn Braund*

102. 2 dogs, 2 bitches	4-17-83	Ct.
2 BROWN		
Charlie de Alvalade	Deyanne F. Miller	
(import) ex		
Fe		
(import)		

103. 1 bitch	5-2-83	Va.
Spindrift Galley	P. Schaefer	
(litter 33) ex		
Keel Torreira		
(litter 20)		

104. 2 dogs, 4 bitches	5-22-83	N.J., N.Y.,
4 BROWN		Pa., Wi.
C.B. Baluarte de Alvalade	Kathryn Bowling Hovey	
(import) ex		
Rosmaninhal do Mar		
(litter 18)		

105. 2 dogs, 4 bitches	5-22-83	Il., Ky., Mi.,
Keel Tonel	Eleanor Dee and Rudy	Oh., Pa.
(litter 20) ex	C. Pierce	
Canopus Galacia, CD		
(litter 59)		

106. 4 dogs, 6 bitches	6-25-83	Az., Ca., In.,
5 BROWN		Ma., N.J.,
C.B. Baluarte de Alvalade	Mr. and Mrs. J. Santos	N.Y., R.I.,
(import) ex		Va.
Rainha do Mar		
(litter 18)		

IMPORTS FROM PORTUGAL

(Wherever possible, imports through 1984 are included. Information is as follows: Name of dog, sex, birth date, sire and dam and owner(s).)

Renascenca do Al Gharb (f), 7/12/68. C.B. Lis Algarbiorum ex C.B. Enga Algarbiorum. Mrs. Deyanne F. Miller, Connecticut.

Anzol do Al Ghard (m), 11/2/69. C.B. Lis Algarbiorum ex C.B. Espada Algarbiorum. Herbert H. Miller, Jr., Connecticut.

Ancora do Al Gharb (m), 11/2/69. C.B. Lis Algabiorum ex C.B. Espada Algarbiorum. Fay C. Harback, New York.

Xino do Al Gharb (m), 6/5/69. C.B. Lo Algarbiorum ex C.B. Escuta Algarbiorum. Natalie B. Rees, New York.

Trovoada de Alvalade (f), 10/19/70. C.B. Lumpi de Alvalade ex Ria. Mrs. Deyanne F. Miller, Connecticut.

Febo do Al Gharb (m), 11/17/72. C.B. Lo Algarbiorum ex C.B. Espada Algarbiorum. John A. Scott, New York.

Daho do Al Gharb (f), 3/10/72. C.B. Lo Algarbiorum ex C.B. Espada Algarbiorum. Natalie Rees and Virginia Stone, New York.

Raja do Al Gharb (m), 7/12/68. C.B. Lis Algarbiorum ex C.B. Enga Algarbiorum. George Wauchope, New York.

Xelim de Alvalade (m), 2/24/73. C.B. Lumpi de Alvalade ex C.B. Truta de Alvalade. Dorothy M. and Eric Pearson, Rhode Island.

Zinia de Alvalade (f), 3/18/75. Taro ex C.B. Truta de Alvalade. Miss Helen Roosevelt, Connecticut.

Zingara de Alvalade (f), 3/18/75. Taro ex C.B. Truta de Alvalade. Mr. and Mrs. James Santos, New York.

Zagaia de Alvalade (f), 3/18/75. Taro ex C.B. Truta de Alvalade. William and Elaine Spaller, Connecticut.

Amorina de Alvalade (f), 4/17/76. Taro ex C.B. Truta de Alvalade. Ingela Gram, Oslo, Norway.

Alvorada de Alvalade (f), BROWN, 7/16/76. Taro ex Zulu de Alvalade. Mr. and Mrs. James Santos, New York.

Alvor de Alvalade (m), 7/16/76. Taro ex Zulu de Alvalade. Peter Lewis, California.

Zaida (f), 5/10/75. Tucho ex Pipa. Raymond Burr, California.

Avante de Alvalade (m), 10/16/76. Taro ex C.B. Truta de Alvalade. Peter Lewis, California.

Fe (f), 6/22/79. Tucho ex Juca. Deyanne F. Miller, Connecticut.

Duke do Jamor (m), 10/2/78. Fofo ex Penny. Catherine E. Meisel, New York.

Alianca do Vale Negro (f), BROWN, 10/19/79. C.B. Baluarte de Alvalade ex Kira. Grace M. Meisel, New York.

Charlie de Alvalade (m), BROWN, 5/16/78. Taro ex C.B. Truta de Alvalade. Deyanne F. Miller, Connecticut.

Dolly de Alvalade (f), 5/4/79. Taro ex Tamar. Manuel Corte, New Jersey.

C.B. Baluarte de Alvalade (m), BROWN, 11/16/77. C.B. Arriba de Alvalade ex C.B. Truta de Alvalade. Mr. and Mrs. James Santos, New York.

Joia de Azambuja (f), 5/19/83. Ruby ex Falesia de Azambuja. Emily A. Moody, Massachusetts.

Heroi do Vale Negro (m), 9/5/83. Macuti ex Areia. Louis B. Gaker, M.D., Ohio.

Amora do Condinho (f), 3/10/84. Navegante do Condinho ex Colette de Alvalade. Alice B. and Norman C. Vicha, Ohio.

Import Zingara
de Alvalade,
foundation bitch
of do Mar,
is shown six
weeks in whelp.

Alvorada de Alvalade, first
brown imported bitch and for
many years the only one.

C.B. Baluarte
de Alvalade
is shown in Portugal
before his
departure for
the United States.

Cristina do Condinho (f), 5/20/84. Cherna Reliant ex Isolda de Azambuja. Alice B. and Norman C. Vicha, Ohio.

Capricho do Condinho (m), 5/20/84. Cherna Reliant ex Isolda de Azambuja. Arlene P. Summers and Alice B. Vicha, Pennsylvania.

Cigana do Condinho (f), 5/20/84. Cherna Reliant ex Isolda de Azambuja. Arlene P. Summers and Alice B. Vicha, Pennsylvania.

Carocha do Condinho (f), 5/20/84. Cherna Reliant ex Isolda de Azambuja. Deyanne F. Miller, Connecticut.

Janota do Vale Negro (f), 6/3/84. Cherna Reliant ex Kira. Deyanne F. Miller, Connecticut.

Fidalgo do Condinho (m), BROWN, 6/28/84. Negrito do Condinho ex Darky de Alvalade. Alice B. and Norman C. Vicha and Arlene Summers, Ohio.

Faisca do Condinho (m), BROWN, 6/28/84. Negrito do Condinho ex Darky de Alvalade. Alice B. and Norman C. Vicha and Arlene Summers, Ohio.

Festa do Condinho (f), BROWN, 6/28/84. Negrito do Condinho ex Darky de Alvalade. Arlene P. Summers and Alice B. Vicha, Pennsylvania.

Tejo (m), 1/9/79. Yacht de Alvalade ex Boia. Alice B. and Norman C. Vicha and Arlene Summers, Ohio.

Verbena do Condinho (f), 4/23/83. Chico do Condinho ex Darky de Alvalade. Alice B. and Norman C. Vicha and Arlene Summers, Ohio.

5

Portuguese Pedigrees Behind American Foundations

WE DEDICATE THIS CHAPTER to Dr. Vasco Bensaude, the Portuguese shipping line owner, well remembered for his advancement of the modern Portuguese Water Dog.

In this chapter it is historically important to show pictures as well as pedigrees of the dogs intimately involved in the rebirth of the breed. Wherever possible, we have reproduced photographs as well as pedigrees. Unfortunately, photographs of some of the early dogs have disappeared. In these cases, pedigrees of early stock stand alone.

The pedigrees are not listed alphabetically. They're listed in order of the dog's birth date. Yet, birth dates of some of the early dogs are not known. Where this occurs, these dogs are listed in the appropriate time frame.

It is not possible to reproduce the pedigrees in standard format. Instead, we list them in text format: Name of dog, sex, birth date, registration numbers, sire and dam, sire's sire and dam, dam's sire and dam.

The breeder's name is only given if it is different from the kennel name. Color comments appear with some of these pedigrees.

Following is an explanation of the symbols which describe the various registries, titles, and explanations of the pedigrees:

A.D.   Ascendencia Desconhecida (ancestors unknown)
C.B.   Champion in Portugal

FCI   Federation Cynologique Internationale

LOP   Livro de Origens Portugues—Clube Portugues de Cani-
        cultura Stud Book

R.I.   Initial Registration with Clube Portugues de Canicultura

To recapitulate, the outstanding Portuguese Water Dog in Portugal was Leao. Born in 1931, he was the founding sire of the modern breed.

On August 30, 1951, C.B. Azinhal Algarbiorum and C.B. Dala Algarbiorum produced Farrusca. She became the dam of the Alvalade line (Dr. A.B. Cabral). On December 18, 1953, this same pair also produced a litter of three dogs and one bitch of whom three—C.B. Palma Algarbiorum, C.B. Pacata Algarbiorum, and Padrao Algarbiorum—furthered the Algarbiorum line.

On July 12, 1968, C.B. Lis Algarbiorum and C.B. Enga Algarbiorum, descendants of the above dogs, produced Renascenca do Al Gharb. She was, as you know, the first dog of Portuguese stock to come to America. Renascenca, who is registered with the PWDCA as PWDCA #1, became the dam of PWDCA litters 1, 6, and 7. C.B. Lis Algarbiorum and C.B. Espada Algarbiorum produced Anzol do Al Gharb, PWDCA #2. Anzol was the sire of PWDCA litters 1, 3, 18, and 25.

The pedigrees that follow, of dogs whose lineage is traceable today, are as complete as possible from available records. If we have erred, however slightly, we apologize.

The Pedigrees

Dina (f). LOP 2.402. AD × AD. Black with white.

Leao (m). 6/31. LOP 2.403. Lontra × Cigana. AD × AD. Black with white on chest and paws.

Tavira Algarbiorum (f). 6/1/37. LOP 2.413. Leao × Dina. Lontra × Cigana/AD × AD. Black.

Venesa (f). LOP 2.445. Landrim × Troia. AD × AD. Gray.

Lontra (m). AD × AD.

Silves (m). LOP 6.318. AD × AD.

Cigana (f). AD × AD.

C.B. Murta Algarbiorum (f). 8/18/38. LOP 2.468. Leao × Venesa. Lontra × Cogana/Landrim × Troia. Black with white on chest and paws.

Guia Algarbiorum (f). 8/14/39. LOP 2.413. Leao × Tavira. Lontra × Cigana/Leao × Dina. Black with white on chest.

Quito Algarbiorum (m). LOP 2.995. Leao × C.B. Murta Algarbiorum. Lontra × Cigana/Leao × Venesa.

Escol Algarbiorum (m). 10/15/40. LOP 2.683. Leao × C.B. Murta Algarbiorum. Lontra × Cigana/Leao × Venesa. Black with white on chest and paws.

Hastil Algarbiorum (m). 7/19/41. LOP 2.837. Leao × Guia. Lontra ×

Tavira Algarbiorum.   *Bensaude Archives*

Silves.   *Bensaude Archives*

Cigana/Leao × Tavira. Black with white chest.

Pata Algarbiorum (f). 4/1/43. LOP 3.156. Silves × Tavira. AD × AD/Leao × Dina. Black with white on chest and paws.

Urze Algarbiorum (f). 11/5/45. LOP 3.597. Quito Algarbiorum × Pata Algarbiorum. Leao × C.B. Murta Algarbiorum/Silves × Tavira Algarbiorum.

C.B. Azinhal Algarbiorum (m). 7/6/47. LOP 4.666. Hastil Algarbiorum × Urze Algarbiorum. Leao × Guia Algarbiorum/Quito Algarbiorum × Pata Algarbiorum. Black.

C.B. Dala Algarbiorum (f). 10/13/47. LOP 4.022. Escol Algarbiorum × Pata Algarbiorum/Leao × C.B. Murta Algarbiorum/Silves × Tavira Algarbiorum. Black with white.

Farrusca (f). 8/30/51. LOP 7.481. C.B. Azinhal Algarbiorum × C.B. Dala Algarbiorum. Hastil Algarbiorum × Urze Algarbiorum/Escol Algarbiorum × Pata Algarbiorum.

Esperdicio (m). RI 3.386. AD × AD.

Algarvia (f). LOP 8.438. AD × AD.

Padrao Algarbiorum (m). 12/18/53. LOP 5.734. C.B. Azinhal Algarbiorum × C.B. Dala Algarbiorum. Hastil Algarbiorum × Urze Algarbiorum/Escol Algarbiorum × Pata Algarbiorum. Black.

C.B. Palma Algarbiorum (f). 12/18/53. LOP 5.733. C.B. Azinhal Algarbiorum × C.B. Dala Algarbiorum. Hastil Algarbiorum × Urze Algarbiorum/Escol Algarbiorum × Pata Algarbiorum. Black.

C.B. Pacta Algarbiorum (m). 12/18/53. LOP 5.731. C.B. Azinhal Algarbiorum × C.B. Dala Algarbiorum. Hastil Algarbiorum × Urze Algarbiorum/Escol Algarbiorum × Pata Algarbiorum. Black.

Gale (f). 3.8.57. LOP 7.487. Silves × Farrusca. AD × AD/C.B. Azinhal Algarbiorum × C.B. Dala Algarbiorum.

C.B. lagos De Alvalade (m). 9/13/58. LOP 10.066. Silves × Gale. AD × AD/Silves × Farrusca. Black.

C.B. Orca Algarbiorum (f). 8/19/58. LOP 7.891. C.B. Azinhal Algarbiorum × C.B. Dala Algarbiorum. Hastil Algarbiorum × Urze Algarbiorum/Escol Algarbiorum × Pata Algarbiorum. Black.

C.B. Silvo Algarbiorum (m). 6/9/60. LOP 9.450. C.B. Azinhal Algarbiorum × C.B. Dala Algarbiorum. Hastil Algarbiorum × Urze Algarbiorum/Escol Algarbiorum × Pata Algarbiorum. Black.

Fuseta de Recaredo (f). 5/1/60. LOP 9.855. Esperdico × Algarvia. AD × AD.

Salema Algarbiorum (f). 6/9/60. LOP 9.452. Padrao Algarbiorum × C.B. Palma Algarbiorum. C.B. Azinhal Algarbiorum × C.B. Dala Algarbiorum/C.B. Azinhal Algarbiorum × C.B. Dala Algarbiorum. Black.

Tabu (m). RI 3.931. LOP 2.995. AD × AD.

C.B. Guincho Algarbiorum (m). 3/7/62. LOP 9.809. C.B. Silvo Algarbiorum × C.B. Orca Algarbiorum. Padrao Algarbiorum × C.B.

CB Lagos
de Alvalade.
Bensaude Archives

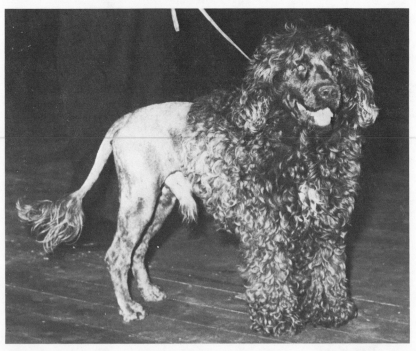

CB Lumpi de Alvalade.

Bensaude Archives

Palma Algarbiorum/C.B. Pacata Algarbiorum × C.B. Palma Algarbiorum. Black.

Lampreia de Alvalade (f). 8/20/62. Quito Algarbiorum × Fuseta de Recaredo. C.B. Leao × C.B. Murta Algarbiorum/Esperdicio × Alvarvia.

C.B. Enga Algarbiorum (f). 9/9/63. LOP 11.086. Tabu × Salma Algarbiorum. AD × AD/Padrao Algarbiorum × C.B. Palma Algarbiorum.

C.B. Escuta Algarbiorum (f). 9/9/63. LOP 11.087. Tabu × Salema Algarbiroum. AD × AD/Padrao Algarbiorum × C.B. Palma Algarbiorum. Black.

C.B. Espada Algarbiorum (f). 9/9/63. LOP 11.088. Tabu × Salema Algarbiorum. AD × AD/Padrao Algarbiorum × C.B. Palma Algarbiorum. Black.

C.B. Lumpi de Alvalade (m). 7/25/65. C.B. Lagos de Alvalade × Lampreia de Alvalade. Silves × Gale/Quito Algarbiorum × Fusetas de Recaredo. Brown.

C.B. Lo Algarbiorum (m). 8/25/66. C.B. Guincho Algarbiorum × C.B. Enga Algarbiorum. C.B. Silvo Algarbiorum × C.B. Orca Algarbiorum/Tabu × Salema Algarbiorum. Black.

C.B. Lis Algarbiorum (m). 8/25/66. LOP 12.929. C.B. Guincho Algarbiorum × C.B. Enga Algarbiorum. C.B. Silvo Algarbiorum × C.B. Orca Algarbiorum/Tabu × Salema Algarbiorum. Black.

Ria [Unofficially, sister to Renescenca do Al Gharb] (f). RI 7.717. C.B. Lis Algarbiorum × C.B. Enga Algarbiorum. C.B. Guincho Algarbiorum × C.B. Enga Algarbiorum/Tabu × Salema Algarbiorum.

6

Current American Breeders of the Portuguese Water Dog

$\mathbf{E}$ACH AND EVERY PORTUGUESE WATER DOG bred in America has helped give eternity to the breed.

At the present time, there is some diversion of type within the breed. Some definite American strains are developing. Dogs from Farmion and do Mar—the two largest kennels—are beginning to display a definite stamp. Using these two kennels as examples in no way detracts from the developing strains of other kennels. Whether a breeder has bred several litters or as few as one, each dog has left a mark upon the breed in some subtle way.

It's interesting to note that while the brown Portuguese Water Dog is still a rarity in the breed (1985), three brown dogs became champions in the first year of AKC recognition. One of these three became the first Best in Show Portuguese Water Dog . . . he is Ch. Charlie de Alvalade, a brown import (Farmion Kennels). At the end of 1984 Charlie was also the most prolific sire and produced the first American brown bitch champion, Ch. Umbrion Kerri (Umbrion Kennels). Ch. Firmamento Kalakua is the first American brown dog champion. Both his parents were bred by James and Sonja Santos (do Mar Kennels). Amazingly, it was only in 1975 that the first brown dog was whelped in the U.S.; this dog was born in a litter owned by Thomas Barrows.

Ch. Charlie de Alvalade, multiple Best in Show winner, demonstrates another best skill, diving under water.   *Steve Krongard*

It's also interesting to note that in the 1970s, American breeders referred to white markings on dogs as follows: white paws were called gauntlets; white hairs on the body or legs were called white threads; and white on the chest was called blaze, crusader's cross, and star.

Avalon

Mr. and Mrs. Philip A. (Diana) Metcalf only wanted a pet for their children. Diana discovered the Portuguese Water Dog in a picture of a black puppy with white chest markings in *Town and Country* magazine. She dreamed about that picture and then called Deyanne Miller. That's how Farmion Nelas, one of the three bitches in Trovoada de Alvalade's litter of 15, came to live with the Metcalfs.

Nelas looked very much like Renascenca. she was mated to Adonis do Mar when she was three years old "to preserve the breed." On August 27, 1980, Nelas whelped seven puppies, 4 males and 3 females. Each has a good temperament. Five of the seven were x-rayed and found free of dysplasia. Each has a correct bite, correct coat and good breed type.

Currently, the Metcalfs own two Portuguese Water Dogs; Nelas and one of her sons. "Our male, Blackie, is robust, our female calm and quiet, even with our three active children. Both will protect our baby at all costs. We find they are excellent guards. They're tremendously close to their owners and are very affectionate."

Diana Metcalf was the PWDCA's corresponding secretary for three years and national membership chairman for three years. She insists she's primarily a pet owner and enjoys helping the breed advance by doing her part in club activities.

Brinmar

Maryanne B. Murray and Linwood A. Kulp, Jr. of Worcester, Pennsylvania went looking to buy a dog that was different, didn't shed, and was intelligent. They came close to purchasing a Standard Poodle. Just before the purchase was made—in January of 1979—Maryanne saw an article in *Life* Magazine on rare breeds. She liked the looks of the Portuguese Water Dog shown in the article, showed the picture to her husband, Linwood, and they went to a rare breed dog show to see one. Both promptly fell in love with the breed.

"Showing wasn't our primary concern when we inquired about breeders. We wanted a good pet. We called a breeder, Jane Kenyon (Trezena Kennels) who had the only litter of Portuguese Water Dogs in the U.S. at the time. She had only two out of nine puppies left. We went to see the two and bought the runt of the litter.

"When our puppy, Brilha (pronounced Bree-uh), now Champion

Trezena Konstelada, was only six months old in August 1979, we entered her in a dog show. We just went to see if we would like showing a dog. She won Best in Show! It's an understatement to say that when she went BIS, showing got into our blood.

"It's gone like that until the present. From buying the runt of the litter, we've come a long way. Linwood is currently President of the PWDCA (1984) and I am Corresponding Secretary (1984).

"We've only had one litter so far. But we'll have more. Our utmost concern in future breeding is furthering good temperament—then conformation. Because if we have to choose one thing it is temperament."

Maryanne Murray and Linwood Kulp have three dogs at home at present and are co-owners of several more. Their stud is Keel Tonel, a black wavy. At this writing, Mr. T, as he is called, is the sire of 52 puppies and is one of the few pure Algarbiorum studs in the country. Brilha, Ch. Trezena Konstelada, is a black curly bitch. She finished in four successive shows with a total of 19 points—all majors—and handled by her owner, Maryanne, who became the first owner-handler to finish a Portuguese Water Dog champion. Brilha was also a two-time Best of Opposite Sex winner at the PWDCA National Specialty—1981 and 1984. Their third dog, Ch. WhiteCap Bianca of Brinmar, is a parti-color (white and black) wavy bitch; the first parti-color champion in the United States.

"We hope," says Maryanne, "that twenty years from now people will say, 'Go to Brinmar for your dog. They breed to the standard.' That's our aim. We hope to maintain what the breed is right now in the standard."

Do Mar

James and Sonja Santos are founding members of the PWDCA. They were long active members of the Long Island Rare Breed Association. They're currently members of the Riverhead KC on Long Island and are associate members of the CPC, FCI and registered breeders with the PWDCA, CPC, and FCI.

Sonja's first Portuguese Water Dog was purchased from the Houghtons of New York in 1965. Her brother-in-law had seen one of Joseph Gratton's English-bred Portuguese Water Dogs on an Albany, New York TV station in early 1960. He told his brother, James, who is of Azorean (Portuguese) descent. James, who saw the ad in the New York Times, immediately took his wife to Bedford Hills to see and then buy a puppy. It was a long automobile trip for Sonja because she had just been released from the hospital and was eating nothing but tea and toast.

"It was worth it," Sonja said as she recalled the afternoon. Fado, one of the puppies, ran to Sonja's feet and stayed close beside her when she sat down to tea and toast at the Houghton's. It was love at first sight for both her and the puppy.

James and Sonja Santos' first Portuguese Water Dog, Fado, bred from English stock.

Real do Mar, sire of two champions in 1984, with owner-breeder, Sonja Santos.

When Fado was two years old, the Santos decided to breed her. Pedro, the intended stud, was a magnificent gray male. Unfortunately, Pedro was not only disinterested but was discovered to be impotent. Fado had two other brothers but the Santos decided against them. The last of the English imports died when Fado passed away in Sonja's arms ten years and ten months later. "She was a wonderful dog," Sonja recalled.

Several months prior to Fado's death—in 1975—the Santos imported a Portuguese Water Dog from Dr. Cabral, president of the CPC and owner of de Alvalade Kennels. The bitch's name was Zingara (meaning Gypsy) de Alvalade. Zingara was black. The Santos had reserved a brown dog but he was shot by a band of roving gypsies as he lay in his kennel. The first time Zingara was put on a plane, the plane was called back when halfway across the ocean because of a bomb scare.

A year later, in October 1976, the Santos imported the first brown from Portugal. She was also from Dr. Cabral's kennels. Her name was Alvorada (meaning dawn) de Alvalade. Because of the political situation, her trip was postponed several times.

Zingara was bred to Anzol do Al Gharb to produce the 18th litter for the breed and do Mar's first. Alvorada was bred to Trezena Monte Clerico to produce the 27th litter. Sonja then bred from members of these two litters. Her kennel was off and running.

The Santos desire to preserve white markings and to breed richly colored brown dogs.

In the middle 1970s, when hip dysplasia was discovered in the breed, Sonja worked hard on the program to help eradicate HD in the Portuguese Water Dog.

She also wants to get gray back into the standard. This color was taken out when the standard was revised by the PWDCA. She sat on the Breed Standard Committee but couldn't save the color. "I saw the most beautiful gray Portuguese Water Dog in 1967; he lived to be 18 years old."

The Santos are cautious breeders. Their do Mar dogs are well put together, nicely balanced dogs.

Sonja beams when asked if she is pleased with the breed's full recognition by the AKC. "I think it's partly through the efforts of every single person who owns a Portuguese Water Dog that we now have a registrable breed."

A founding member of the PWDCA, Sonja served for years as a Director of the club, and for several years as Vice President. She also audited the registry, was Assistant Foreign Registrar, and wrote the PWDCA Policy Book.

Regala

Mr. and Mrs. Rudy C. (Eleanor) Pierce of Bethel, Pennsylvania are owners of three Portuguese Water Dogs who won their championships in 1984.

Yet three years ago (1981), there wasn't a dog in their household.

"I always wanted a dog," Eleanor says. "The type I wanted was a medium size, intelligent dog—something like the Irish Water Spaniel, a breed I admired. I not only wanted a pet, I wanted to show the dog I would buy.

"I saw a Portuguese Water Dog at a dog show and knew immediately this was going to be my breed. The rarity of the breed didn't draw me to it—what did was the intelligence and superb temperament."

Eleanor Pierce and family now own six Portuguese Water Dogs, four females and two males. That's a crowd of dogs for any family.

"This energetic breed is not a dog for a person who wants a quiet house dog—the Portuguese Water Dog has to be in the thick of things at all times."

Eleanor and family are breeding for temperament, type, and structure. They prefer the black Portuguese Water Dog best.

Seawolf

Dr. Richard and Dawn Woods may well be called the pioneers of the breed in the west. Although they didn't become owners of a Portuguese Water Dog until 1981, they have introduced the breed to fanciers throughout the southwest.

The Woods purchased Corky, a wavy adult male, from Deyanne Miller in 1981. "I knew what we were getting when we bought an adult, rather than a puppy," says Dawn.

"I love the joy of every one of these dogs . . . each is really happy," says Dawn in describing the character of the breed. Dawn herself is joyful. "I love the way they think. I love the way they stay close to people."

Shanesca Pico Alto, CD was Best in Show at a California Rare Breeds Association match in 1983. He became a champion in 1984.

Skipper (Ch. Bandido do Mar), their second male, came from do Mar Kennels. The Woods wanted a bitch but got a male instead. Skipper became a champion at 14 months. He was born in June, 1983 on Dawn's birthday.

The Woods started out in dogs with Kerry Blue Terriers in 1948. They loved them, "except for their wet whiskers and because they challenged other animals." They next got into Malamutes and have had six generations of champions. They have also owned Irish Wolfhounds and Papillons. They still own two Papillons.

Starview

Bobbe Kurtz, past owner of the Pet-Pourri, a grooming parlor and pet food store in Fairhaven, Washington, discovered the Portuguese Water Dog in *The Uncommon Dog Breeds*. She had to have a pup. And in 1980, a fat and "absolutely gorgeous" eight-week-old male with a magnificent curly coat entered her life. Even after a day-long airplane trip, he hadn't soiled his crate. In every way, he was just what she had ordered.

"How fortunate I was," Bobbe reminisces. "After smothering him with hugs and kisses, I handed him to my friend who had come to the airport with me. He put his head next to her neck and never moved for the 30-minute ride to her home."

In 1983, Avalon Yestrela (this pup) became father to four puppies. Since 1976, several other Portuguese Water Dogs have been flown into Seattle from the east to Starview.

In late 1984, Bobbe moved to southern California. There she will continue breeding Portuguese Water Dogs.

Spindrift

Ed Whitney and his wife, Barbara, were first-time dog owners when they purchased a Portuguese Water Dog to accompany them on their sailing trips; at the time the Whitneys owned a 30-foot sailboat. They no longer own the boat; they still own Portuguese Water Dogs!

Their first dog was Farmion Algoz. He was killed by a car. Heartbroken, they beseeched Deyanne Miller to please send them another dog. The only dog available was Farmion Alfambra. Deyanne had recently rescued Alfambra—she was a returned dog and was ill. But the Whitneys wanted her. They bred her, "to preserve the breed."

Alfambra's daughter, Spindrift Kedge, UD became the first obedience titled dog for the breed and the first CDX and UD titled dog. Kedge was also the dam of litters 33 and 50. The Whitneys had two Specialty match winners from these litters, Ch. Spindrift Galley, CD and Ch. Spindrift Genoa, CDX.

The Whitneys became so interested in dogs that in 1976 Ed helped found the Long Island Rare Breed Association (LIRBA). He then became president of this club, as well as a participant in rare breed matches held all along the eastern seaboard. When the LIRBA began awarding obedience titles, conforming to all AKC obedience regulations, Ed Whitney's wife, Barbara, won both a CD and CDX title on Kedge at matches.

"We have had the fun and challenge of being personally involved in trying to save an endangered species," says Ed, "the pride of being the first one on the block to own this dog, and the reward of seeing the breed gain acceptance in the dog world."

Trezena

Jayne Kenyon (the distaff side of Mr. and Mrs. E. Niles), Sewickley,

Judge Langdon L. Skarda awarding Avalon Yestrella the Miscellaneous Class ribbon at a Washington show in 1982. Bobbe Kurtz, owner, is standing alongside handler D. Castro.

Barbara and Edward Whitney's four Portuguese Water Dogs: Spindrift Kedge, UD (mother), Ch. Spindrift Genoa, CDX (daughter), Ch. Spindrift Galley, CD (son) and Farmion Alfambra (grandmother).

Pennsylvania, has a historic first in her kennels. Her bitch, Trezena Meia Praia whelped the first parti-color Portuguese Water Dog in the United States. Sire was Priscilla Roosevelt's Portimao do Peixe.

Jane Kenyon's first bitch, Famion Defeza, was the dam of the 13th litter and helped Jayne select her kennel name. *Trezena* means 13 in Portuguese. The litter had 13 puppies. The 13 puppies were born in 1976, America's bi-centennial year. Two-hundred years ago there were 13 colonies in the nation. Farmion Defeza, an improperly coated bitch, has always thrown excellent coats. Trezena Monte Clerico, Pam Schneller's famous "Cappy," was born in this 13th litter.

Umbrion

Umbrion is the kennel name of Mr. and Mrs. Michael J. (Una) O'Neill of Manhasset, New York. Una says, "I'm not really a show person. I got into breeding because I owned a Portuguese Water Dog and felt it was an obligation to the breed and to Deyanne Miller to breed my Bria (Farmion Umbrias) once. I've now bred her three times—the first time was in 1978.

"I absolutely adore the breed. Its intelligence is overwhelming—its exuberance, enthusiasm, dedication to family and work—to guarding and being concerned is fabulous.

"Bria's first litter was sired by Minfeia Herculano and was the first all-brown litter in the United States. Ch. Charlie de Alvalade sired Bria's second and third litters.

"We only have Bria but are looking forward to another dog in the future. With four children to bring up, one dog has been enough. When circumstances allow, we'll have more. We certainly will keep breeding.

"We are proud to have bred the first champion brown bitch, Ch. Umbrion Kerri (Asta). We are proud Asta took BOS to her famous Dad, 'Charlie', at the Philadelphia KC show the day following the Centennial."

Varina

"I still don't know if I'll ever breed my bitch again," smiles Mrs. George (Jayne) McCarthy of West Islip, New York. She will.

Jayne and her husband bred their bitch Bittersweet Herdade in 1981. She had eight puppies. They kept a puppy bitch, Varina Hastada, and spayed the mother. They bred Hastada in 1984 and kept one of her nine puppies, Varina Hospedira.

"Now we have three and three is a crowd. We keep our dogs in the house and, of course, litters are lots of work.

"We just absolutely love Portuguese Water Dogs. Their temperaments are fabulous!"

The McCarthys look like they'll keep on breeding.

Farmion Umbrias, as a puppy, became the foundation matron of Umbrion Kennels.

Ch. Firmamento Kalakua (ChuChu), first American-bred brown champion, relaxes at home.

White Cap

Pam and Jon Schneller discovered the Portuguese Water Dog after reading a newspaper article and after reading *The Uncommon Dog Breeds.* Soon afterwards, they purchased their first dog from Jane Kenyon.

Sailors and water lovers, they purchased a dog that could swim, was odor-free, and would not shed. He was Trezena Monte Clerico (Cappy). When Cappy grew up he won the National Specialty fun matches three out of the four times he competed. He also won many Bests in Show at rare breed shows. Kurt Unkelbach chose Cappy to represent the Portuguese Water Dog in his book, *The Best of Breeds Guide for Young Dog Lovers.*

Even before Cappy died at age five from cancer, Pam and others called him an "immortal Portuguese Water Dog." He was the sire of four litters by dams Alvorada de Alvalade (3 pups), Ramo do Mar (10 pups), Spindrift Keel (7 pups), and Keel Torreira (7 pups). Pam kept the pick female out of Keel Torreira's litter. Named Keel Beleza, CD (Bo), she is the Schneller's foundation bitch and was bred for the first time in 1981. Her puppies have done well in the ring with four of them becoming champions in 1984: Ch. White Cap Chamejar of Regala, Ch. White Cap Capitao do Monab, Ch. White Cap Chloee, and Ch. White Cap Capriccio.

Pam Schneller has served in many capacities for the PWDCA; she was president in 1981 and 1982.

Other Friends of the Breed

These are stories of only a few of the current breeders.

There are also many Portuguese Water Dog owners who have helped advance the breed by allowing their pets to have one litter so these pups could carry on the breed's seed. Each has made a contribution to the breed. Please study the pedigrees as listed in Chapter 4, and remember that although these pages aren't edged in gold, the names of the breeders should be.

We'd like to give you an idea of how intense the interest is among these owners—those who prefer not to breed but just enjoy their dogs. The authors sent out a questionnaire and we've included some of the responses here. There are many rare breed clubs whose members share the same feelings about "their" breed.

From *Sarah A. Holder, Raleigh, N.C.* "I could not resist writing to you since my interest is so keen. We had been married for 26 years and never had a dog. When my twins celebrated their 13th birthday last year we told them they could have a puppy and with that our research began . . . we find our Portuguese Water Dog to be totally dedicated to all members of our family. The first time we took him on our boat and the children were water skiing we thought he was going to jump in and help. Yes, he's an excellent swimmer.

Trezena Monte Clerico.

Four pups—Gnoum, Geronimo, Ghafan, Galileo—from Carolyn Meisel's Canopus Kennels. Carolyn Meisel was the 36th breeder in the United States, importing two dogs from Portugal.

"The word that I think best describes our dog is robust. When I asked the twins, they said awesome."

From *Mrs. Phillip Kessler, Westport, Conn.* "He's so affectionate with people he knows. He's unpredictable to others. Loyal. Tremendous physical strength. Highly intelligent. Protective. Loves Mexican Chili and Italian tomato sauce. There is not a day that passes on our walks that somebody—a perfect stranger—doesn't stop and tell us what a beautiful and handsome dog Sasha is."

From *Mrs. Donna Buckenmaier, Westport, Conn.:* "Describing the character of our Portuguese Water Dog, she always wants to please. She goes swimming by herself in the pool. Whenever someone's head goes under water, she immediately tries to rescue the person by circling overhead, and offering her tail (or hips) as a tow when the person's head appears again. She was never taught to do this."

From *Mrs. Ronald Ronzoni, Manhasset, N.Y.* "Intelligent. Bogart has a white chin, chest and white on front of each paw. These markings are, I think, desirable."

From *Mrs. Rita Sylvia (Praia Kennels),* owner of Cherna Praia da Rocha, CD (Flor): "I was happy to exhibit my Portuguese Water Dog in Miscellaneous class and at matches to acquaint people with this beautiful and rare breed. Flor is a great ambassador for her breed. She is outward-going and likes people and other dogs immensely. In fact, at times she is too friendly and shows no timidness or fear. When I do the wash she is assigned the chore of carrying a towel or facecloth to the basement as I carry the basket. She's wonderful."

Rita Sylvia's poem about Flor sums up the feeling owners have for Portuguese Water Dogs.

"People watch me obey in English and Portuguese
I even lift my paws and hug them to please
Sure, I'll reach out and give you a handshake
And then stand prettily while my picture you take.

"Presently comes our first time in the show ring
Whoops! I have to stand, not sit, for this breed thing
A sweet look at the judge, but to no avail—
Seems she wants to see more happy curl in my tail.

"What's this, a gray ribbon and only fourth place
My mistress is smiling, so it can't be such a disgrace
For our first try, she says, we did just fine
Maybe we'll even win first prize, if given more time.

"So for now, I'll continue with what I like and do best
To introduce you to one who is different from all the rest
It's lonely being the only one here of our kind
But with this great attention, maybe I really don't mind.

"So, if around the dog show you went for a walk
Stopped by this one curly black dog to stare and to talk
Marveled at how I stay without chain or cage
Looked at my picture on N.E.O.N's cover page.

"Then proceeded to ask my mistress how in the water I act
While she talked and elaborated on fact after fact
'Flor is a Cão De Áqua,' she states with pride and with glee
And now you've seen all the other 1,438 dogs at the show . . .
And ME!"

Cherna Praia Da Rocha, CD (Flor), owned by Rita O. Sylvia.

7

Evolution of the Portuguese Water Dog Standard

NO DOG IS BORN PERFECT, just as no human is born perfect.

The standard of a breed describes the best characteristics of the breed and normal features, but also describes weaknesses.

Study a dog's breed standard very carefully; it is a textbook on form and function. The standard teaches you how to recognize the good and bad characteristics of the breed.

The standard is judiciously followed by conscientious dog breeders who want to develop better dogs. It gives them a breeding ideal to aim for.

Without breed standards, there would be no specific breed as a Basset Hound or a Dalmatian. There would just be breed conglomerates. All dogs would be composed of various breeds.

A breed isn't developed in one generation. It comes about after many generations when the animals develop distinctive characteristics. The evolution of a breed is a slow process and the Portuguese Water Dog owes his existence to early breeders who patiently mated like to like.

The evolution of this breed is believed to have taken place many centuries ago when his function was pastoral rather than nautical.

When Portugal became his homeland, he learned to herd fish instead of sheep. He was taught to retrieve lost tackle rather than lost lambs and to carry messages rather than bags of wool.

Many cynologists now believe that the Cão de Áqua was the same celebrated water dog claimed to have been used by sportsmen to enrich breeding lines in many old world sporting dogs.

And, as with most dog breeds prior to the twentieth century, the British were often the first to record much of what we presently know about the formation of various races. Most breeds became known by what these Britons wrote about them.

Since few Englishmen or Europeans knew the Water Dog as he lived in Portugal, the breed was largely ignored until well into the twentieth century. Most of the breed had already died out when Vasco Bensaude rescued several specimens in the early 1930s.

With the purchase of Leao, a fisherman's dog, in the Algarve district, Bensaude began a revival of the breed. He knew that if the Cão de Áqua was to survive in its pure state, recognition was imperative, and so he made this his goal.

Leao, fortunately, besides being a great working dog, was an excellent specimen. And he was prepotent. The bitches Vasco Bensaude bred to him threw puppies that mirrored their sire's type and temperament.

Development of the First Standard

Vasco Bensaude put two of his friends, medical veterinarians Professor Manuel Fernandes Marques and Capitao Frederico M. Pinto Soares, to work. He asked them to write a standard for the Cão de Áqua. In 1938, the standard was completed and then approved by the Clube Portuguese de Canicultura and published.

Here is the text of Professor Marques' and Capitao Soares' standard translated into English. While this work has been translated into English a number of times, none of the writers could agree on some of the definitions. This is because the Portuguese word, as the Portuguese sentence, does not always follow English rules. We think you will find it interesting to view the translation in this light.

Professor Marques, whom, it is reported, did the bulk of the work, entitled the standard, *O Cão D'Áqua, Estalao da Raca,* meaning *Standard of the Race for the Water Dog.*

The accompanying chart presents the standard in Portuguese.

Review the standard. You'll agree Professor Marques' points are well defined. You'll also agree the AKC standard following adheres to his in all but terminology.

This close relationship pays tribute to doctor Marques' scientific study of the breed. Without doubt, he was well qualified to define characteristics breeders could follow.

116

ESTALÃO DO CÃO DE ÁGUA

STANDARD DU CHIEN D'EAU PORTUGAIS

STANDARD OF THE PORTUGUESE WATER DOG

The standard in Portuguese.

Bensaude Archives

ESTALÃO DO
CÃO DE ÁGUA PORTUGUÊS

APROVADO PELA

SECÇÃO DE CANICULTURA

DO

CLUBE DOS CAÇADORES PORTUGUESES
Membro da Fédération Cynologique Internationale

E PROPRIETÁRIO DO

LIVRO PORTUGUÊS DE ORIGENS

———

RESUMO DOS TRABALHOS ELABORADOS
pelos Médicos Veterinários
Capitão FREDERICO M. PINTO SOARES

e

Professor MANUEL FERNANDES MARQUES

———

TRADUCTION FRANÇAISE, PAGE 15
ENGLISH TRANSLATION, PAGE 29

118

ESTALÃO DO CÃO DE ÁGUA

DESCRIÇÃO GERAL

Solar e sua distribuição geográfica. Em épocas muito remotas o Cão de Água teve o seu solar em todo o litoral português. Hoje, pela contínua modificação da arte da pesca, encontra-se principalmente no Algarve, região esta que é o seu actual solar.

A sua presença nas costas de Portugal deve remontar a épocas muito idas, devendo o Cão de Água ser considerado como uma raça do país.

Lugar nas classificações científica e utilitária. Cão mesomorfo, sub-convexilínio com tendências para rectilínio; tipo bracóide.

Nadador e mergulhador exímio e resistente, inseparável companheiro do pescador, a quem presta inúmeros serviços, tanto na pesca como na guarda e defesa do seu barco e propriedade.

Durante a faina da pesca atira-se, voluntàriamente, ao mar para apanhar e trazer o peixe escapado, mergulhando se for necessario, e procedendo da mesma forma se alguma rêde se parte ou algum cabo se solta.

É empregado também como agente de ligação entre o barco e a terra, e vice-versa, mesmo quando a distância é apreciável.

Animal de inteligência invulgar, compreende e obedece fàcilmente e com alegria a todas as ordens do seu dono.

Temperamento, carácter, etc. Animal de temperamento ardente, voluntarioso e altivo, brigão por índole, sóbrio e resistente à fadiga. Tem a expressão dura e um olhar penetrante e atento.

Possui grande poder visual e apreciável sensibilidade olfactiva.

É dócil e obediente para quem dele cuide e com frequência o acompanhe.

Conformação. Tipo mediolínio, harmónico de formas, equilibrado, robusto e bem musculado. Nota-se nele o desenvolvimento muscular devido à constante natação.

DESCRIÇÃO DETALHADA

CABEÇA

Bem proporcionada, forte e larga.

Crânio. Visto de perfil o seu comprimento predomina levemente sobre o do chanfro. A sua curvatura é mais acentuada posteriormente e a crista occipital é pronunciada.

Visto de frente os parietais têm a forma abobadada com leve depressão central; a fronte é ligeiramente escavada, o sulco frontal prolonga-se até dois terços dos parietais e as arcadas supra-ciliares são proeminentes.

Chanfro. Mais largo na base que na extremidade. A chanfradura nasal é bem definida e situada um pouco atrás do canto interno dos olhos.

Narinas. Largas, abertas e de fina pigmentação. De cor preta nos exemplares de pelagem preta, branca e suas combinações. Nos acastanhados, a cor segue a tonalidade da pelagem, mas nunca deve ser almarada.

Beiços. Labios fortes especialmente na parte da frente. Comissura não aparente. Mucosa bocal (céu da boca, debaixo da língua e gengivas) acentuadamente pigmentada de preto.

Maxilares. Fortes e correctos.

Dentes. Bons e não aparentes. Caninos fortes e desenvolvidos.

Olhos. Regulares, aflorados, arredondados, afastados e levemente oblíquos. A coloração da íris é preta ou castanha e as pálpebras, que são finas, orladas de preto. Conjutiva não aparente.

Orelhas. Inserção acima da linha dos olhos, colocadas contra a cabeça, levemente abertas para trás e cordiformes. Leves e a sua extremidade nunca ultrapassa a garganta.

CORPO

Pescoço. Direito, curto, redondo, musculado, bem lançado e de porte alto, ligando-se ao tronco de uma forma harmoniosa. Sem colar nem barbela.

Peito. Largo e profundo. O seu bordo inferior deve tocar o plano do codilho. As costelas são compridas e regularmente oblíquas, proporcionando grande capacidade respiratória.

Garrote. Largo e não saliente.

Dorso. Direito, curto, largo e bem musculado.

Lombo. Curto e bem unido à garupa.

Abdómen. Reduzido volume e elegante.

Garupa. Bem conformada, levemente inclinada, ancas simétricas e pouco aparentes.

Cauda. Inteira, grossa à nascença e de fina terminação. Inserção média. O seu comprimento não deve ultrapassar o curvilhão. Na atenção enrola-se em óculo, não indo além da linha média dos rins. É um precioso auxiliar na natação e mergulho.

MEMBROS ANTERIORES

Fortes e direitos.

Espádua. Bem inclinada de perfil e transversalmente. Forte desenvolvimento muscular.

Braço. Forte e de comprimento regular. Paralelo à linha média do corpo.

Antebraço. Comprido e de forte musculatura.

Carpo. Forte ossatura, mais largo de frente que de lado.

Metacarpo. Longo e forte.

Mão. Arredondada e espalmada. Dedos pouco arqueados, de comprimento médio. A membrana digital, que acompanha o dedo em todo o seu comprimento, é constituída por tecidos flácidos e guarnecida por abundante e comprida pelagem. As unhas pretas são as preferidas, mas, segundo as pelagens, também são admitidas as brancas, raiadas ou castanhas. Unhas levemente afastadas do solo. Sola rija no tubérculo plantar e de espessura normal nos tubérculos digitais.

MEMBROS POSTERIORES

Bem musculados e direitos.

Coxa. Forte e de regular comprimento. Muito bem musculada. A rótula não se afasta do plano médio do corpo.

Perna. Comprida e muito bem musculada. Não se afasta do plano médio do corpo. Bem inclinada no sentido antero-posterior. Toda a estrutura ligamentosa é forte.

Nádega. Comprida e de boa curvatura.

Tarso. Forte.

Metatarso. Comprido. Nunca há dedos suplementares.

Pés. Em tudo idêntico às mãos.

APRUMOS

Os aprumos dos membros anteriores e posteriores são regulares. Admitem-se os membros anteriores levemente estacados e os posteriores um pouco acurvilhados.

ANDAMENTO

Movimentos desembaraçados, passo curto, trote ligeiro e cadenciado, galope inérgico.

PELAGEM

Todo o corpo encontra-se abundantemente revestido de resistente pêlo. Há duas variedades de pelagem: uma mais comprida e encaracolada e outra mais curta e encarapinhada.

A primeira variedade é ligeiramente lustrada e fofa, a segunda atochada, baça e reunida em mechas cilindriformes. À excepção dos sovacos e virilhas os pêlos distribuem-se por igual em todo o tegumento. Na cabeça tomam o aspecto de trunfa, na pelagem encaracolada; de carapinha na outra variedade. O pêlo das orelhas adquire maior comprimento na variedade de pelagem encaracolada.

A coloração da pelagem é simples ou composta; naquela existe o branco, preto e castanho nas suas tonalidades; nesta, misturas de preto ou castanho com o branco.

A pelagem branca deve existir sem albinismo, pelo que as ventas, bordos palpebrais e interior da boca devem ser pigmentados de negro.

Nos exemplares onde entram as cores preta e branca a pele é ligeiramente azulada.

Pelugem não tem.

É característica nesta raça a tosquia parcial da pelagem quando esta se torna muito comprida.

A metade posterior do corpo, o focinho e a cauda são tosquiados, ficando todavia nesta uma pequena borla na ponta.

ALTURA

Nos machos a altura típica é de 54 cms., admitindo-se à classificação um mínimo de 50 cms. e um máximo de 57 cms.

Nas fêmeas a altura deve ser de 46 cms.; o mínimo e máximo respectivamente de 43 e 52 cms.

PESO

Nos machos deve variar entre 19 e 25 quilos; nas femeas entre 16 e 22 quilos.

DEFEITOS QUE IMPLICAM DESQUALIFICAÇÃO

Cabeça. Muito longa, estreita, chata e afilada.

Chanfro. Muito afunilado ou ponteagudo.

Narinas. Almaradas no todo ou em parte.

Olhos. Gázeos, claros, desiguais na forma ou no tamanho, muito salientes ou muito encovados.

Orelhas. Má inserção, muito grandes, muito curtas ou dobradas.

Cauda. Amputada, rudimentar ou não existente. Pesada, caída na acção ou erecta perpendicularmente.

Pêlo. Diferente dos tipos descritos

Pés. Existência de pesunhos.

Albinismo.

Gigantismo ou **Nanismo.**

Prognatismo. Em qualquer das maxilas.

Surdez. Congénita ou adquirida.

TABELA DE PONTUAÇÃO

Pontos positivos

	Machos	Fêmeas
1. Cabeça e seu porte, crânio, orelhas, olhos, chanfro, boca, chanfradura nasal, ventas	20	20
2. Pescoço, garrote, espáduas, membros anteriores	10	7
3. Peito, rins, linha superior e inferior do corpo	15	15
4. Garupa, bacia, membros posteriores	10	13
5. Pés, dedos, unhas	10	10
6. Cauda e seu porte, forma, inserção	5	5
7. Pêlo e sua textura, cor, densidade	5	5
8. Aspecto geral, harmonia de formas, andamento, corpulência, caracteres sexuais	25	25
	100	100

Pontos negativos

1. Apresentação má ou deficiente	10
2. Hérnias	10
3. Leves defeitos, deformações acidentais ou congénitas	7
4. Massas tumorais	20
5. Mau estado de nutrição da pele e mau pêlo	25
6. Pequenas lesões de carácter transitório	3
7. Raquitismo manifesto	25
	100

This picture of Sagres, Leao and Olhao—Algarbiorum dogs—shows the look-alike results Vasc Bensaude had in preserving the Cão de Áqua in its original form. Olhao is a silver-grey.

Bensaude Archiv

Compare this picture of Farmion Albuferia (taken in 1971) with that of Leao in Chapter 2, proving the same characteristics pass on.

He wrote:

With the publication of this work, those whose interests have been awakened by this magnificent race, as well as it ought to be, can now orient their creations in the sense of breeding exemplary dogs, for it is our conviction that for now the standard, when it does become official, should not differ much from what we have written down.

Thanks to Capitao Soares, and to the Portuguese fishermen who created the definite Cão de Áqua type from ancient type in the image and likeness of the sea life and sea work they shared, the breed is healthy and growing today.

Thanks also to Vasco Bensaude, who saved the Portuguese Water Dog in his original form. Obviously, these twentieth century Portuguese Water Dog pioneers did everything possible to maintain the remarkable breed's natural and unique working and structural qualities.

STANDARD OF THE PORTUGUESE WATER DOG

(Marques/Soares)

Origin and geographical distribution—In bygone times this race existed everywhere along the coasts of Portugal. Today, owing to modifications in the fishing systems used, the race has become restricted practically to the province of Algarve which should now be considered its home.

The presence of these dogs along our coast can be traced back to very remote times and entitles them to be regarded as a purely Portuguese breed.

Scientific and utilitarian classifications—Meso-morphal, sub-convexilinial type showing tendencies towards the rectilinial; bracchoid form.

A swimmer and diver of quite exceptional qualities and stamina, this dog is the inseparable companion of the fisherfolk to whom it is of great utility not only during fishing but also as a guard to defend their boats and property.

Whilst his master is fishing the dog is attentive and, should a fish escape (from hook or net), jumps, voluntarily, into the sea to retrieve it, diving under water if necessary. It also swims out to retrieve any broken net or loosened rope end.

These animals are also employed as couriers between boat and land, or vice-versa, even when the distance is considerable.

A dog of exceptional intelligence it obeys any orders given by its master with facility and apparent pleasure.

Temperament, character, etc.—An animal with a fiery disposition and self-willed, brave and very resistant to fatigue. It has a hard-penetrating and attentive expression, splendid sight and a fair nose. It is absolutely docile and obedient with those who look after it and with whom it works.

General form—Mediolinial type, well-balanced, robust and well-muscled. The muscular development due to constant swimming is noticeable.

Head—Well-proportioned and massive.

Skull—Seen in profile it is slightly longer than the muzzle, its curvature more accentuated at the back than in front and it possesses a well defined occiput. From the front the parietal bones are seen to be domed-shaped and to have a slight depression in the middle. The forehead has a central furrow for two thirds of the length of the parietals and the frontal bones are prominent. **Muzzle**—Is narrower at the nose than at its base. The stop, which is well defined, is slightly further back than the inner corner of the eyes.

Nose—Wide. Nostrils well open and finely pigmented. Black, in animals with black, black and white or white coats. In browns the nose is of the same colour as the coat. Flesh-coloured or discoloured noses are a disqualification.

Lips—Thick, especially in front. Inner corner of lips not apparent. Mucous membrane (roof of mouth, under the tongue and gums) well ticked with black or quite black.

Jaws—Strong and neither over- nor undershot.

Teeth—Not apparent. Canines strongly developed.

Eyes—Medium-sized, set well apart and a bit obliquely, roundish and neither prominent nor sunken. Brown or black in colour. The eyelids, which are of fine texture, have black edges. No haw.

Ears—Leather heart-shaped, thin in texture and set well above the line of the eyes. Except for a small opening at the back, the ears are held nicely against the head. The tips should not reach below the beginning of the neck.

Body—

Neck—Straight, short, nicely rounded and held high. Strongly muscled. No mane and no dewlap.

Brisket—Wide and deep, reaching down to the elbow. Ribs long and well-sprung.

Withers—Wide and not prominent.

Back—Short and nicely joined to the croup.

Abdomen—Held well up in a graceful line.

Croup—Well-formed and only slightly inclined, with hips hardly apparent.

Tail—Not docked, thick at the base and tapering; medium setting. It should not reach down below the hock. When the dog is attentive the tail should be held in a ring, the front of which should not reach beyond the line of the kidneys. The tail is of great help when swimming and diving.

Forelegs—Strong and straight.

Shoulder—Well-inclined and very strongly muscled.

Leao, groomed in Lion Clip for a dog show, is a study of the well-balanced, robust and well-muscled body of the ideal Portuguese Water Dog. *Bensaude Archives*

This picture of Leao shows him still wet from swimming in the ocean. The ideal skull shape and obliquely placed, roundish eyes are not obscured by the coat.

Bensaude Archives

Upper Arm—Strong and of regular length, parallel to the medial body line.

Forearm—Long and strongly muscled.

Knee—Heavy-boned, wider in front than at the side.

Pastern—Long and strong.

Forefeet—Round and rather flat. Toes not too knuckled up and not too long. The membrane between the toes, which reduces the tip of these, is of soft skin well covered with hair. Black nails are preferred but whites, browns and striped are allowed according to the colour of the coat. Nails held up slightly off the ground. Central pad very thick, others normal.

Hind Legs—Straight and strongly muscled.

Thigh—Strong and of regular length. Very strongly muscled. Thigh bones parallel to the medial body line.

Second Thigh—Long and strongly-muscled, parallel to the medial body line. Decidedly inclined from front to back. All the tendons well developed.

Buttocks—Long and well curved.

Hock—Strong.

Metatarsus—Long. No dewclaws.

Hind Feet—Similar, in all respects, to the fore feet.

Position of Legs—Regular. It is admissible for the front legs to be held so that feet are slightly in front of the perpendicular and the back legs, from the hock downwards, also a bit forward.

Movements—Gay, short steps walking, a light trot and an energetic gallop.

Coat—Profuse coat, of strong hair, covering the whole body evenly except for the under-arms and groin where it is thinner.

There are two varieties of coat.

In one: the hair is fairly long, wavy, rather loose with a slight sheen. The hair on the top of the head is upright and that on the ears decidedly longer than the leather.

In the other: the hair is shorter, forms compact cylindrical curls, thickly planted and somewhat lustreless. On the top of the head the hair is similar to that of the rest of the coat, whereas that on the ears is, sometimes, wavy.

Colours are black, white and various tones of brown; also combinations of black, or brown with white.

A white coat does not imply albinism provided nose, mouth and eyelids are black.

In animals with black, white, or black and white coats the skin is decidedly bluish.

There is no undercoat.

As soon as the coat grows long the middle part and hind quarters of

e strong hindquarters and well-muscled thighs of this Portuguese Water Dog about to leap off the
ck are typical features of dogs of this breed.   *Wayne Arnst*

ro, an Algarbiorum dog, showing the clip the Portuguese used, with the middle part as well as the
dquarters clipped.   *Bensaude Archives*

131

these dogs, as well as the muzzle, is clipped. At the end of the tail the hair is left at full length.

Height—

Males between 19.68 inches (50 cms) and 22.44 inches (57 cms); the ideal height being 21.25 inches (54 cms).

Females between 16.92 inches (43 cms) and 20.47 inches (52 cms); the ideal height being 18.11 inches (46 cms).

Weight—

Males between 41 pounds 14 ounces and 55 pounds 2 ounces (19 to 25 kilos).

Females between 35 pounds 4 ounces and 48 pounds 8 ounces (16 to 22 kilos).

Disqualifications—

Head—Very long, narrow, flat or pointed.

Muzzle—Funnel-shaped or too pointed.

Nose—Flesh-coloured or discoloured, totally or in part.

Eyes—Light-coloured, different to each other in form or size; sunken or bolting.

Ears—Wrong setting, very big, very small or having folds.

Tail—Docked, rudimentary or non-existent. Heavy, droopy in action or held perpendicularly.

Hind Feet—Existence of dewclaws.

Coat—Different from the types described.

Albinism

Over- or undersized animals

Undershot or overshot jaws

Deafness—Either inherited or acquired.

Scale of Points

Positive Points—

1. Head and how held, skull, muzzle, stop, nose, mouth, eyes and ears. Males 20; Females 20.

2. Neck, withers, shoulders and forelegs. Males 10; Females 7.

3. Brisket, loins, upper and lower line of body. Males 15; Females 15.

4. Croup, pelvis, hind legs. Males 10; Females 13.

5. Feet, toes, nails. Males 10; Females 10.

6. Tail and how held, form and setting. Males 5; Females 5.

7. Coat and its texture, colour, density. Males 5; Females 5.

8. General aspect, harmony of form, movement, corpulency, sexual development. Males 25; Females 25.

Total positive points, 100.

Nero, showing the length of hair on a typical curly coat before trimming.

Bensaude Archives

Leao is measured by Fausto.

Negative Points—

1. Deficient or bad presentation, 10.
2. Rupture, 10.
3. Small defects, accidental or congenital, 7.
4. Tumours, 20.
5. Bad coat or deficient nutrition of the skin, 25.
6. Small injuries of a transitory nature, 3.
7. Rickets and their after affects, 25.

Total negative points, 100.

The Standard is Translated

Marques' and Soares' standard was updated in 1951 when it was translated into English. The changes made were in sentence structure.

The English version of this revised standard was accepted in January 1974 by the Clube Portuguese Canicultura (CPC) having reciprocal agreements with the Kennel Club of England. One change was made at this time. Deleted was the phrase *brawler by nature*. The Portuguese Water Dog is not a brawler by nature!

This translation was then approved by the Federation Cynologique Internationale (FCI), also in January 1974. This version then became FCI's official standard for the breed.

In March 1974, when the Portuguese Water Dog Club of America, Inc. (PWDCA) was two years old, it adopted this standard. The club revised it in October 1980, clarifying some foreign words and phrases. The "clarifying" words and phrases did not concern themselves with physical characteristics of the dog; they merely gave better English phrasing of the words used to describe him. As an example, the words "strong and wide" head was substituted for "massive head."

The PWDCA again revised the standard in December 1980, making two more minor word changes. They made this revision in the expectation that the American Kennel Club (AKC) would approve the breed for its showcase class of rare breeds, called the Miscellaneous class.

And on June 3, 1981, after several more minor changes were made to satisfy AKC requirements, the breed was accepted in the Miscellaneous class at AKC all-breed dog shows. Portuguese Water Dogs then became eligible to earn Obedience and Tracking titles at AKC obedience trials.

The AKC suggested several more nomenclature changes before the standard could be accepted. Approval of the PWDCA standard by the AKC Board of Directors came on May 10, 1983 in anticipation of the breed being granted full registration privileges.

These changes were made. They are word changes and correspond with the accepted definitions as listed in AKC's *The Complete Dog Book.* We list them although not all of the terms were utilized. They are listed in

An improper Portuguese Water Dog coat.

An improper Portuguese
Water Dog coat.

An improper Portuguese Water Dog coat.

An improper Portuguese
Water Dog coat.

the order in which they were to appear in the currently approved standard.

From	To
buttocks	rump
dome-shaped	domed
The forehead	Above the eyes (AKC did not need to change)
forehead	frontal bones (AKC did not need to change)
Abdomen	Tuck-up
knee	carpals
Hamstrings	All structural ligaments (AKC did not need to change)
membrane	webbing
under-arms	forearm meets the brisket

With these changes made, the AKC then authorized the opening of the AKC Stud Book to the Portuguese Water Dog in the Working Group effective August 1, 1983. The AKC also approved the offering of regular show classification for the breed as of January 1, 1984. It set a March 1, 1984 closing date for registering the breed's foundation stock.

With AKC approval, we publish its currently approved standard.

Official Standard for the Portuguese Water Dog
as approved by The American Kennel Club, May 10, 1983

The Board of Directors has approved the following Standard for Portuguese Water Dogs. On and after January 1, 1984 regular show classification for the breed may be offered at all-breed shows.

General Appearance—Medium build, well-balanced, robust, and well-muscled. The muscular development due to constant swimming is noticeable. The breed is shown in its natural stance which is for the front legs to be positioned so that the feet are slightly forward at the shoulders and the hind legs are positioned approximately under the rump.

Head—Well-proportioned, strong and wide.

Skull—Seen in profile it is slightly longer than the muzzle, its curvature more accentuated at the back than in the front, and it possesses a well-defined occiput. The top of the skull appears to be domed and to have a slight depression in the middle. The forehead has a central furrow for two-thirds of the distance between the forehead and the occiput. The forehead is prominent.

Muzzle—Is narrower at the nose than at its base.

Stop—The stop is well-defined.

Nose—Wide. Nostrils well-flared and finely pigmented. Black in animals with black, black and white, or white coats. In brown, the nose is the same color as the coat.

Teeth—Not visible when the mouth is closed. Canines strongly developed. Teeth meet in a scissor or level bite.

Jaws—Strong and neither over nor under shot.

Eyes—Medium size, set well apart, roundish and neither prominent nor sunken. Brown or black in color. The eyelids, which are of fine texture, have black edges. The haws are dark and are not apparent.

Ears—Leather heart-shaped, thin in texture and set well above the line of the eyes. Except for a small opening at the back, the ears are held nicely against the head. The tips should not reach below the lower jaw.

Lips—Thick, especially in front. No flew. Mucous membrane (roof of mouth, under the tongue, and gums) well-ticked with black, or quite black, in black or white dogs. In brown same as coat.

Body—*Neck*—Straight, short, nicely rounded and held high. Strongly muscled. No mane and no dewlap. *Brisket*—Wide and deep, reaching down at the elbow. *Ribs*—Long and well-sprung. *Back*—Short and meets the croup smoothly. Good tuck-up.

Croup—Well formed and only slightly inclined, with hip bones hardly apparent.

Tail—Not docked, thick at the base and tapering, medium setting. It should not reach down below the hock. When the dog is attentive, the tail should be held in a ring, the front of which should not reach beyond the forward line of the hips. The tail is of great help when swimming and diving.

Forequarters—The forelegs are strong and straight. *Shoulder* is well inclined and very strongly muscled. The upper arm is strong. The forearm is long and strongly muscled. The carpus is heavy-boned, wider in front than at the side. *Pasterns*, long and strong. *Dew-claws* may be removed.

Hindquarters—The thigh is very strongly muscled. When viewed from the rear, the thigh bones are parallel. Second thigh, long and strongly muscled, decidedly inclined from front to back. Hamstrings are well developed. The rump is long and well-curved. Hock is strong. When viewed from the rear, the hind legs are straight and very strongly muscled. Metatarsus, long and *no dew-claws. Feet*—Round and rather flat. Toes not too knuckled up and not too long. The webbing between the toes, which reaches the tip of these, is of soft skin well covered with hair. Black nails are preferred, but whites, browns, and striped are allowed according to the color of the coat. *Nails* held up slightly off the ground. Central pad very thick, others normal.

Coat—Profuse coat, of strong hair, covering the whole body evenly except where the forearm meets the brisket and the groin where it is thinner. There is no undercoat, mane or rough.

There are two varieties of coat:

Wavy: fairly long, wavy, rather loose with a slight sheen. The hair on the top of the head is upright and that on the ears is decidedly longer than the leather.

Curly: the hair forms compact cylindrical curls, thickly planted and somewhat lusterless. On the top of the head the hair is similar to that for the rest of the coat, whereas that on the ears is, sometimes, wavy.

Clips—Two clips are acceptable:

Lion Clip: as soon as the coat grows long, the middle part and hindquarters of these dogs, as well as the muzzle, are clipped. At the end of the tail the hair is left at full length.

Working-Retriever Clip: in order to give a natural appearance and a smooth unbroken line, the entire coat is scissored or clipped to follow the outline of the dog leaving a short blanket of coat no longer than 1 inch in length. At the end of the tail, the hair is left at full length.

Colors: are black, white, and various tones of brown, also combinations of black or brown with white. A white coat does not imply albinism provided nose, mouth, and eyelids are black. In animals with black, white, or black and white coats, the skin is decidedly bluish.

Gait—Short, lively steps when walking, at a trot it is a forward striding, well-balanced movement.

Height—Males between 20 and 23 inches. Females between 17 and 21 inches.

Weight—Males between 42 and 60 pounds. Females between 35 and 50 pounds.

Faults—Any deviation from these specifications is a fault; the degree to which a dog is penalized is dependent upon the extent to which the dog deviates from the standard and the extent to which the particular fault would actually affect the working ability of the dog.

Temperament—A dog of exceptional intelligence, it obeys any orders given by its master with facility and apparent pleasure. It is obedient with those who look after it and with those for whom it works. An animal of spirited disposition, independent, brave and very resistant to fatigue, it has a hard, penetrating and attentive expression, splendid sight and a fair nose.

8

The Portuguese Water Dog Standard Defined

WHY DO WE DEFINE the words in a breed standard? Don't the words in the breed standard sufficiently explain what the dog should look and act like? Well, the words in standards are guideline words, open to interpretation. Unless you know a breed intimately, words really don't tell you all you need to know.

After all, a breed standard is of little value unless you understand exactly why it's written the way it is, what it means, and how practical it is. We will define it so that you'll be able to better understand the Portuguese Water Dog. If, for instance, the Portuguese dog fanciers who rescued the breed from oblivion—Vasco Bensaude (Algarbiorum Kennels) and Dr. Antonio Cabral (de Alvalade Kennels) weren't able to revive the breed according to the physical and mental characteristics called for in Portugal's original standard, breed type would have been lost. Extinction of the Portuguese Water Dog would have followed quickly.

When Deyanne F. Miller, America's first lady of the breed, read about the breed and then studied the Portuguese standard, she next had to see the dog in its home environment. Personally observing the dogs gave her a substantial feel for the breed. It brought it alive for her.

This is what we want to do here, in this chapter. We want to make the standard come alive for you. Consider the llama.

Recently, llamas stormed the livestock arena contests in the western United States. Enthusiasts of this cousin to the camel sell llamas as pack animals; they are extremely easy keepers. At the first livestock contest held for llamas in Montana (Great Falls, 1984), the judge said, "There really aren't any standards for llama judging yet. My opinion is it." This judge, in exercising his personal preference in awarding best llamas in the show, followed some of the "trends" the bigger breeders were doing.

We won't follow trends here. While llamas are comparatively new to the livestock contest scene and a standard for judging and breeding has yet to be defined, purebred dogs have reached excellence because for a very long time, creators of type in dogs have followed standards, not trends, in both breeding and judging.

Here is an example of how helpful understanding a written standard is.

In Portugal, when an unregistered Portuguese Water Dog is located, it is up to the Clube Portuguese Canicultura's breeding commission to authenticate that the dog meets characteristics of the breed before they will grant him an Initial Registration (R.I.). The commission is made up of five experts. Two are veterinarians. In examining the dog, they adhere strictly to the Portuguese breed standard. They'll only say, "Yes, this *is* a Portuguese Water Dog," if he has breed type, soundness, and temperament.

If the unregistered dog passes the commission's examination, he is given an R.I. Many European countries grant such secondary registrations. Registering kennel clubs in the United States do not do so and the PWDCA chose not to do so.

To continue—when the dog or bitch is approved with the R.I., each dog in a litter sired or whelped by this particular dog may then be given an R.I. when each is shown under three different judges and is accorded an excellent rating by each judge. Each gains the R.I. on individual merit.

To breed dogs in Portugal, the breeder has to fill out the intent to breed within a fixed period and the breeder has to register all the dogs in the litter and their markings within a fixed period. Until recently, no pet shop in Portugal was allowed to carry dogs that were not fully registered.

European registration is, in many ways, stricter than in the United States. Europeans don't allow litters to be born on "puppy farms." Because there are no puppy farms in Europe, registering organizations don't have to send out representatives to ascertain if pups to be sold are purebred, and if so, of what breed!

The more you know about a standard the more successful you'll be in choosing, breeding and judging dogs.

First, let's look at breed type, soundness, balance and temperament. While good dogs of all breeds possess all these traits, individual breed type, soundness, balance and temperament is what keeps the total picture of the dog in view.

Here are four breed musts.

Type

Breed type, as defined in the glossary of the AKC's *The Complete Dog*

Book, is "The characteristic qualities distinguishing a breed; the embodiment of a standard's essentials."

Type is what makes a Portuguese Water Dog look as it does and not like a Dalmatian. Type is the distinguishing feature of a breed.

Before beginning a breeding program, good breeders look for dogs with typey heads, typey structures, typey coats, typey tailsets and typey temperaments. These breeders feel there is no point of breeding one dog to another unless they mirror fundamentals of breed type.

Nevertheless, type within a breed varies slightly from strain to strain; some breeders, to improve head type, concentrate on heads; others concentrate on coat; still others on tail carriage. But as the concentration on heads, for instance, continues, type should conform to the standard.

Structural Soundness

When a dog is structurally sound, he has good shoulders, legs, paws, hindquarters, top line, and chest—all in line with the standard of the breed. After all, if the dog has faulty breed structure, he may not be able to perform the work for which the breed was bred. Remember, all dogs within a breed deviate somewhat from ideal structure. They deviate because no dog is born perfect. Better dogs have fewer faults. When you hear the term "a well-knit dog," it means the dog is put together right.

Physical Soundness

This means the dog has inherited a sound nervous system, lungs, has a thrifty coat, has good digestion, skin health and all factors that enable a dog to live a normal, healthy life. Physical soundness also stands for good mental health (temperament). Breeders have to breed for sound temperament as well as sound structure. The aim is to breed dogs people can live with 365 days of the year.

Balance

Every part of a Portuguese Water Dog should fit together in rectangular balance with every other part of the dog. His height and length should balance. His bone substance should be in harmony with his symmetrical lines. His head must look like it belongs on his body and on nobody else's body. Also, front and rear angulation must support his body in a balanced ratio.

Some flawed dogs may have possessed breed type, structural and physical soundness, and balanced form at birth, however, *after* they were born they acquired unsoundness either through an accident or through bad care. These dogs, while not show dogs, certainly can be bred. They still make wonderful pets.

Read the standard, and compare it to the Portuguese Water Dogs you have seen or will see. Examine photographs. These show type and balance; they can never show structural or physical soundness. Nevertheless, by examining photographs as well as live dogs, and then comparing both to the standard, you can visualize the ideal Water Dog. Then, when you look at a dog, you can judge him honestly according to your own ideal. That is what must count with you.

General Appearance—Medium build, well-balanced, robust, and well-muscled. The muscular development due to constant swimming is noticeable. The breed is shown in its natural stance which is for the front legs to be positioned so that the feet are slightly forward of the shoulders and the hind legs are positioned approximately under the rump.

The Portuguese Water Dog's appearance reflects his purpose. His health is reflected in his physique. He's a sturdy dog. He has stamina. He's a happy dog. He's a dog who can respond with intelligence and eagerness. You know that even if he never leaves your fireside, fine; but if you choose, he could take his place at your side by a lake or stream or ocean and do your bidding.

One obvious characteristic of the breed is his curly or wavy coat. It's a single coat and non-shedding. Dead hairs are removed by regular grooming with comb and brush. He has a well-balanced body; his strong head and teeth suggest excellent grasping abilities. The dog's stance shows off his deep broad chest and powerful legs. This is one dog, more than any other, that looks directly into your eyes when you're talking to him. Most dogs turn away slightly when you address them, showing submission. They prefer not to look directly at you. This dog looks right into your eyes. His movement shows his happy yet stoic attitude. This is what enables him to get along with people and other animals. We can only surmise that he developed this cooperative spirit after centuries of living in close quarters on a small fishing boat. Certainly, no fisherman would have the time or inclination to train a dog for water work unless he was eager to cooperate. Any other attitude should be faulted.

Ideally, the Portuguese Water Dog male stands about 22 inches tall at the withers; females stand 20 inches tall. The ideal dog is in perfect rectangular balance from the front of his chest to the end of his rump. His coat is black, brown, or in combinations of black or brown with white. His eyes are medium in size and set obliquely in the head. It's important to remember they are not round eyes set well apart looking out at you. They are eyes set obliquely (slanted) in the head.

His head is carried high on a short, extremely muscular neck. His chest is wide at birth. You may see deep chests on some wee pups, although most drop as the dogs reach maturity. Like fine wine, chests improve with age. Exercise and food also contribute to good development of chest. Shoulders are firmly placed and slope onto his back smoothly. This is why he's able to reach well forward with his front legs when striding or swimming. He has a straight topline without any dip where his withers meet his back. His loin is short, tough and firm. It meets his croup with a slight arch, a necessary feature in an excellently constructed dog. His tail is hung on his rump at a medium setting. A finger followed down the topline of a good dog shows that the tail is set on right up in there; it should never be set low. Not enough attention is paid to tail sets; the way the Water Dog's tail is set is important because he uses it while swimming. His tail is shaped like those of most dogs. It is thick at the base and tapers to the end.

His paws are webbed, rather flat. The pads are thick with the central pad pronounced in its thickness.

You'll like the way the Portuguese Water Dog moves. He does so in a free and energetic yet lively ground-covering glide. The word lively defines motion not attitude. His tail is not normally carried high over his back in a ring when he moves. Sometimes, he prefers to fling it straight out behind him, waving it like a flag in a stiff breeze. It's only when he is looking at something intently that he lifts his tail over his back.

All in all, the Portuguese Water Dog impresses your eye with beauty, strength and his naturally happy attitude.

> **Head**—Well proportioned, strong and wide. *Skull*—Seen in profile it is slightly longer than the muzzle, its curvature more accentuated at the back than in the front, and it possesses a well-defined occiput. The top of the skull appears to be domed and to have a slight depression in the middle. The forehead has a central furrow running for two-thirds of the distance between the forehead and the occiput. The forehead is prominent. *Muzzle*—Is narrower at the nose than at its base. *Stop*—The stop is well-defined.

His head is chunky; it's not refined like a Poodle head. It shows plenty of brain room in the skull and plenty of gripping power in the muzzle. He usually carries his head high. Hair should not cover his eyes.

In the original English translation of the Portuguese standard, accomplished by a committee of the Federation Cynologique International (FCI) in Belgium, the word "massive" was used to describe the shape of the head. Now, while the Portuguese Water Dog's head may appear massive when thick curls, waves or groomer-designed topknots cover it, his skull is not massive. Put your hands down through the shaped curls and you'll find it is, just as the standard says it is, "well-proportioned, strong and wide." For comparison, it is wide like the head of the Puli, the Labrador, the Golden Retriever and the "Landseer" Newfoundland. When you put your hands on a good head, you'll feel the pronounced rise of the occipital crest, you'll trace the depression running from the occiput to the nose. Slide your fingers over his stop, the depression slashed across his face between his eyes. This is well-defined but not overly cliffed as in the Bulldog or all but missing as in the Bedlington Terrier. Some heads and their stops don't mature until the dog is close to two years of age.

In other words, the stop is definite, but never sharply angular. Neither is it in an absolutely straight line from the tip of his nose to his forehead.

The degree of stop, of course, should be in balance with the dog's head. Remember that the head must be in balance with the total dog.

The Portuguese Water Dog's head is evenly rounded, the occiput is prominently raised, the depression running from occiput to nostril leather is well defined, the eyes are well-spaced and obliquely placed, the brow is protective, the skin is tight, and the foreface is narrower at the tip of the nose than at its base right below the stop.

Head faults are very long, narrow, flat, or pointed skulls. Muzzles must never be funnel-shaped, too-pointed or snipy.

> *Nose*—Wide. Nostrils well-flared and finely pigmented. Black in animals with black, black and white, or white coats. In brown, the nose is the same color as the coat.

Well-flared is another term for wide. Wide nostril placement is attractive and in balance with the correct muzzle of the Portuguese Water Dog. Dogs without complete black- or brown-colored noses—that is, dogs with some flesh-color in their nose leather—have noses that lack pigment. This is a fault.

> *Teeth*—Not visible when the mouth is closed. Canines strongly developed. Teeth meet in a scissor or level bite.

A scissors bite, where the upper front teeth slightly overlap the lower teeth, is preferred. The level bite, where the front teeth meet with no overlapping, does not wear well as dogs get older. The CPC standard calls for a level bite, but most international kennel clubs prefer the scissor bite which is healthier. Teeth should be strong and healthy.

> *Jaws*—Strong and neither over nor undershot.

There are some undershot jaws in the breed. The majority of these jaws are strong and have the capacity for carrying heavy fishing gear as well as fish, even though the under teeth overlap the upper more than as in the scissors bite. The late English international judge, Arthur Westlake said a breed's first sign of deterioration came when the jaw became undershot. However, Hayes Hoyt, the American international judge commented to Deyanne Miller at the first PWDCA match that any dog expected to retrieve tackle might need a longer and stronger under jaw than other breeds do. She believed fishermen would breed dogs to be slightly undershot for this reason. Fishermen may have even deliberately bred these dogs to be undershot. The reader may come to his own conclusion. Owners of puppies with show potential should watch the puppy's mouth when the first teeth erupt. If any appear crooked, one or more should be pulled. Then the second teeth waiting down in the gums will emerge with ample room to grow up straight.

> *Eyes*—Medium size, set well apart, roundish and neither prominent nor sunken. Brown or black in color. The eyelids which are of fine texture, have black edges. The haws are dark and are not apparent.

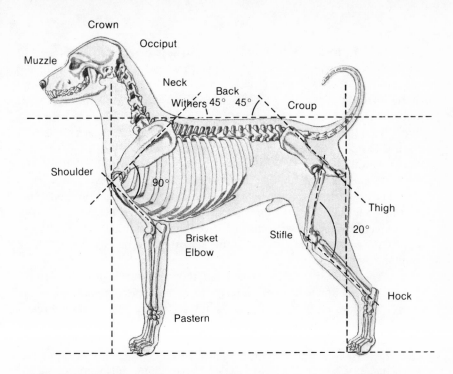

Every part of a Portuguese Water Dog should fit together in rectangular balance with every other part of the dog.   *Elaine Sorenson*

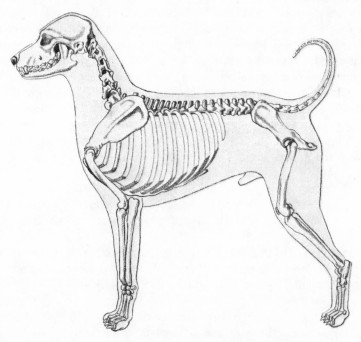

His bone substance should be in harmony with his symmetrical lines.

Elaine Sorenson

A genetic feedback program conducted in 1978 records that 14 percent of the breed in America had light eyes. So we wonder. Is the Portuguese Water Dog standard stuck with a lot of old wives tales and myths? Remember the centuries' old myth that a horse with a watch (light) eye was to be reckoned with? You would be afraid of him. You weren't to trust him. Well, from that myth came the human emotion of not trusting a horse with a different-colored eye. Could the dog fancy's belief that dogs of most breeds should have dark eyes emanate from that myth?

Eye placement is oblique. Eye shape is roundish.

The breed does not have eye problems, although several animals have had juvenile cataracts. Portuguese Water Dogs may get cataracts as they get older; however, that is normal with aging animals. Eye faults are light-colored eyes, eyes different from each other in either form or size, and sunken or protruding.

>*Ears*—Leather heart-shaped, thin in texture and set well above the line to the eyes. Except for a small opening at the back, the ears are held nicely against the head. The tips should not reach below the lower jaw.

Look carefully at the ears. Their set should be high. When the dog is alert, the base is on line with the top of the skull. Leather should hang close to the head. When the dogs are working in the water, it is believed the ear flap fits tightly against the ear. When Portuguese Water Dogs come out of the water their ears are dry inside.

An artist who drew ears of 52 different breeds, said the Portuguese Water Dog's ears appear to be shaped differently than those of any other breed she had studied. Perhaps the shape is the reason the ears remain dry.

Like the Poodle and Kerry Blue Terrier and many Spaniel breeds, hair grows on the inside of the ear. Nature may put heavy hair there to help keep water out. In present day dogs, the hair is removed from ears for cleanliness. With most of this hair removed, the ears can be inspected and thoroughly cleaned. And when the Portuguese Water Dog is shown, hair on both inside and outside flaps is trimmed even with the edges of the leather. If the lower end of the trimmed ear flap is even with the outside corner of the eye, the length is correct.

>*Lips*—Thick, especially in front. No flew. Mucous membrane (roof of mouth, under the tongue, and gums) well-ticked with black, or quite black, in black or white dogs. In brown same as coat.

Dogs that work in the water and carry things in their mouths certainly do not need excess skin around the mouth. This would keep them from grasping swimming fish. Skin should be thick, tough, and tight.

>**Body**—
>*Neck*—Straight, short, nicely rounded and held high. Strongly muscled. No mane and no dewlap.

The neck is strong and muscular, and it sits smoothly on the dog's shoulders in perfect balance with the head. The strong neck allows the dog to lift his head to look around in the water. It allows him to drag boat gear. Even small dogs and bitches have strong necks. His neck blends smoothly into both head and topline. The Portuguese Water Dog's neck has no mane or loose skin to slow him down in the water.

Brisket—Wide and deep, reaching down at the elbow.

The brisket is well-developed and well-defined. It is wide, but moderately wide, else the dog would not have endurance. It is well filled and should show depth down to the elbows. This gives him room for large lungs. As the ribs approach the brisket, they should be nearly flat. They must never be rounded like barrel hoops. Excessive width hinders free forearm movement, so necessary to a strong swimmer.

Ribs—Long and well-sprung.

If the Water Dog is deep in ribs, he obviously has excellent depth of chest to do his work.

Back—Short and meets the croup smoothly. Good tuck-up.

The back from withers to hip bones is short, yet in balance with the total dog. Females are usually slightly longer in back so that they can more comfortably carry unborn pups. There is good height to the Portuguese Water Dog's withers. The back should not curve toward the loin as seen in a roached back; it needs to be good and square, the loin strong, broad, muscular and taut so it can tense and flatten easily. If it isn't taut, the dog loses stamina. A strong loin also enables the dog to turn quickly under water. The Portuguese Water Dog has to have an eminently practical back. A long back, straight shoulders, and faulty rear movement are undesirable. Good tuck-up doesn't mean extreme development as with a Greyhound. The bottom line should slope gently upward in a firm but moderate "waist." The Portuguese Water Dog's deep, broad chest and muscular loin endows him with a firm, graceful tuck-up.

Croup—Well formed and only slightly inclined, with hip bones hardly apparent.

The croup, in connection with the loin, performs a major function in a dog's movement. It is the source of rearing muscles and propulsive effort. In the Portuguese Water Dog the croup is rounded and wide with muscles extremely well-developed.

Tail—Not docked, thick at the base and tapering, medium setting. It should not reach below the hock. When the dog is attentive, the tail should be held in a ring, the front of which should not reach beyond the forward line of the hips. The tail is of great help when swimming and diving.

When the dog is at attention or on alert, the tail is circled over the back. Even at attention, the tail should never be tightly curled. The dog should carry it over his back in an arc with a high-flying tuft. When relaxed,

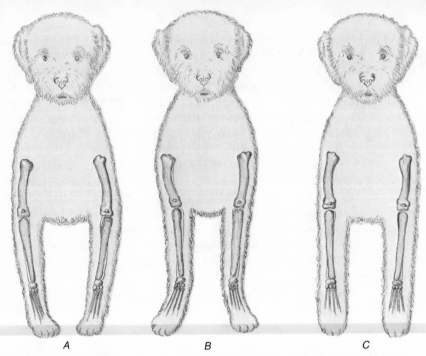

The Portuguese Water Dog's forequarters give the impression of power combined with excellent reach and freedom of leg movement as shown in *C*. *A* shows a dog with a bad front—toeing-in—and *B* shows a dog toeing-out.

Elaine Sorenson

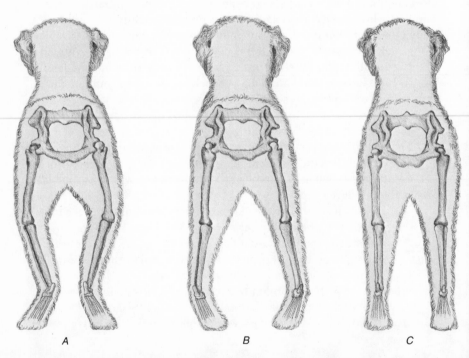

When viewed from behind, as shown in *C*, hock joints do not lean in or out. Bone is of good substance. *A* shows a cow-hocked dog while *B* shows a spraddle-hocked dog.

Elaine Sorenson

the dog holds it straight out behind him or he allows it to hang straight down.

His tail, thick at the base and tapering toward the end, is used for balance and a rudder. He uses it to gain equilibrium when diving, swimming, or running. In swimming, he uses it as a rudder. It also shows his feelings. He wags it in long, horizontal sweeps when he is happy. When he thinks he has done something wrong, he wags it quickly, side to side. When diving, his tail is the last part of his energetic anatomy to disappear beneath the waves. This may be why fishermen left the tuft on the end of the tail; it may help the dog use its tail as a rudder. The tuft, however, should never be exaggerated so that the dog looks like a clown or shaped like a pompon as in a Poodle.

Tail faults include a docked tail, rudimentary or nonexistent tail, one that is heavy, droopy, or one held perpendicularly. Uncharacteristic tail set and action detracts from the style of the dog, and destroys lateral stability, so important to this breed.

> *Forequarters*—The forelegs are strong and straight. *Shoulder* is well-inclined and very strongly muscled. The upper arm is strong. The forearm is long and strongly muscled. The carpus is heavy-boned, wider in front than at the side. *Pasterns,* long and strong. *Dewclaws* may be removed.

The Portuguese Water Dog's forequarters give the impression of power combined with excellent reach and freedom of leg movement. His shoulder blades are set farther apart than those of racing dogs. The blade should be firmly set in muscles. Shoulder angulation should be sloping to supply him with necessary reach. The upper arm (humerus) should come down at a 90 degree angle. Elbows are held close to the chest. Pasterns, while long and strong, have to be somewhat sloping to allow for endurance.

> *Hindquarters*—The thighs are strongly muscled. When viewed from the rear, the thigh bones are parallel. Second thighs, long and strongly muscled, decidedly inclined from front to back. All structural ligaments are well developed. The rump is long and well-curved. Hocks are strong. When viewed from the rear, the hind legs are straight and very strongly muscled. Metatarsals, long and *no dewclaws.*

The Portuguese Water Dog has breadth across the pelvis. His strong, lithe hindquarters are there to manufacture power. When viewed from behind, hock joints do not lean in or out. Bone is of good substance, with muscles well developed and powerful. Thighs are long, stifles well bent. Look carefully at the angles of the bones. While back legs need angulation, this should be moderate. Moderate angulation is synonymous with agility. If the Portuguese Water Dog has too straight a stifle, he is robbed of driving power; he may even hop in the water. Push comes from behind. The hindlegs produce power and send it to the forequarters.

Hocks are well developed. High hocks may give initial speed but lower hocks add endurance. The ideal hock starts two-thirds down from the hip.

Feet—Round and rather flat. Toes not too knuckled up and not too long. The webbing between the toes, which reaches to the tip of these, is of soft skin well covered with hair. Black nails are preferred, but whites, browns, and striped nails are allowed according to the color of the coat. Nails held up slightly off the ground. Central pad very thick, others normal.

The Portuguese Water Dog is definitely web-footed. The webbing is thick and comes out to the end of the toes. The paws (feet) are round and spreading. The dog is rather flat-footed. His pads are thick and fleshy, never thin. Toes are slightly arched. Both front and rear feet are extremely powerful. A heavy growth of hair protects the webbing on the bottom of the feet between toes. The tops of the toes are covered with wavy, rather than curly hair even in dogs with curly coats. Paws are paddles and thick hair aids the paddling. Dewclaws on the hind feet is a fault. Although it is not mentioned in the standard, splayed feet would also be a fault.

Coat—Profuse coat, of strong hair, covering the whole body evenly except where the forearm meets the brisket and groin where it is thinner. There is no undercoat, mane or rough. There are two varieties of coat:

Wavy: Fairly long, wavy, rather loose with a slight sheen. The hair on the top of the head is upright and that on the ears is decidedly longer than the leather.

Curly: The hair forms compact cylindrical curls, thickly planted and somewhat lusterless. On the top of the head the hair is similar to that of the rest of the coat, whereas that on the ears is sometimes wavy.

The adult Water Dog's coat is strikingly beautiful in both texture and quality. Sometimes a puppy's coat will not settle down: One moment it is scraggly; another it is thick, then thin, or bushy. Happily, most coats settle down by the time the pup reaches a year of age.

Two types of coats are described in the American standard: curly and wavy. In Portugal, a third type is accepted in the breed ring. It is the curly-to-the-corded coat.

The texture of the wavy coat is soft and silky. It shines. It's glossy. The texture of the curly coat ranges from soft to lusterless. It has a matte finish. The curly coat usually has no sheen. In some dogs, curls feel wooly like the curls on the Curly-Coated Retriever or the Irish or American Water Spaniel. The Portuguese Water Dog is also said to be an ancestor of the Kerry Blue Terrier; the similarity in coat type gives rise to the possibility.

Both coat types may grow equally long. The curly coat usually appears thicker than does the wavy. Both coats shed water well.

Coat types are not judged separately in the breed ring.

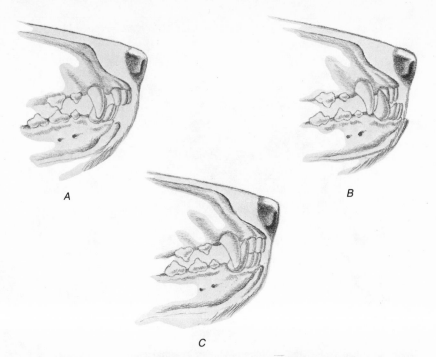

A scissors bite, as shown in *C,* where the upper front teeth slightly overlap the lower teeth, is preferred. *A* shows an overbite; *B* shows an underbite. Dogs having bites like *A* or *B* must be faulted.   *Elaine Sorenson*

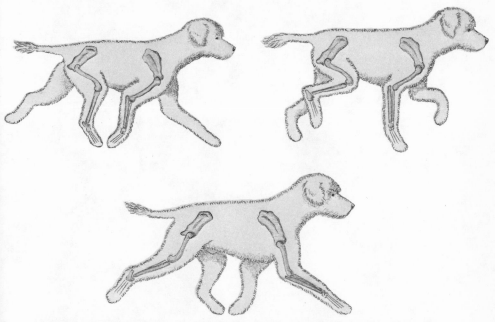

The well-constructed Portuguese Water Dog combines beauty and efficiency in his movement.   *Elaine Sorenson*

The Portuguese Water Dog is properly shown in either the Lion clip (above) or the Working Retriever clip (below). In either clip, the dog should impress the observer with an equal blending of beauty and strength. His attitude—an enthusiastic love of life—completes the harmonious picture of a distinctive dog breed. *Elaine Sorenson*

The coat should not only be thick but should be of good quality and texture. For work on land, the coat should be maintained very short—if long it picks up burrs, foxtails and weeds. In winter, long coats gather snowballs.

The Portuguese Water Dog's thick coat doesn't hamper his swimming ability because of its single, water-resistant nature. Water droplets don't cling to it, as they will to dogs with double coats (undercoats), but a long coat may hamper his water work. For example, untrimmed hair from the skull may irritate his eyes and keep him from seeing clearly underwater. Kathryn Braund's Portuguese Water Dogs living in Montana are comfortable diving and swimming in freezing or warm water.

The Portuguese Water Dog's coat dries quickly, and the oil in it repels water. If he is left alone, his waves or curls fall into place naturally without brushing or combing. If his hair is too long, it holds sand and forms mats easily.

There's an old belief that the "water dog could maneuver in water easily if his coat was clipped in a Lion clip." Too much hair in front could help drag the dog down when wet, rather than give the dog buoyancy. The shorter Working clip protects the entire body from the cold yet allows the dog to slip through the water with ease.

The Working Retriever clip is the most similar to the clip used by Portuguese fishermen. The country's stamp depicts the breed in Working clip.

Fausto, trainer for Vasco Bensaude, told Deyanne Miller he was terribly sorry he had not clipped Leao for the bellwether dog's now-famous photos. Leaving Leao's hair long, Fausto said, gave people the wrong impression of the breed. The fishermen, he said, always sheared their Portuguese Water Dogs in the spring when the sheep were sheared.

Some dogs change their coats once a year, usually in late winter. Some bitches shed just before or just after they come into season and again after they have had puppies. This is normal.

There are improper coats in the breed. Farmion Defeza, dam of Trezena Monte Clerico, had an improper coat. So did Inia de Alvalade, dam of Bittersweet Hypolito. It's interesting to note that these offspring won BOB at PWDCA Specialties. Clerico won three out of four times shown and Hypolito won twice. The gene for improper coats is probably in every dog but only a few puppies in the succeeding generations will have bad coats.

Clips—Two clips are acceptable:
Lion clip: As soon as the coat grows long, the middle part and hindquarters of these dogs, as well as the muzzle, are clipped. At the end of the tail the hair is left at full length.
Working Retriever clip: In order to give a natural appearance and a smooth unbroken line, the entire coat is scissored or

clipped to follow the outline of the dog leaving a short blanket of no longer than 1 inch in length. At the end of the tail, the hair is left at full length.

There has been much confusion as to how to clip to the standard. Let's simplify it.

Lion clip: When the coat is long, the muzzle and hindquarters from the *first rib back are clipped. The tail is clipped to within three inches of the end,* where the hair is left at full length. Some people interpret the middle part as from the first rib and clip accordingly and others interpret it to mean the third or fourth rib from the rear or first rib.

Working Retriever clip: The entire coat, *including head, face and legs* is clipped or scissored to follow the outline of the dog leaving a short blanket of coat *appearing* no longer than one inch in length. Three inches from the end of the tail, the hair is left at full length.

Colors: are black, white, and various tones of brown, also combinations of black or brown with white. A white coat does not imply albinism provided the nose, mouth, and eyelids are black. In animals with black, white, or black and white coats, the skin is decidedly bluish.

At one time in Portugal, blazes, white on the tip of a tail, large patches of white on the chest and along the back were considered undesirable. Dogs showing substantial white areas were disposed of and a parti-color is still rare today. In 1981, two dogs whelped in litter 73, from black parents, were largely white parti-colors, much to the surprise of breeder, Jayne Kenyon. Consequently, a University of Pennsylvania veterinarian, Dr. Donald Patterson, was consulted. Dr. Patterson voiced the opinion that white dogs with black markings were genetically *black* dogs carrying parti-color (PP) or Irish spotting (IP) genes which produce black dogs with small white markings of black with two-thirds white. Nevertheless, genetically they are black dogs.

In 1984, two parti-colored dogs made their championships.

Petra Schaefer, who has studied color for the PWDCA, says brown is recessive to black but that black is not dominant over all colors. Parti-color, when it is in the homozygous form (PP), that is genetically black dogs, is dominant over all solid colors. Irish spotting (IP) is dominant over all solid colors, unless parti-color is in the homozygous form (PP).

In Portugal, silver-gray is seen. Robert Fries in *Origin of the Weimaraner* refers to silver-gray as a dulled brown obtained through a process of color degeneration. He also believes silver-gray is brought about by the lack of vitamin D. It is thought that the Portuguese Water Dog, like the Irish Water Spaniel, does not carry a graying factor. But the Poodle has a graying factor which occasionally shows up when breeding blacks to browns.

Most Portuguese Water Dogs in the United States today are black or black with white markings. They're also found in various shades of brown as well as in combinations of white with black or white with brown. In all animals, the standard says, the skin should be decidedly bluish. However, with white markings that will remain white for life, the skin underneath is pink.

During the summer, sun and salt water may rust a black coat and fade a brown coat.

There is Irish spotting in the breed; Irish spotting means two-thirds of each dog is black with as much as one-third white. A parti-colored dog would be two-thirds white with spotting of other colors.

Gait—Short, lively steps when walking. At a trot it is a forward striding, well-balanced movement.

The well-constructed Portuguese Water Dog combines beauty and efficiency in his movement. He moves with his head held high and his tail swinging. Lively describes motion, not attitude. When moving at a moderate stride, his backline remains level as he flows smoothly over the ground. At both trot and gallop his action is long and free. When running, his front legs are placed beneath him, not to the side. When looking at the dog from the front, his legs swing straight forward, with good reach. There is no interference or twisting in or out at the elbows. From the side, his leg action flows rhythmically: 1, 2, 3, 4 in exact balance. The legs don't overreach or strike together. When looking at his gait from the back, his hocks are parallel. He drives forward without his rear feet too close together. Neither do his back legs adjust for thrust to gain good front movement.

Height—Males between 20 and 23 inches. Females between 17 and 21 inches.

It will be noted that there is considerable variation in the breed's size. There is a reason for this. In Portugal, fishermen using small boats, called caiques, containing one, two or three men sensibly required small dogs. Those who fished from larger vessels required larger dogs. We still encounter some dogs that measure over the standard's acceptable height. At one time it was not uncommon to find dogs as tall as 26 to 28 inches. Faults are oversized or undersized animals.

Weight—Males between 42 and 60 pounds. Females between 35 and 50 pounds.

Weight should be in balance with the dog's bone and muscular structure. If a dog is balanced in both vertical and horizontal dimensions and possesses bone in keeping with his size, he is certainly to be preferred over one who is out of balance but within the correct weight limit.

Faults—Any deviation from these specifications is a fault; the degree to which a dog is penalized is dependent upon the extent to which the dog deviates from the standard and the extent to which the particular fault would actually affect the working ability of the dog.

Temperament—A dog of exceptional intelligence, it obeys any orders given by its master with facility and apparent pleasure. It is obedient with those who look after it and with those for whom it works. An animal of spirited disposition, independent, brave and very resistant to fatigue, it has a hard, penetrating and attentive expression, splendid sight and a fair nose.

Because the Portuguese Water Dog was the fisherman's helpmate, he is a swimmer and diver of quite exceptional quality. He has stamina. He has spirit. The late philosopher, Edmond Bordeaux Szekely said, "Intelligence is the ability to adapt oneself adequately to unexpected changes in the environment." This is certainly true of the Portuguese Water Dog. Highly adaptable, he's able to live amicably in confined quarters with others, be they people or animals.

Even if another dog attacks, he'll keep trying to become friends, fawning if he must. At times, this may become a problem.

While he's not a quarrelsome breed, he is a guard dog. He likes to get along, yet he likes to be in command. This is why this dog needs to be taught manners early so he learns how to be aggressive only when asked.

The words in the standard, "splendid sight and a fair nose" are English terms. Ask for a cookie in England and you get a biscuit. When the British say, "That's a fair nose," that's a British understatement! They mean that this is a nose to be reckoned with. The breed has an excellent nose. When diving, the Portuguese Water Dog can pick out a stone thrown for him from others on the bottom just by the smell. Their sight is also excellent as long as hair is kept away from their eyes.

Brigao in Portuguese means stout-hearted, courageous. It also means "brawler by nature." When the standard was initially translated into English, the translators took brigao to mean "brawler" rather than "courageous" or "stout hearted." The word was finally deleted from the standard because it is not accurate. The dog will not attack without cause.

9

The Character of the Portuguese Water Dog

NOW THAT YOU KNOW the history of the Portuguese Water Dog, let's look at his character. Once in a while, people buy a dog and then say, "He's too much for me." It's wise to prepare for the pleasures and possible problems of owning a Portuguese Water Dog before acquiring one.

The Portuguese Water Dog is not a mild dog. He's robust, willing, strong, and sturdy. He's full of the "Let's do it!" temperament of a happy working dog. He wants to be active. His blithe spirit is a grace for owners who are young in heart. For them he makes an ideal pet.

On the other hand, many of the breed's traits parallel those of the Portuguese fishing people. Both male and female are warm, loving and affectionate dogs; they're also dignified, sensitive and thoughtful. While friendly and cheerful to everyone, they're loyal only unto their own. Many Portuguese Water Dogs work out well as "land-lubber" apartment dogs.

The daily hardships the Portuguese fishermen suffered in their dangerous lives at sea are reflected in the breed's almost stoic acceptance of whatever fate has in store for him. Let children pull his hair, let puppies climb all over him, even let a master abuse him—he endures.

Once, on a visit to Deyanne Miller, Kathryn Braund's Portuguese Water Dog, Diver (Ch. Farmion Geo, CDX), had to ride in a car on a trip a distance of 7200 miles—from Montana to Connecticut and back. Yes, he was able to stretch his legs at rest and gas stops. Yes, he was walked in the

His blithe spirit is a grace for the young in heart.   *Pamela Schneller*

He accepts whatever fate has in store for him.

mornings, afternoons, and evenings and, sure, he played on the floor in motel rooms. But daily, hour upon hour, while we drove, he had to be content to ride in a confining crate. His spirit never dimmed. He never sulked. He was a confident, willing pup.

When a Portuguese Water Dog is being worked as a retriever, at times he may appear to be an indifferent observer. Hah! Call to him. He jumps up eagerly, his beautiful eyes telling you he's eager to please. You know his heart is beating wildly. You know he wants to retrieve for you.

If he's being groomed for show, he'll put up with several hours of tedious grooming, accepting the ministrations in a completely relaxed attitude. But when the brushing and combing and scissoring are over, he comes alive with a bounce!

In obedience performances, he rivets his eyes on his handler. He tail whips with pleasure as he works.

The Portuguese Water Dog is remarkably adaptable to whatever is asked of him. Faye Just of Oxnard, California told Deyanne Miller in a letter:

> Everyone loves Frosty. My husband says that he would like to have another just like him. And my husband hasn't had a dog since 1938. My mother is considering dog-napping him and she has *never* liked a dog before.

Yet, sometimes, when pressed, he may become temperamental. Yes, he misbehaves. He's an inveterate tease who enjoys testing your patience. He also accepts correction gracefully. It's just that right after his scolding, he'll attempt once more to get his own way.

His persistence is a plus in his work, but in teaching him consistency in household manners, it may be a pain in the neck.

He wants to be friends with other dogs. He adores their companionship. If some won't tolerate his friendly overtures, he fawns on them. Endlessly he wags, kisses and subjugates himself, ignoring their growls and snarls. One wonders: does he try to get along because centuries ago, on small crowded boats, he had to cooperate to survive? One also wonders if once he's grabbed attention (good or bad) and walks away—is that saunter really a strut?

He comes often to his humans for their love because he wants to be near them. He is jealous. He needs to be noticed. He's a very demanding and affectionate dog. You simply can't put him in a corner and not expect him to protest. He will.

His bark is unique. It goes up and down the octave. To go outside, he yips once or twice at high C. When he begs, he does so politely, right in the middle of the scale. When guarding, he yodels. He'll yip when he's separated from his favorite people.

He's a guard dog. His strong protective instincts don't usually emerge until he reaches maturity. As a pup, he's likely to jump up on strangers happily. However, he may learn to bite to get his way unless taught not to do so.

His life is centered around his master. He's devoted to his whole family.

His playing can be annoying. He paws people. He pushes doors open by attacking them with his feet. He kicks tennis balls in front of him as if he were playing soccer.

His memory is outstanding. He never forgets a face or a smell. He's not likely to forget an unhappy incident either. Therefore, use a positive approach when working him. He does need a firm hand. If he doesn't believe he should be made to do something, he clamps his teeth together refusing to cooperate, smiling all the while. That's why some people say he's as tenacious as a Bulldog. This tenacity can be used to advantage when training him. Teach him to perform a job and his desire is so great, he'll never forget how.

He seldom makes a happy kennel dog. Although he likes the outdoors, he needs to be doing something with somebody (if possible) every moment. He's a fun-loving dog.

He lords over the house if he's allowed to do so. Teach him not to get up on the furniture and he obeys—at least while you're present. Leave the room and you'll return to find the imprint of his warm body on your favorite cushion.

He's not a wanderer. He likes to stay close to home.

When you're away from home, he bides his time in a chair by the window. Left in the yard, he waits at the gate. While guarding the car or boat, he watches the world go by from the driver's seat or captain's chair.

He has two awful habits. He leaps up on people when greeting; when young and left alone in the yard, he enjoys chewing the trees and shrubs. These habits are difficult to break. He needs firm and repeated corrections before he learns exactly what can and cannot be done.

Give a Portuguese Water Dog pup a chunk of tree limb to play with. He'll rip the bark off with his teeth, expose the spine and proudly show you the remains. He also likes to make holes in lush lawns. Why? He digs down to eat the grass roots. He chews shoots off bushes, eats ends of branches of precious young trees and buds off flowers. He believes that young and tender growing greens were planted for his taste buds. Heritage plays a part here. In the Algarve, in the winter when the sea was too rough for a small boat to go out, the Portuguese Water Dog often herded sheep. He appears to mimic their eating habits.

Paradoxically, chewing is not a problem inside. In the house, he can be taught to discriminate quickly. He knows his toys and he knows yours. Yours are untouchable. Okay!

He's happy outside. He doesn't mind a change in weather. He rushes outside in rain, wind and snow as readily as he does on a warm, sunny spring morning.

He is normally friendly with other dogs.   *A.G. Prangley, Jr., MD*

Farmion Xavier, who lives in North Carolina, demonstrates the joy of living typical of the breed.   *B.J.S. Adams*

In the summer, he's not bothered by most insects. They have a tough time trying to penetrate to his skin, but mosquitos can bite him when he's in heavily infested areas. Some Portuguese Water Dogs may be allergic to fleas. Ticks can hide well in his heavy coat.

When it's hot, he doesn't need to be reminded to seek the shade. But when snow lies on the ground, he does have to be kept from playing too long. If his coat is too long, snowballs form on his legs and chest and weigh him down.

Since the Portuguese Water Dog originated in the mountains of central Asia, he evolved a heavy coat and he retained it even when the Algarve became his home. There, "snow" falls only in the form of white blossoms from the thousands of almond trees. His heavy coat proves good protection from sea winds and from the cold waters. The coat also protects him from the hot sun.

As a puppy, he's a *klutz*! He trips over everyone and everything. He never stops walking on people's feet, bumping into their shins, or falling out of boats! Once he matures, however, owners and friends may miss the frivolous creature who chewed plantings and scratched the oak doors.

He's so fond of water—even as a puppy—that keeping the area around his water dish dry is a never-ending chore. He just naturally wants to learn about water. He'll constantly test the water in his bowl with his front paws. Then if there's any left, he'll push his muzzle in and drip the rest of it over the rugs.

His first excursion into the water is an adventure for his owner as well as for him. Even if he's never been near water before, a Portuguese Water Dog seldom tests it. He leaps in. If the water is over his head, he may sink to the bottom. If so, he'll reappear shortly, gulping for air, his eyes rolling. He'll appear quite astonished at his predicament, yet, he'll jump right back in and learn to swim.

He should have a plastic tub in which he can wade, dig water toys from the bottom, or lie in on a steamy summer day. And ah! If there's a swimming pool nearby, he'll leap the otherwise unleapable fence for his daily swim, even if the pool's posted: "No dogs allowed." When trained correctly, he'll respect pool hours standing by waiting for water fun.

As stated earlier, the cold doesn't bother the Portuguese Water Dog. Work the garden on a blustery spring day with a sweater over your shirt, a parka on top, a hood covering your head, and long-johns under your jeans; he'll seek out the nearest patch of snow to lie upon and supervise your work. No coats or hoods for him, thank you. He is amply provided with same—naturally.

If you go fishing and your small fishing boat has no shade, lay a thin layer of water along the deck. He'll thank you by sopping up the water with his coat as he stretches in comfort.

If his coat is too long, snowballs can form on his legs and chest, weighing him down.   *Kathryn Braund*

The same dog, in photo above, in a shorter trim, runs freely in snow, unencumbered by snowballs.   *Stuart White*

The Portuguese Water Dog's heavy coat provides good protection from sea winds.

A.G. Prangley, Jr., MD

He should have his own pool to wade in, as Ch. Natale do Mar is doing here.

Catherine M. Kalb

At thirty below when the wood fire keeps the house cozy, he finds the crack in the door and lies there. He likes the frigid air.

He likes to retrieve almost as much as he likes to swim. Retrieving is his heritage. It's simple to teach him to ride a surfboard, fetch the paper, the children's shoes, the socks you left behind.

In Europe, the Portuguese Water Dog was brought up to live with people and go with them wherever they went. That's the reason for Farmion's famous Charlie Brown's (Ch. Charlie de Alvalade) celebrated personality. And when picked up at New York's JFK Airport after his initial flight from Portugal, how else should he sit, but as he sat in his crate—looking utterly bored and very at ease as befits a gentleman who travels about. He received his owners' entire vocabulary of Portuguese and French in the first 15 minutes while they tried to make him feel less strange.

Initially owned by M. and Mme. Jean-Pierre Naudin, Charlie was born in Portugal. He spent some of his youth in Sao Joao Estoril. He travelled to Nigeria, and spent many hours riding in cars to Paris and home again. With all the travelling and all the miles that Charlie logged, the transition from sea heritage to air and land passage wasn't very difficult.

When the Naudins, because of career commitments, could no longer keep Charlie, the Millers welcomed him. Deyanne Miller had judged Charlie as a puppy in Portugal in 1978. The next time she judged him in Portugal, she awarded him an excellent. He came to live with Herb and Deyanne Miller in 1980.

In the years he flew with his Miller family from Bridgeport, Connecticut to Nantucket, Massachusetts, he rushed for the passenger seat the moment he got on the plane. You could see what was going through his mind. Was he going to have the seat or was he going to have the floor? If somebody was going to sit in the seat, he took the floor, resigned. A couple of times he viewed the world from the co-pilot's seat. If his lot was the floor he was sound asleep before the plane took off from Bridgeport. When it landed, he yawned and stretched. He was laid-back in every respect. Why not? Travel was part and parcel of his heritage.

One Portuguese Water Dog character evaluation comes to us from owner Janice Ronzoni of Manhasset, New York. Janice hadn't planned to buy a dog when she went to breeder Una O'Neill's home to help her bathe a litter of brown Portuguese Water Dog puppies. The puppies were to appear in a story in a local newspaper. Here is her story.

> I volunteered my time and it was love at first splash! I went to help Una secure in knowing I never wanted to own another dog. After seeing them for some reason I felt I had to own one of these puppies—any one would do! To make it short, the male pick of the litter became ours.
>
> Bogart was quite aggressive with his litter mates; no question about it, he was a tyrant. We heeded Una's advice to take charge, even if he was so cute.

Bogart has a fantastic disposition.

It's simple to teach him to ride a surfboard. Farmion Neptuno (Tuna) has fun with the Grauer (Mr. and Mrs. Donald Grauer) children.

Bogart is, however, a very social animal with a fantastic disposition. I felt I wanted a dog to co-exist with us. So Bogart was crate trained, but our children spent much time holding, cuddling, brushing and playing with this fluffy brown animal. The children are now nineteen, twenty and twenty-one years old and talk about owning their own Portuguese Water Dogs some day. I feel the love and affection, not just attention, that they showed is returned by this dog. He's no longer the tyrant.

We love to watch the dogs on our block frolic with Bogart. They come to our yard to loll in the sun or romp through the snow. Bogart demonstrates he is not aggressive in the least, he is very docile.

The one word I use to describe Bogart is *intelligent*. He is a very friendly, affectionate dog who has a collection of stuffed animals. When we brought him home at eight weeks he slept in his crate with a teddy bear. He has never destroyed any of his collection. He greets anyone at the door with his teddy and has on occasion taken one of them for walks by carrying a teddy in his mouth. We sometimes think he is embarrassed when the other dogs see him with his teddy! Bogart always props his head on the bear and sleeps this way. When the light goes out and we leave the family room he collects his teddy to go to his sleeping place. I find that he will not jump to greet people if he is carrying one of his animals.

Bogart "works" by herding me to the kitchen at precisely 5:15 p.m. if I'm not already there preparing dinner for my family. One of the funny things he does is to let me know he has finished his meal by very adeptly placing his paw in the handle of the storage drawer where his vitamins are kept. He then proceeds to pull the drawer open and waits for his vitamin.

Bogart swims when we are at the beach, for us, Long Island Sound. He most enjoys running on the sand bar.

He is always walked on a leash. This is when many people stop me to inquire about his breed and training.

I enrolled with Bogart in the adult education class run by our school district entitled "Dog Training." It was suggested the dog should be more than a year old. Bogart was just seven months and performed magnificently. As a novice trainer, I was impressed by what I had learned, but Bogart was so eager to be put through the paces. Una was right about training at an early age. It was a most delightful experience. It is now my great pleasure to walk him daily.

The Portuguese Water Dog is a very handsome breed and not only a "real man's dog" but a true family dog.

10

Grooming Your
Portuguese Water Dog

L EARN TO GROOM your Portuguese Water Dog yourself. Whether he is wavy or curly coated, set aside time at least three days a week to groom him.

Grooming is fun when you start out right—it's a relaxing time for both of you even though you may have a busy daily schedule. Developing your skill so your dog is comfortable and attractive in "clothes" that fit nicely makes the effort most worthwhile.

The Portuguese Water Dog's coat is one of the best advertisements for the breed.

Let's talk about the breed's show clips and about a mini version of one of these clips. You might even want to keep him in this in his daily life. He is shown in the breed ring in either of two clips: the Working Retriever clip or the Lion clip.

Historical Perspective

The Working Retriever clip originates from his use as a fisherman's dog. Centuries ago in Portugal, along the Algarve, the fishermen sheared him along with the sheep each spring. They sheared him all over, except for a tuft on the end of his tail. The fishermen also kept the hair around his eyes trimmed so he could see well enough to perform his work.

The Lion clip also originated centuries ago. The Romans maintained

170

their Lion Dogs this way. Many small dogs were maintained in a Lion clip throughout the centuries; the clip wasn't limited to any particular breed. This was the clip in which Vasco Bensaude showed his Portuguese Water Dogs. In this clip, the hair on the dog's face and for one inch above the eyes is trimmed. So is all the hair on the dog's body behind his ribs, as well as the hair on his hind legs. Again, hair is left full length on the last three inches of the tail.

Either clip is acceptable and handsome. Either clip is comfortable for the dog, and both are comparatively easy to maintain

The Benefits of Good Grooming

The owner of a pet who wants to keep his dog in a low-maintenance clip should use a 4F blade, clip the dog all over except for the tuft on the end of the tail. Allow the hair to grow out. This takes about two to three months. When the coat has grown out clip again, and be sure to follow the other suggestions on grooming and coat management in this chapter. Professional groomers might want to use a 1½ inch snap-on plastic comb with a No. 40 blade. When using this combination, be sure to bathe and blow dry the dog's hair so it is absolutely straight before clipping. Otherwise the snap-on comb and No. 40 blade will snag any wave or curl and may damage the coat.

Many people purchase a dog never realizing that coats need care. It's nearly as important to groom the dog properly as it is to feed him. No dog can brush or comb himself. All he can do is clean himself with his tongue, rub, scratch, scoot, or bite himself.

Any dog that remains ungroomed soon becomes a host to fleas, lice, ticks, or mites. He often develops dandruff and his deteriorating coat and skin condition makes him testy and irritable. Obviously, the problem is worse for any long-coated breed.

Some potential dog owners try to circumvent the dog grooming chore by purchasing short-haired dogs. They believe that then grooming will be minimal. But even short-haired dogs shed.

Portuguese Water Dog grooming is minimal compared to the parallel needs of many long-coated breeds. The healthy Portuguese Water Dog doesn't shed. This is one reason the breed does well with allergic people. But when his hair is long, he certainly does decorate carpets with grass clippings, burrs, weeds, and sand if he isn't cleaned up after outdoor play. And if the Portuguese Water Dog is not brushed, combed and bathed regularly, dirt gets into his skin. Dead hair, which he cannot remove by himself, begins to annoy him. When he scratches himself, his hair may mat. Too much scratching may also leave sore patches.

These are the reasons grooming is so important. Really, by establishing the habit, grooming can be a relaxing, pleasant time for both you and your dog. If you have the grooming done by a professional, have it done often. But at least try to do some brushing and combing yourself.

Dogs respect those who groom them, just as they respect those who train them. Grooming enhances the close bond that should exist between you and your dog.

To groom your dog yourself you'll need the necessary tools shown in the accompanying illustrations. Only three of the tools are expensive: the Oster small animal clippers, the grooming table, and the small animal hair dryer. Perhaps you don't need to purchase some or any of these. However, each will pay for itself in convenience. Prices of scissors vary. You'll be giving scissors lots of heavy use in the years to come, so purchase the best you can afford.

Let's groom.

First Day's Grooming

The ideal time to begin grooming your Portuguese Water Dog puppy or adult is when he first comes home. Start his first grooming session *after* he's settled in and been introduced to his family.

Your Portuguese Water Dog may become frightened the first time you lift him onto the grooming table. This is natural. With a little tender loving care, he'll relax. Puppies fuss when you try to work with them on a table. Patiently ignore his protests.

If you have bought an adult dog, treat him as you would a young pup receiving his first grooming.

1. After sitting your dog on the grooming table, place your arm around him so that he cannot move away.

2. Standing in front of him or at his side, place your hands against his ear flaps. In a circular motion, rub them gently against his head. Talk to him softly as you rub. You're relaxing him.

3. Next, stand beside him so that his head is to your right. Stand him up. He'll stand easily if you place your right hand under his muzzle and your left hand under his body in front of his rear legs. As you raise him, tell him, "Stand." If he becomes fearful and resists, do the best you can, while speaking gently to him, telling him how pleased you are that he is cooperating (even if he isn't).

4. Once you have him standing, rub his belly to relax him. Spend from five seconds to about a half a minute, if the puppy is fussing. Try to hold onto his muzzle with your right hand. He should gradually relax. Next, lightly massage his body with your fingers. If he yawns or shivers, he is nervous. Sit him gently. Most dogs are more confident when sitting. Massage him gently to keep him relaxed.

5. End the grooming session by praising him and giving him a snack from the treat cannister. Place him on the floor.

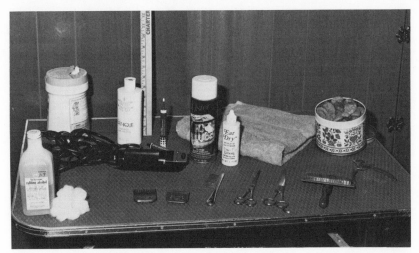

A grooming table laden with grooming tools. The cookie bone cannister is also an important grooming "tool." *Wayne Arnst*

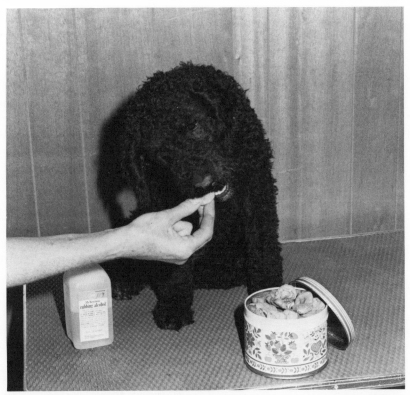

End every grooming session with praise and a treat from the cookie bone cannister. *Wayne Arnst*

Grooming Tools

FOR	NECESSARY	OPTIONAL	NOTE
EARS	RUBBING ALCOHOL OTI-CLENS COTTON BALLS DRYING POWDER	MINERAL OIL	
TEETH	CLOTH OR GAUZE		THE CONDITION OF AN ADULT DOG'S TEETH USUALLY DEPENDS ON HIS DIET AND WHAT HE HAS BEEN ALLOWED TO CHEW. YOU MAY CLEAN THE TEETH OR GUMS PERIODICALLY WITH A DAMP CLOTH MOISTENED IN SALT WATER (1 TABLESPOONFUL TO A PINT OF WATER). TARTER REMOVAL FROM THE DOG'S TEETH, ON A DAILY BASIS, IS BEST REMOVED BY FEEDING HIM ONE LARGE MILK BONE.
			IF HIS TEETH BEGIN TO ACCUMULATE TARTER OR YOU SUSPECT TOOTH DECAY MAKE AN APPOINTMENT AND SEE YOUR DOG'S VETERINARIAN. TARTER RE-MOVAL, ON A LIFETIME BASIS, IS BEST ACCOMPLISHED BY THE VET. HE HAS THE INSTRUMENTS TO REMOVE TARTER AND HE CAN CHECK YOUR DOG'S MOUTH FOR TEETH DECAY OR DISEASE.
EYES		STERILE OPHALMIC SOLUTION	USE TO CLEAR DUST-LADEN OR SUN-BURNED EYES. USE ONLY WHEN PRESCRIBED BY THE VETERINARIAN.
FEET	TOENAIL CLIPPERS	GRINDER	THERE ARE TWO TYPES OF CLIPPERS: THE GUILLOTINE TYPE OR THE HEAVY-DUTY PLIERS TYPE. THE LATTER IS IDEAL FOR PORTUGUESE WATER DOGS WITH HARD NAILS.
COAT	STRAIGHT SCISSORS CURVED-END SCISSORS SLICKER BRUSH PIN BRUSH THINNING SHEARS	BLUNT-END SCISSORS TEASING COMB	DOG SHOW EXHIBITORS OFTEN TIDY THE DOG'S SHOW COAT WITH A PIN BRUSH AND TEASING COMB BEFORE THEY ENTER THE RING AT SHOWS.
	COMB		THERE ARE TWO TYPES: A HALF-COMB AND A FULL COMB. THE FIRST NAMED HAS A HANDLE. THE LATTER HAS NO HANDLE; IT IS A FULL COMB WITH ONE HALF OF ITS TEETH COARSE AND THE OTHER HALF FINE.

Grooming Tools (Continued)

NECESSARY	OPTIONAL	NOTE
SPRAY (MIST) BOTTLE	MATTING COMB SMALL ANIMAL CLIPPER; OSTER A-5 WITH A NO. 4, NO. 4F, NO. 10, AND NO. 7 BLADES.	IT'S GOOD TO INVEST IN A SMALL ANIMAL CLIPPER. EVEN IF YOU INTEND HAVING YOUR DOG GROOMED BY A PROFESSIONAL GROOMER, YOU SHOULD PRACTICE CLIPPING HIM WHEN HE'S A PUP. YOU MIGHT BECOME AN EXPERT.
HAIR DRYER		IT'S BEST TO PURCHASE A SMALL ANIMAL HAIR DRYER. HAIR DRYERS SOLD FOR HUMAN USE EMIT A HIGH-PITCHED WHINE ON HIGH HEAT THAT BOTHERS A DOG'S SENSITIVE EAR DRUMS. IF YOU USE A HUMAN HAIR DRYER, KEEP IT ON LOW.

Other Grooming Tools

NECESSARY	OPTIONAL	NOTE
CANNISTER OF BABY-TYPE DISPOSABLE WASH CLOTHS		USE THESE FOR CLEANING AROUND EYES, VULVA, SCROTUM, ETC.
KWIK-STOP		USE THIS STYPTIC POWDER TO STOP BLEEDING, SUCH AS WHEN CUTTING INTO A NAIL QUICK.
GROOMING TABLE		THIS IS A WISE BUY. YOU MAY CHOOSE TO USE THE TOP OF A CRATE, AN ORDINARY TABLE. WHEN USING A CRATE OR TABLE, BE SURE TO PLACE THE NON-SLIP RUBBER MAT ON IT SO THE DOG HAS SECURE FOOTING. DON'T ATTEMPT TO GROOM YOUR DOG ON THE FLOOR. BOTH OF YOU WILL FIND THE GROOMING PROCEDURES UNCOMFORTABLE AND GROOMING YOUR DOG WILL TAKE ON THE ASPECTS OF A CHORE.
	GROOMING SLING	THIS IS AN ARM WITH A NOOSE 9COLLAR0 ATTACHED TO HOLD THE DOG'S HEAD STEADY WHILE YOU GROOM HIM.
RECTAL THERMOMENTER		WHEN YOUR DOG IS SICK, YOU MUST TAKE HIS TEMPERATURE.

Other Grooming Tools (Continued)

NECESSARY	NOTE
RULER OR TAPE MEASURE	YOU WANT TO KEEP A RECORD OF HOW YOUR DOG GROWS.
BATH SCALES	
CANNISTER OF DOG BISCUIT TREATS	YOU WANT TO REWARD YOUR DOG WITH TREATS AT THE END OF EACH GROOMING SESSION.

Bath Tools

NECESSARY	OPTIONAL	NOTE
BATHTUB		
HAND SPRAYER OR SMALL FLEXIBLE SPRAY HOSE WITH ADJUSTABLE HEAD OR PAN USED TO POUR WATER OVER DOG FOR RINSING		
NON-SLIP RUBBER OR SYNTHETIC BATH MAT		
pH BALANCED CONDITIONING SHAMPOO FOR DOGS	SMALL-ANIMAL INSECTICIDE SHAMPOO OR DIPS	THESE SHAMPOOS ARE HARD ON DOGS' COATS. USE THEM ONLY WHEN NECESSARY FOR PARASITE CONTROL (FLEAS, TICKS, ETC.)
COTTON BALLS		
VASELINE OR MINERAL OIL		
FACE TOWEL		
LARGE BATH TOWELS		

Easy, wasn't it.

During the first two weeks your Portuguese Water Dog lives with you, groom him daily. Because grooming makes him feel good, he'll look forward to it. Later, when you head for the grooming table, he'll get there first and be standing on top waiting for you.

If, after the first two weeks you decide he doesn't need daily grooming, change the schedule to fit his needs. The habit of grooming will have been established.

Whatever your decision, never neglect either the weekly or the twice-monthly health check. These are important lifetime grooming checkpoints.

Daily Grooming

1. Place the dog on the grooming table.

2. EARS—Rub his ears. This relaxes him and loosens dirt that might be clinging to the underside of his ear flaps. Next, lift the flaps and look at both ear leather and inside ears for dirt.

If the ear is dirty, clean it using a cotton ball moistened with "Oti-Clens," a multi-cleansing ear solution obtainable at your veterinarian, or with alcohol. Squeeze the excess alcohol from the cotton ball. Carefully wipe the earlobe clean. Rub his ear again while the alcohol dries. Follow the same procedure for the second ear. Don't probe when cleaning the inside of a dog's ear or go deeper than your finger can reach. We don't advise using cotton-tipped sticks. The pointed tips may damage a dog's ear, even though the ends are wrapped with cotton.

If you can't get an ear clean or if an ear emits an odor, take your dog to your veterinarian. The dog may have an ear infection. An infection can "blow up" a dog's ear within 24 hours. He may have picked up ear mites, which are highly contagious among puppies. In the warm months, foxtails and plant awns may get stuck deep inside a puppy's ears. If this happens, soften the sharp pointed stickers by moistening them with cooking oil. To do this, put about a teaspoonful of the oil on a cotton ball and squeeze into the ear. Then get your dog to your vet. Stickers may penetrate his eardrums. Only veterinarians have the proper instruments to probe ears and the skill to use them.

3. EYES—Using a disposable washcloth, gently wipe dirt from the inside corner of each eye, using a clean portion of the washcloth for each. By removing dirt and normal discharge, hair loss caused by these irritations should be minimal.

4. BODY—Move your fingers over the dog's body. Check for burrs, mud or parasites that might be caught in his coat or be clinging to his skin. Check carefully under elbows, along his underside and under his back legs. While you search, massage him. Check for mats. The most obvious places are behind and under the ears, under elbows, under the rump and on legs

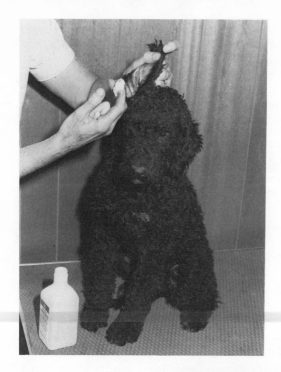

If the ear is dirty, clean it only with an alcohol-moistened cotton ball. *Wayne Arnst*

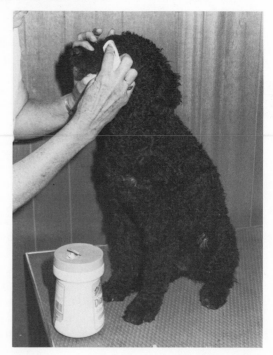

Using a disposable wash cloth, gently wipe dirt from the inside corner of the eye. *Wayne Arnst*

178

and paws. The Portuguese Water Dog's hair is thinner on his underside.

With regular grooming, mats seldom form. If they do appear and you cannot brush them out, pull them apart with your fingers—gently please. Then comb the rest of the hair around the mat. If you still can't remove it, strip the mat out with the thinning shears.

Brush your curly-coated Portuguese Water Dog well with the slicker brush. Brush the wavy-coated dog with a pin brush, especially on show coats. Finish with the comb.

While you groom the dog, alternately stand and sit him. Have him lie down. Each time you change his position, tell him what you are doing. Emphasize the command and bolster him with the praise. "Stand, good puppy, g-o-o-d! Sit, g-o-o-d." "Lie down, good." Praising him while sitting, standing, or lying down teaches him what the command means.

5. RECTUM—Clean the anus and reproductive organs with a clean washcloth. With scissors, carefully trim the hair so the dog can keep the area clean.

6. COMPLETION—Sit him on the table and admire him. This special attention gives him added confidence and pride.

End the grooming session by praising him for cooperating and reward him with a treat.

Weekly Grooming

1. EARS—Portuguese Water Dogs will grow excess hair inside their ears if the growth is not checked. This hair may prevent air from reaching the inner ear; a damp inner ear channel can lead to infection. To avoid infection, regularly pluck this excess hair from the ears. Sprinkle a little ear powder inside, then pluck excess hair out with your fingers. It'll come right out. What doesn't, isn't meant to. Professionals often use round tipped tweezers or blunt-edged scissors to trim inner hair, rather than plucking. Some dogs, whose ear hair is plucked constantly, may develop an infection if the ear isn't cleansed properly. But you must be careful in using scissors. You don't want the blunt scissors to injure his ears. Ears are very delicate.

2. PAWS—Cut his nails often. There are two ways to do this: either sit him or lay him on his side on the grooming table. If you want him to lie down and you're right handed, lay him on his left side; if you're left handed, lay him on his right side. It'll be easier for you to manipulate the clippers. As you lay him down, teach him the command, "Down . . . good boy." Always cut nails on hind paws first. Your dog won't be as likely to protest because he can't see exactly what you're doing. When you get to the front paws, most dogs want to watch and draw their front paws away in anticipation of discomfort. He'll soon get used to having his nails cut.

Each nail on a dog's foot has a live portion, or quick. Because the nails on your Portuguese Water Dog's toes may be colored black or brown,

Brush your dog well with a slicker or pin brush. *Wayne Arnst*

depending on his coat color, it's not easy to tell where the quick begins. And if you cut into it, bleeding results and the dog will be in pain. This discourages many dog owners from cutting nails. It shouldn't.

If you're fearful of cutting into the quick, shine a flashlight under the nail to show you where the quick ends. If you're still unsure, just snip the outer edge of the nail. Don't cut close to the quick. It's better to take off a little and clip twice as often than to cut into the quick. With weekly practice, you'll soon gain the necessary confidence.

If you accidentally cut into a quick, don't apologize. If you do, your dog will try to prevent you from cutting other nails. Instead of apologizing, simply say, "Oh oh, that's too bad." Let it go at that. Apply a coagulant powder to stop the bleeding. Continue cutting his nails. Be firm.

If he fights your attempts to make him lie still, rebuke him sternly. Every dog must allow his owner to cut and file his nails. Place him back into position. Teach him that you are boss. This will pay off. He's learning to become obedient.

Some dogs may try to bite when their nails are cut. If the dog turns his head toward you to bite, rap his muzzle firmly with your finger and tell him sternly, "No."

Many dog owners wonder why their dogs' nails have to be cut so often. If they're cut frequently, only a little needs to be taken off each time. With regular cutting, the quick recedes, so there's less chance of cutting into it. The wild animal's nails stay short because he wears them down running free. If a dog's nails grow too long, the toes may spread (splay). Splayed paws are very ugly; in addition, the dog will be handicapped. He can't walk well, run well, or swim well with this condition. Incidentally, dogs kept in cement runs may develop splayed feet. Taking your dogs on leash to run often on grass and sandy beaches helps tighten the pads.

3. SCISSORING FEATHERING ON BOTTOM OF PAWS— Hand scissor the excess hair (feathering) from under his foot pads with small blunt-end scissors. You'll eliminate many possible paw irritations from burrs, small stones, foxtails, mud and other debris by doing this.

4. MEASURING AND WEIGHING—Measure your puppy by laying a tape measure or yardstick against his side at his point of withers (tip of shoulder). Do this throughout his life, even after he's full grown. This accustoms him to being touched and to being measured, a requirement in advanced AKC obedience classes.

5. COMPLETION—Complete the grooming session by praising your dog and giving him a treat.

Twice-Monthly Grooming

Bath time!
You may have read that dogs should only be bathed twice a year. It's

not so. A dog should be bathed when he is dirty. Healthy, clean pores are necessary for a healthy coat. Frequent baths may cause skin problems. But this is only true if the soap used is too harsh and rinsing is incomplete. If you want the dog to have a good coat, never leave a trace of soap scum on the dog's body.

Kathryn Braund raises Dalmatians along with Portuguese Water Dogs. While Dalmatians have short coats, they shed fine white hair in all seasons. Dalmatian hairs get all over the house. The non-shedding Portuguese Water Dogs lie down on the carpets but the Dalmatian hair doesn't cling to their coats. The oil in the Portuguese Water Dog coat repels the hairs.

But the Portuguese Water Dog still gets dirty. He should be bathed at least once a month during the winter and twice a month during the summer. Take common-sense precautions in bitter weather so that he doesn't become chilled after his bath. Don't allow him out of the heated house until he is thoroughly dry.

Portuguese Water Dogs may like water, but they merely suffer their bath. Few dogs enjoy having their faces soaped, even though pH canine balanced soaps are tear-free.

Bathing your dog:
1. On the grooming table, brush dirt out of the coat. Look for tangles and mats. If you find any, comb them out.

Never scissor or clip your dog when he is dirty. Dirt dulls both scissors and clippers, giving them shorter lives. It may split hair ends as well.

2. You may fill the bathtub with water up to the dog's elbows or use a spray attachment. Be sure the water is warm.

3. Place a non-slip rubber mat in the bathtub.

4. Place a cotton ball inside each ear to keep soap out.

5. Place a dab of vaseline or mineral oil in the corner of each eye. This protects the eyes from soap.

6. Now place your dog in the bathtub. Wet him down thoroughly. Start soaping him from the neck back. Massage the soap onto his coat well. Scrub his feet. Wash his tail. Wash his hindquarters and belly. Finally, soap and wash the top of his head and muzzle.

7. When he's been well scrubbed, rinse him. Use warm water to rinse. Cold water doesn't remove soap. The soap must be thoroughly rinsed off for his coat to maintain luster.

8. Resoap him. This soaping removes dirt that the first soaping softened. Some canine shampoos must be left on the dog for from 5 to 10 minutes during the second soaping so conditioners can penetrate the hair shafts. While you wait, rinse his head and face. Clean his anal glands, if necessary. Anal glands of most dogs have to be squeezed periodically to clear them.

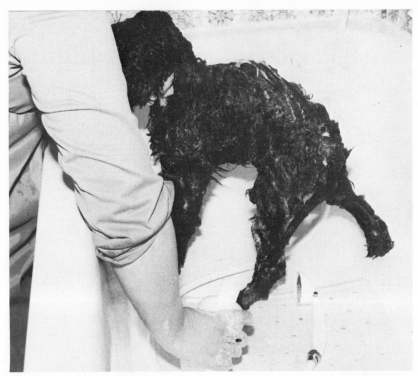

Start soaping from the neck back.   *Wayne Arnst*

Clean the anal glands,
if necessary.
Wayne Arnst

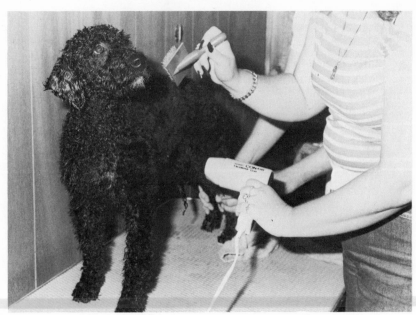

To tidy, clip and scissor, you must first straighten the hair by blow-drying. *Wayne Arnst*

Here is Diver (Ch. Farmion Geo, CDX) in a mini-version of the Working clip, highly suitable for an active dog *and* for show. He was trimmed with a plastic snap-on comb over a No. 40 blade. Leg hair is left at two inches.
Stuart White

NOTE: Never attempt to empty your dog's anal glands until you've been instructed by your veterinarian. He will be glad to teach you how to do this since this is not a function most veterinarians have time to perform regularly. After you've been instructed, it's easy to expell excess fluid from the dog's anal glands when you are giving him a bath. If the dog sits down and drags his anus along the ground he may need his anal glands cleared. He may also do this to clean himself after defecating. Occasionally, anal glands emit a strong odor if they need cleaning. If he licks his anal area too often, you may want to check his anal glands.

9. Using warm water, rinse him again and again. Remember, soap residue is responsible for setting up many skin irritations. It may also split hair ends when you clip or scissor. A final cool rinse gives added gloss.

10. Before taking him out of the tub, dry his head with a face towel. Remove the cotton balls from his ears and dry the ears gently yet thoroughly. Then place a large bath towel around his body. The towel will discourage him from shaking himself when he is allowed out of the tub. It also absorbs excess moisture. Some professional groomers use sponges to pat a dog dry. Take him out of the tub and put him on the grooming table.

11. Now, let him shake. Help him learn the command by telling him "shake" each time he does. Shaking helps his coat spring back to its natural curl or wave immediately. Let him dry.

12. To tidy, clip, and scissor, you must first straighten his hair by blow-drying it. While blow-drying, brush his hair with the grain. On his sides, brush at an angle. On his legs, particularly at his stifle, brush at an angle. Under his elbows, brush against the grain. Hold the back legs up so you can get underneath when brushing.

Do one small section at a time. Begin from the back and work forward. Dogs are usually easier to handle from the rear. It is impossible to clip, scissor, or trim evenly unless you blow dry first because blow-drying straightens the coat so you'll see unevenness or high and low places.

13. Don't clip until the hair is dry. You won't shock yourself. Clippers run more easily through straightened hair.

14. The accompanying photographs show the proper way to hold both scissors and clippers. They'll also guide you in learning how to groom your Portuguese Water Dog. Please don't expect to do a good job until you've had ample practice. Allow yourself at least a dozen trimming sessions to begin to master the art of clipping and scissoring a dog. The most difficult parts will be under the elbows, groin, hindquarters, and back legs. None of these surfaces are straight. Even though you may have a grooming arm to hold your dog fairly steady, dogs twist their heads and pull their legs away as you work on them.

If you have doubts that you can master this art, hire a professional to scissor, at least once a month. But with practice, you can keep your dog in nice shape for home, if not for a regular program of shows.

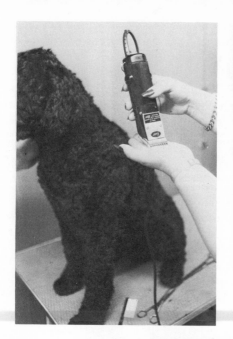
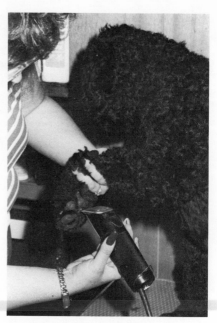
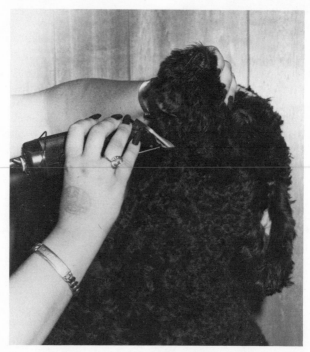

This group of photographs shows the proper way to hold clippers and dog for the grooming procedures.

Wayne Arnst

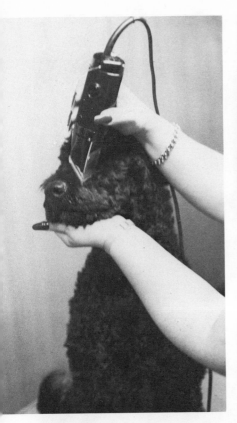

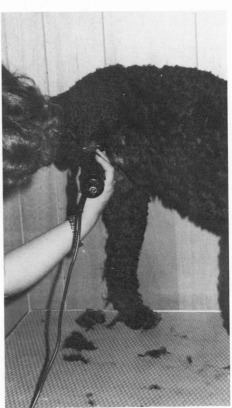

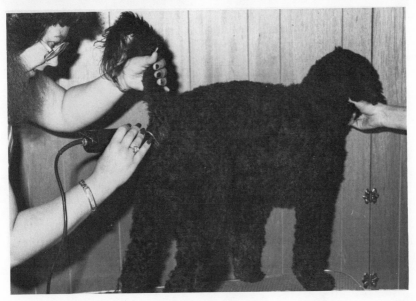

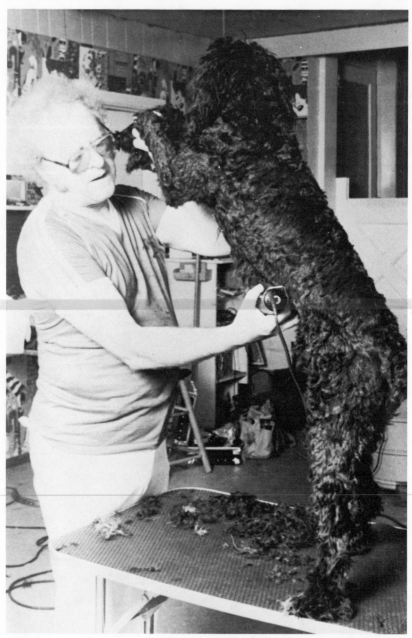

If you have doubts you can clip and scissor, hire a professional. Here Ed Griffith clips one of Deyanne Miller's dogs.

15. Here are points to remember when handling clippers:
    a) Keep a flexible wrist when working.
    b) Don't dig into the dog's skin.
    c) Follow the grain of hair on body and face, go at an angle on legs and sides, and go against the grain under arms and legs.
    d) Finish by scissoring.
    e) Finally, use the scissors to shape the hair on the dog's paws.
    f) Don't worry if you make mistakes. The hair soon springs back into a curl or wave, hiding incorrect snips. Normally the hair grows quickly to cover more serious errors.

Working Retriever Clip

The entire coat including head, face, and legs is clipped or scissored to follow the outline of the dog, leaving a short blanket of coat appearing no more than one inch thick. Three inches from the end of the tail, the hair is left at full length.

Use the No. 4F blade to clip his hair about 5/8 inch long. Clip his body, legs, feet, head, muzzle, ears, and tail—to three inches from the tip.

Clip the dog's ear flaps inside as well as outside.

Attach the No. 10 blade to the clippers. Trim belly hair, hair under elbows, and hair around the genitals. Teach the dog to lie down quietly for this part of the clipping procedure.

Now, with the scissors, shape his coat evenly, snipping off scraggly hairs. Finish trimming hair around the genitals with blunt nosed scissors.

Scissor-trim the edges of the ear leathers. Do so, using your thumb and index finger, moving to the end of the ear leather. Then scissor. If you cut too closely, you'll be apt to nick your finger, not the dog's leather. Trim even with the ear leather. Tidy hair on the outside of his ears.

Scissor-trim scraggly curls on his tail, but not beyond the last three to five inches. A tuft must remain on his tail. Why do we say three to five inches and not a definite three or a definite five? Each dog is an individual and is groomed to make him look his best.

Scissor-cut hair for an inch around his eyes to a half inch in length. Without this halo trim, the Portuguese Water Dog's eyes soon become lost under a mass of hair that obstructs his vision.

Lion Clip

When the coat is long, the muzzle and hindquarters from the middle part of the dog, usually the third or fourth rib from the last rib back, are clipped. Three inches from the end of the tail, the hair is left at full length.

First, allow the dog's hair to grow to a length of from three to four inches. Then after bathing, blow drying and brushing, attach the No. 10

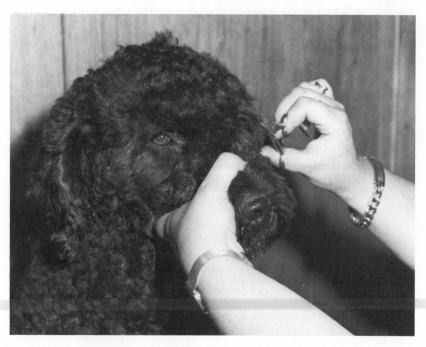

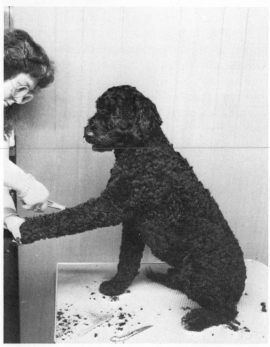

Finish by scissoring.

Wayne Arnst

blade to the clippers. Clip him from the third or fourth rib from the last rib back. In the clipping, include all of the hind legs, feet and tail—with the exception of the last three to five inches. Here, leave the hair its natural length.

Using the No. 10 blade, clip his face from his throat to ears. Don't clip above his eyes.

Hand scissor the remainder of his coat to a length that looks best on him.

Hair Growth

Like human hair, dog hair grows approximately 1/2 inch a month. During late spring and early fall growth is slightly faster. As days lengthen in the spring, the daylight stimulates hair growth. When temperatures drop in early fall, colder weather stimulates hair growth. A young dog's hair grows faster than the hair of an older dog. Dogs on vitamin supplements and other supplements tend to have faster hair growth than dogs on maintenance diets. Also, dogs kept outside and dogs who swim often grow hair more rapidly. Most animal coats are thinner in the summer, lusher in the winter.

Grooming for the Show Ring

Now that you have been grooming your Portuguese Water Dog on a daily, weekly, and twice-monthly basis, apply your new skills and groom him yourself for the show ring.

The first step in preparing to groom him for the show ring is to hang a photograph of an ideal Portuguese Water Dog in the clip you prefer—Working Retriever or Lion—near the grooming table. Groom your dog to the ideal.

If you're going to show him in the Working Retriever clip, you'll want to scissor him. Clipping may straighten curls or waves too much. If you clip, you must do it at least several months before being shown. Tidy a Working Retriever clip several weeks before showing.

If you're going to show your dog in the Lion clip, you must first allow his hair to grow long. This may take as long as four to five months after his last clipping.

Show Ring Working Retriever Clip: During the last two weeks before showing your dog, spend a half hour a day thoroughly brushing and combing him. If your dog has a curly coat it will look more like a wavy coat after several days of this intense grooming. Regardless of coat type, the show dog's coat should be very clean and tangle free.

The night before the show, bathe him. Allow him to dry naturally. If he's curly, place a towel around him and leave it on him overnight. His hair will curl tightly and evenly. Just before entering the show ring, brush and then comb the hair on his head and legs. Snip off body curls that appear scraggly. Take a mist bottle to ringside and mist his body coat lightly and press scraggly curls just before your class is called.

If he's wavy, everything is essentially the same, except you must blow dry him after each bath. You don't need any coat oil or mist as his wavy coat is naturally glossy. Several hours before ring time, mist (spray) him all over and allow him to dry naturally. Then, with a teasing comb, gently lift his hair. You do this because the wavy hair tends to lie flat.

Show Ring Lion Clip: Follow the same brushing and combing procedure as with the Working Retriever clip. Clip with the No. 10 and No. 7 blades where necessary several days prior to showing him. Bathe your dog the night before the show and brush him well.

Some groomers say it takes three days for natural curl or wave and coat oil to return; however, by following the above brushing procedures, no coat oil will be lost. It's much nicer to enter the ring with a sparkling clean dog.

Food Supplements For Healthy Coat Growth

Animals, as well as humans, are a reflection of both heredity and environment. A dog's coat is nourished from the inside. Build its quality with proper food and exercise.

Fresh food supplements such as ocean fish, meat, eggs, fruit and green vegetables will be reflected in coat condition. Canine nutritionists claim these may be safely added to a complete and balanced dry dog food in a 20 percent ratio. Be sure the dry meal you feed your dog is labeled "complete and balanced."

Do give your Portuguese Water Dog vitamin-mineral supplements daily. Ask your veterinarian which supplements he recommends.

Add oil to your dog's diet as well. A good rule of thumb to follow is this: 1) summer—one teaspoonful of oil daily for every thirty pounds; 2) winter—one tablespoonful of oil or one teaspoonful of cod liver oil. Do not use cod liver oil in the summertime. If you do, you're taking a chance on oversupplying his vitamin D requirements. During summer, the sun's rays ordinarily supply him with ample vitamin D. Another excellent source of oil is wheat germ. Wheat germ oil contains a healthy supply of vitamin E. Be careful not to overdose. An excess of this oil-soluble vitamin may cause hair loss. All oil stimulates intestinal activity and may cause diarrhea or loose stools. Too much oil increases the dog's requirement for vitamin E.

Lack of biotin may be one of the reasons some Portuguese Water Dogs are prone to coprophagy (stool eating). To help eliminate coprophagy in all dog breeds, dog food manufacturers routinely add biotin to dry meals. Biotin's best natural sources are brewer's yeast, brown (untreated) rice, liver, and kidney.

192

Clam juice, which contains an ample amount of vitamin B, may be fed twice weekly to aid in growing a lustrous coat. When Portuguese Water Dogs have lost their coats because of illness or pregnancy, clam juice has worked miracles.

In Portugal, salt water (ocean) fish was a staple. There have been only a few generations of dogs born since this breed's diet became processed. We believe some health problems may be caused by the inability of the digestive system to adapt quickly.

We suggest feeding your Portuguese Water Dog a teaspoonful of brewer's yeast daily. Brewer's yeast may help control fleas. In a study conducted by Richard E. Bradley, DVM, Ph.D., of the University of Florida, College of Veterinary Medicine, dogs given brewer's yeast at the rate of 110 mg/kg a day had a deterrent of up to 54.4 percent fewer fleas. Brewer's yeast tablets delivering as much as 60 mg thiamine hydrochloride/day worked about as well.

He concluded: "Although the manner in which brewer's yeast reduces flea populations is unknown, the routine use of brewer's yeast as a dietary supplement for dogs apparently provides some degree of flea control."

Finally, don't underestimate the value of sun conditioning. Vitamin D is absorbed from the sun's rays. Be aware too much sun may also dull or rust mature hair. When is hair on a Portuguese Water Dog mature? When it has grown to about 1½ inches in length and remains uncut and exposed to weather for several months.

To inhibit rusting, some breeders limit the Portuguese Water Dog's sun bathing to a short interval each day. But Portuguese Water Dogs themselves, if allowed, limit the effects of too much sun. They seek the shade when the sun bears down hard on them for any length of time.

Frequency of Clipping

How often should you clip or scissor your Portuguese Water Dog?

The standard calls for the Working Retriever clip to "follow the outline . . . leaving a short blanket of coat no longer than one inch in length." This is ambiguous. Although we highly defend the standard, it should read "appearing no longer than one inch in length." Two inches of coat compressed into one inch leaves a short blanket of coat appearing no longer than one inch in length.

Those who prefer the Lion clip aren't given exact specifications. The standard states the hair may be clipped "as soon as the coat grows long."

Remember, this is a working dog. The Portuguese Water Dog's all-weather, non-shedding, well-groomed coat is one of the breed's best advertisements.

Happy grooming.

11

Lifetime Care of the
Portuguese Water Dog

$\mathbf{I}$N THIS CHAPTER, we're going to take you through the life cycle of the Portuguese Water Dog.

We're going to concentrate on his life from the moment he is conceived—a tiny germ plasm programmed with a remarkable canine potential for love and loyalty—until he departs the world leaving behind glorious memories. We'll spend more time on his puppy phase because the puppy's care and environment largely forms the adult dog.

Before Birth

This is how a Portuguese Water Dog comes to life.

His mother goes into her normal estrus cycle or heat by discharging blood from her uterus. This cycle ordinarily occurs about every six to eight months and lasts a full 21 days. Within the cycle there is a short three- to six-day ovulation period, commonly called "standing heat." During this period, some of the eggs fall off the wall of the ovary and float down into two passageways, called the fallopian tubes. These tubes lead to the uterus. There, the eggs mature. When the bitch is mated during her standing heat, the mature ova (eggs) are fertilized by the male's sperm. In most bitches, standing heat begins about the 12th day of estrus and ends about the 15th. In some, ovulation may begin as early as the eighth day; in still others, it may not begin until the 15th or 16th day. This is why the breedable bitch must be confined for most, if not all, of each 21-day heat cycle whether or not she's to be bred. The bitch need not be confined during the first six days.

The determining factor of litter size is the number of mature ova that the bitch has waiting to be fertilized. She, therefore, determines the litter size. The dog's sperm cells contain the chromosomes that determine sex. He, then, determines the sex of each pup in the litter. As in humans, females determine number and males determine sex. Each egg develops with the genes for structure and physical characteristics inherited from both parents.

Each fertilized egg finds sanctuary in one of the two uterine horns, the bitch's insulated incubators.

In normal pregnancy, each pup reaches the size of a walnut about 26 days after conception. The pups may often be felt as hard nodules. Only skilled hands, such as those of a veterinarian, should be allowed to palpate the bitch. Unnecessary probing and prodding by inexperienced hands may displace the pups and make survival difficult.

Just when palpating is easiest, a sac of fluid begins to form around each pup. It quickly encases him, protecting his growing body as the mother moves about. It is difficult to palpate once the sac forms.

After the pup has spent eight weeks inside his mother, he's almost ready to emerge into the world. His skeleton is formed and muscled. During the last week of incubation finishing touches are added—hair, toenails, and eyelashes.

This is an exciting week: he's full of action. His mother feels him move; you can feel and see him move. He kicks his feet, turns his head and may even wag his tail. Shortly before birth he slowly drops down toward the birth canal from where his mother had him hidden, high under ribs or abdomen. His entrance into the world is imminent. He is born from 59 to 66 days after he has been conceived.

While the bitch may suffer during delivery, most pups enter the world without any sign of distress. They arrive well protected inside their private fetal sac, which is doubly protected by being enclosed in a private water bag. Until they reach the outside world, the pups remain connected to their mother by umbilical cords.

The pups enter the world one at a time from their individual incubators in opposite uterine horns. Sometimes, when descending the birth canal, a pup becomes twisted; if he doesn't emerge shortly, he dies. Another may inhale fluid from an unexpelled afterbirth which seeps into his fetal sac. If the pup inhales this into his lungs, he dies. These are birth tragedies certainly, but most pups arrive unharmed.

After the pup is born, most bitches immediately remove the fetal sac which has protected her developing infant but which now prevents him from breathing. If she doesn't, the owner must help. Next, she snips off his umbilical cord. She then cleans him, her abrasive tongue stimulating his blood circulation. When she is done tossing him about to make sure every inch of him is dry—he tests his lungs by crying. The sparkling clean, sweet-smelling, newborn Portuguese Water Dog then immediately crawls to the warmth of mother's breast to feed.

The First Weeks—Helplessness

At birth, he can cry; he can crawl; he can smell; he can suckle. The remainder of his motor responses are sluggish, some largely undeveloped. He can't see and he can't hear. His eyes and ears are glued shut. He can feel cold and heat, but he can't protect himself from the cold; neither can he generate warmth within himself. He is born before his heating mechanism has developed.

His very helplessness protects him. By staying close to his mother, he stays close to his source of heat and food. He nurses almost continuously while awake. He sleeps the rest of the time and grows continuously.

Rate of Growth

For the first seven weeks, or until fully weaned, a healthy Portuguese Water Dog's rate of growth is dependent on birth weight. If, for instance, he's eight ounces at birth, he'll gain about five more ounces in the first week. Most Portuguese Water Dog pups triple their birth weight in the first three weeks. Optimum weight gain during the early and helpless weeks is dependent upon the following:

1. Size of litter and availability of nipples plus quality of milk. Pups in small litters gain more quickly because of less competition for food. Pups in large litters gain more slowly.

2. Physical health of individual puppy.

3. Sucking capability. Some puppies are slow to develop sucking power.

4. Amount of protein in the bitch's milk. Weight gain is proportionate to the quality of the bitch's food.

5. Heat regulation of litter box. A newborn puppy has a temperature of only 90 degrees F (32.2 degrees C). His temperature increases very slowly, reaching a normal canine temperature of from 100 to 102.5 degrees F (37.7 to 39.1 degrees C) when he's approximately five and one half weeks old. This is the reason it's absolutely necessary to keep the puppy's environment at from 85 to 90 degrees F during the first week of life and 85 degrees F during the second. Standard procedure at Farmion Kennels during the first 15 days of a litter's life is to use two space heaters and two small humidifiers in the whelping room. The heat in the room is then balanced with the proper ratio of humidity. This is easy to check by a hardware store heat and humidity indicator placed on the floor of the whelping box. During the entire third week, keep the temperature at 75 to

196

80 degrees F. Ideal temperatures during the fourth and fifth weeks is 70 degrees F. After pups are five and one half weeks of age, they can be sensibly introduced to fluctuating temperatures. It's well to note that although pups do survive in lower temperatures during the helpless weeks, they don't thrive as well as those kept at the ideal temperature. Those maintained in ideal environments don't have to waste energy trying to keep themselves warm.

Puppy Deaths

Deaths occurring during the first weeks of life frequently stem from structural malformations such as hare lip, cleft palate, heart defects or anal malformations, congenital diseases such as digestive, circulatory or respiratory; infectious diseases; injuries, chilling and malnutrition.

The first signs of distress in ill puppies are excessive crying and salivation along with the inability to crawl.

Please refer to another Howell book, *Dog Owner's Home Veterinary Handbook,* by Delbert G. Carlson, DVM and James M. Giffin, MD (Howell Book House, Inc.) for detailed information on possible puppy deaths.

Dam's Diet During Pregnancy and Nursing

From the moment of fertilization, the puppy is fed by the mother. Therefore, the quality of his mother's food is important.

Pups draw little sustenance from their mother until they are about four weeks into incubation. From then on, extra protein should be added to the mother's regular maintenance diet.

Canine nutritionists claim fresh food may be safely added in quarter increments; such as one quarter meat, fish, eggs, or milk to three quarters *complete and balanced* dog meal. The nutritionists claim that then there is little chance of unbalancing the dog's nutritional requirements. We believe puppies develop their full potential by the addition of quality food in the above ratio. For sample diets and how to feed please refer to the chapter on nutrition.

Care of the Newborn

First Week—Be sure to keep a dim light on 24 hours a day in the whelping room. You want the bitch to be able to see her puppies at all times so she can avoid laying on them.

The breeder can see in the simple lines of the wet newborn Portuguese Water Dog puppy a glimmer of the future adult structure.

As soon as whelping is over, the bitch and whelping box must be thoroughly cleaned. Remove soiled newspapers. Place puppies in a pad

He tests his lungs by crying.

Newborn puppies get better footing on blankets than they do on newspapers.

and blanket-lined cardboard box warmed with an electric blanket underneath.

When the whelping box is clean, cover the floor with newspapers and place a clean soft blanket over them. A flannel bedsheet is excellent. The blanket will have to be changed several times daily because the bitch will drip a bloody discharge for at least a week, perhaps longer. Also, puppies' urine will spot it. Why then, place a blanket on the floor and not newspapers or carpeting? Newborn puppies get better footing on blankets than newspapers. They learn to crawl faster because they get more exercise. Puppies housed on blankets rather than newspapers develop better legs. Blankets may be washed and dried and replaced quickly. Newspapers are slippery and most carpeting is treated with chemicals toxic to a baby animal.

The soft texture of a blanket has an additional advantage; it offers the bitch a body cushion; it helps prevent pressure points from building on hips and thighs. It also prevents her hair from matting or rubbing off there. Carpet pile is usually rough to a puppy and will rub hair off the pup. Don't house puppies on hay or wood chips either. These materials may cause future allergic reactions in puppies.

When a blanket is replaced with a clean one, puppies examine it with noses. Even day-old puppies give every indication they can scent and feel.

The first week of a healthy puppy's life is spent eating, sleeping, and growing. It is important to watch the whelping box constantly so that the bitch doesn't inadvertently lie on or crush pups against walls or under side railings. The Portuguese Water Dog is still a primitive breed. While this can be seen in easy whelping, it can also be seen in the first days the pup is alive. If the pup whines or cries too much, in her anxiety to placate him, she may grab him with a paw and roughly pull him to her. Puppies and dam should be watched constantly during this period.

The bitch stimulates all elimination with her tongue and injests it, keeping her puppies clean and sweet-smelling.

Second Week—The bitch still stimulates each pup with her tongue so it can eliminate. Toward the end of this week, some pups begin to move away from the bitch, urinating on their own at the far side of the box.

As soon as you see this occurring, fold the blanket covering the floor so that it covers about half of the whelping box. Then spread newspapers over the other half. Housebreaking benefits from this texture division; the puppies quickly learn to crawl to newspapers to urinate.

Eyes begin to open from at the inside corners anytime from the seventh day forward. When this occurs, draw the curtains or shades on the windows in the puppies' room. In the wild dogs' den, darkness protects newly opening eyes. In the modern home and kennel, bright sunlight may stream into the whelping box. Turn off bright lights altogether and protect nature's deliberate slow and delicate eye opening procedure. Use a 25-watt bulb in a well-shaded lamp. Avoid fluorescent lighting. Some ophthalmologists claim the lower frequency of fluorescent lights is harder on eyes.

Ears begin to open at about the same time. Many puppies hear sounds at about ten days. To test this possibility, whistle or coo softly when approaching and look for an ear flap to twitch or even partially rise in answer to the sound. If it does, examine the closure under the ear flap and you'll see a minute opening.

Keep house noises soft. Don't slam doors. Don't shout. Sound shyness in dogs often begins in the whelping box! Sound-caused aggressiveness may also begin here. All sound stimulation during this important imprinting period should be positive. Don't scare your puppies with loud or unpleasant sounds.

Third Week—Puppies have developed a puppy smell. It is soft, furry-like and milky. It's a clean, lovely smell.

Pups now eliminate by themselves. It's so easy to help them learn clean bowel habits. Pick up and replace newspapers as soon as they are soiled. Some pups are developing excellent control. They'll sleep on the blanket, get up from their bed and walk over to the newspapers to eliminate.

If food has been introduced to pups during this week, most bitches stop ingesting their pups' excrement. A few continue to do so as long as pups nurse. If yours has stopped cleaning up after her pups, it now becomes your duty. A meticulously clean whelping box discourages coprophagy (stool eating) among curious pups.

Clipping pups' toenails should now be a weekly task. Blunt-nosed scissors do the job quickly.

Milk teeth may appear through gums. A few pups are restless, because their gums hurt. Teething is relieved by mouthing and biting litter mates. This is an ideal time to place hard nylon bones and large hard rubber balls in the litter box for pups to mouth. Other excellent teething aids are old pieces of toweling and damp wash cloths. A suggestion: wring out a wet wash cloth and place it in the freezer for several hours. This makes an excellent teething aid. Pups also like to teethe on small marrow bones, such as roundsteak bones. Place a fresh one in the whelping box and watch the pups scramble to it. Whelping box toys help teach the pups which objects belong to them and which do not. Farmion Delgades believed in retrieving and collected tennis balls and put them in the whelping box when her pups were about three weeks old.

Fourth Week—Each puppy's face takes on a unique expression. Each is a miracle of response. All systems are go!

When eyes lose the glassy stare, shades may be lifted and lights turned back on. Most eyes are colored baby blue. They'll gradually darken until they achieve their true color at from six to nine weeks of age.

If stains form under eyes and the bitch does not remove them, wipe eyes clean with a water-dampened washcloth. Don't rub. Remember, puppy eyes are delicate.

Ears are wide open. Pups hear well. Even if you don't suspect hearing problems, give each pup a simple hearing test. Isolate him; when he isn't looking at you ring a bell, sing a few words of a song, whistle, rattle a pan. When he's away from his littermates, the pup can't follow their movements. If you suspect a pup's hearing isn't what you think it should be, repeat the simple hearing tests daily. Each day test the pup in a different area.

Pups often scratch their ears during this period. This is natural. It's not a sign of ear problems. However, begin checking ears daily for cleanliness.

You must now provide each pup with individual investigative experiences, both inside and outside the house, weather permitting. Be careful you do not place the pup on grass if there is any possibility of fleas or ticks. Introduce him to new places gradually. Be very protective of the pup so he gains, never loses, confidence.

Have fun. Place food treats or toys on a string and pull them along in front of the puppy to encourage his ability to follow a trail. You are teaching him to play.

Fifth Week—Pups are now well up on their paws. Begin stacking (standing) each pup daily. When you first place a puppy on a table, he'll be fearful of the height. He might roach his back or stretch his front legs forward tensely. Gently rub his tummy as you stand him, grasping his neck firmly with the other hand. Massage his back with your fingers. Then give him a small meat treat and place him back on the floor. The introduction to the grooming table should take no longer than 20 seconds. As the days go by, lengthen the time he is held there. Follow the same procedure. He'll begin to look forward to being placed on the table.

This is the week you'll want to take pictures of the puppies. They now stand in good physical balance. If you're going to stack the puppy on the table for the picture, before you do, focus the camera on a black or brown cloth placed at the exact spot you'll stand the puppy. Be sure to wear a contrasting color if you're in the picture, or use a blue or green cloth as a background. Blue or green refracts light better, making the black or brown puppy stand out. Focus the camera on the puppy, and be sure that he, not the background, fills the camera frame. Eliminate background clutter.

Sixth Week—The bitch's maternal instincts are diminishing. If other dogs live in the house, she won't fuss when they come to the whelping room to nose the infants through the gate. She wants them to play with her pups outside. In fact, those bitches who continue to clean up excrement and enjoy nursing their pups the longest are usually the first ones to welcome other dogs' attentions. Nevertheless, continuous supervision is the key in allowing other dogs to play with the puppies. As a rule, older Portuguese Water Dogs are excellent baby sitters; they're very gentle with infant puppies. Some lie down and let them climb all over their bodies and pull their fur and tails.

One of the most important mother and puppy play periods takes place this week. In her play, she exhibits profound tenderness, yet never hesitates to chastise. She teaches in such a tolerant manner, the observer isn't always certain if her corrections are mock or real. If, however, there isn't ample room, she doesn't give pups these lessons. Some people claim, "My bitch never played with her puppies." The reason may be that the whelping room was too small for her to stretch out and feel free.

Sixth, Seventh and Eighth Weeks—We have briefly covered some of the growth and care of puppies in the helpless weeks.

The ideal time to completely wean puppies from bitch's milk is as soon as feasible after the bitch regurgitates food for them. Most bitches do this sometime during the sixth week. Others wait until the seventh week. A few never regurgitate food. Some may regurgitate food, although you may never see them do it.

We suggest waiting because the healthy bitch's instinct is sure. Puppies weaned at the proper time appear to develop more serene dispositions than those weaned early.

Puppies are ready for new homes within a week after they are fully weaned. It's wrong to send them away too soon. The first week after weaning is a stressful transitional period. It's better to allow them to adjust at home.

Puppies become very active during weaning. Good breeders provide a wide variety of positive experiences for pups during this period.

If the pup is going to travel to his new home in a crate, prepare him by accustoming him to napping in the crate for several days beforehand. Placing a crate in the whelping room is an excellent way to introduce it to puppies. Some will get inside and bark at others walking by; all will take turns napping inside.

Drive him around in your car for short distances, two or three blocks at first.

You've been encouraging housebreaking. Now take more active steps. While pups don't have complete muscle control until about 12 weeks of age, many are able to "hold it" long enough to rush to the door. You must watch each pup carefully as you allow him to run around the house. When you see him squat, pick him up quickly but gently and take him outdoors. Put him in the area you want used. After many times the pup will know where the door is and why he goes outside. Always praise the pup when he is finished outside and then bring him right back inside.

It's important to guide Portuguese Water Dog puppies in this simple training before they leave for new homes. Puppies who have had improper whelping box training are the ones who usually end up at humane shelters. Don't think this fate can't happen to a Portuguese Water Dog puppy.

Selecting a Puppy

If you decide you want a Portuguese Water Dog puppy, how should you select one? Where will you locate a litter?

We'll answer the last question first since you want to choose a pup in person, if at all possible.

If there are no breeders close by and you cannot travel to select a pup, then you'll probably have to have one shipped to you.

The best way to locate Portuguese Water Dog breeders is to write or call the AKC Librarian at the American Kennel Club (AKC), 51 Madison Avenue, New York, NY 10010, 212-696-8200. Ask for the address of the current Corresponding Secretary of the Portuguese Dog Club of America, Inc.

When you receive the information, write to the secretary and ask for a list of breeders, preferrably ones close to where you live. When you receive this answer, write or telephone each one, explaining what you are looking for in a Portuguese Water Dog pup. If they have what you want, they will set up a convenient time for you to see their pups in person. If you can't visit, they will ask you for information about yourself. Later, they will mail you pictures of pups they feel you might like.

There are several other ways to find breeders. One way is through advertisements in canine magazines or newspapers. Visit the public library or your local veterinary office. The library might have a file of canine publications. The magazine *Dog World* lists a great many breeder advertisements. Another magazine which carries breed advertisements is *Pure-Bred Dogs—American Kennel Gazette*. The address is the same as the American Kennel Club's, listed before.

You must decide whether you want a male or female. Dogs of both sexes inherit the happy, affectionate Portuguese Water Dog character. Both sexes thrive on work. They enjoy retrieving and swimming. They like to become close companions and guard dogs. Most females are as strong-willed as males but are milder and assume ladylike behavior long before males shed boyish exuberance. Otherwise, there is not much character difference. Sexual characteristics, of course, are different. Here you must decide which you want: 1) a female breedable twice a year during her heat or 2) a male able to sire pups at any time during the year. With common sense care neither sex poses problems. A female must be confined during most of her three-week heat. A male must never be allowed to wander or to mark his territory in your house with his urine.

If you don't want to breed or show, and don't mind a small breed defect, look for soundness of temperament and intelligence above everything else. You want your pet to have a willing disposition, and when grown, to guard without becoming too aggressive.

If you select your puppy by mail, by all means check the breeder and

At five weeks, pups stand in good physical balance. *Kathryn Braund*

In selecting a puppy, remember that dogs o both sexes inherit the happy and affectionate Portuguese Water Dog character. *Jim K*

litter out with intelligent questions. Trust the breeder. He has probably spent much time breeding quality dogs and he wants to help buyers select the right dog for them.

Going to a New Home

Crates—How should a Portuguese Water Dog puppy be housed in your home?

Keep your Portuguese Water Dog in your home. Then your puppy will become part of the family, a companion dog.

A puppy must never have free run of the house 24 hours a day. Just like humans, your Portuguese Water Dog pup needs his own space in which to relax and to be alone. His space should be a place he can go to when he wants to find toys, and to nap. It's also a place you can put him when you want him out of the way, yet without feeling guilty that you've excluded him from gatherings he simply can't attend.

The best inside dog house is a crate. Purchase one you can also put in the car. The adult height of a Portuguese Water Dog male ranges between 20 and 23 inches, and that of a female between 17 and 21 inches. Therefore, if you own a male purchase a 21 × 30 × 24 inch crate. If you own a female, purchase a 17 × 24 × 20 inch crate. A crate should be large enough so the adult dog may lie comfortably stretched out on his side and be able to sit up without his head hitting the top of the crate.

While your Portuguese Water Dog is still a puppy, build a temporary wall inside the crate so he is not allowed more space than his length. Then he won't use part of the crate to eliminate in. Move the partition as he grows.

Don't purchase a crate thinking that it's cruel to enclose him. Of course, you want to give your dog freedom such as you enjoy. But the dog is not equipped to live in houses and yards and act with human manners. No puppy, and few adult dogs, can handle the myriad curious things found in a home without doing some creative and possibly destructive investigation. When you have to go to town without him for several hours, he'll be safe in a crate resting. Your house and property will be safe. A crate gives your pup supervision while you're away. As the den was the wild dog's sanctuary, the crate becomes your pet's sanctuary.

When crating a puppy under 12 weeks of age, never leave him in the crate more than an hour at a time during the daylight hours. He hasn't developed full control. Neglect now may cause problems later on.

A puppy 12 to 16 weeks of age may be left inside a crate for two to three hours at a time. He'll sleep. At 16 weeks of age, the pup has full bladder and bowel control. He may now be left for four hours at a stretch. But no dog should be left in a crate for more than four hours, except during the night. If you work and intend to crate your Portuguese Water Dog during the day, you must get someone to let him out after four hours.

Yard Space—Another consideration you must make for your puppy is yard space. If you live in an apartment and have to take your dog outside to eliminate, you'll have to consider the amount of time necessary to walk your dog several times daily.

If you have a fenced yard, you may want to fence only part of it for your Portuguese Water Dog's private outside space. If so, add the price of an outside kennel run and dog house in the price of the puppy before you purchase him. Kennel runs big enough to house a Portuguese Water Dog may cost up to one thousand dollars. A home-made dog house will cost considerably less (about $50) than one ready-made ($80 to $150). The dog house should be constructed with protection—not looks—in mind. It must have protection against both heat and cold. A dog house constructed like an "A" frame and an open front gives little protection.

If you purchase a kennel run be sure to place a bench or dog table inside on which he can sit and contemplate the world.

Flooring for a kennel run is an important consideration. There are good and bad features in all types.

Concrete is easiest to maintain. When built and slanted slightly with a drainage ditch on one side, about all one has to do to maintain cleanliness is to hose it down periodically. The water drains. Unlike some soils, which may sour, clean cement is comparatively sweet. But it has drawbacks. Cement is hot in the summer and cold in the winter. This may set up arthritic conditions in dogs which are constantly exposed to its surface. Cement helps wear down paw pads. When dogs lie on cement for any length of time, they develop pressure points on elbows and thighs. Bald spots and callouses appear there. Dogs housed on cement must, therefore, have daily free time on turf, gravel or other natural terrain. Cement is not a good choice for Portuguese Water Dogs. It ruins their coats.

Another popular flooring is crushed stone or gravel. Like cement, this is also easy to maintain when the run is graded properly and if the lining under the gravel consists of several feet of rock. Gravel keeps dogs on their toes, therefore feet do not splay as they are prone to do on cement. But dogs sometimes eat the crushed stone or gravel. A rambunctious Portuguese Water Dog may push the gravel about so much that you'll have to rake it often. Gravel may also injure the hair fibers on his coat is he lies on it too long.

Grass makes fine flooring, but only for about four to six months. Grass doesn't hold up under constant usage. If you prefer a grass run, before placing down turf, test the soil. If it's clay, you'll have to clean the ground often with a lime treatment to keep the soil from turning sour. Urine doesn't drain in a clay soil. For this reason, consider building two kennel runs; then you can alternate by placing the dog in one for a month while allowing the other to rest.

Sand drains well and would be ideal except in climates which harbor

206

fleas. A Portuguese Water Dog housed on sand requires frequent baths. Sand coats his skin and cuts his coat.

The ideal soil for a kennel run is loam. Water drains well and loam is soft. Again, dirt runs mean dogs require frequent baths.

Face the kennel run to the south. Winter sun is cleansing to a run's flooring, no matter what type; it is also drying and warming. Be sure to plant deciduous trees and bushes on the south side of the run. It will then be shaded in summer and protected from prevailing storms both summer and winter.

An admonition. Portuguese Water Dogs are not good kennel inhabitants. They should be house dogs.

Housebreaking—Housebreaking is not the horrible task it is purported to be.

Like all animals, dogs can keep track of time. Enlist this knowledge to aid you in housebreaking him quickly. Feed him at the same times, walk him at the same times, take him to the same places at "Chore Time." Be consistent. Command simply, saying "Do your chores," or a similar phrase each time. Praise you pup each time he performs correctly.

Your puppy will catch on surprisingly fast. Just remember that preventing a mistake is half the battle.

Puppy Manners—When the puppy is not sleeping or resting in his crate, keep him within eyesight every minute. Steel, plastic, and wooden gates are available which you can place at doorways. If you're not in the same room with him, his curiosity might tell him to pick at loose threads in the carpet, at tucks in the cushions on the couch, or at the buttons on the upholstery. When he's in your eyesight, it's easy to discourage him with a "no," and offer him a small toy of his own. But out of eyesight—that's another story. Puppies aren't deliberately naughty. You must teach them how to behave.

Many Portuguese Water Dog puppies bite their owners in play. They also bite children. Some of this may be in retaliation for a child's unthinking roughness. A puppy's bite may be cute. But when he grows, it becomes annoying. Many dogs are given away or put down because "he bites." Yet his biting began in puppyhood and was termed "cute." Each time the puppy play mouths an adult, take him by the scruff of his neck (as his mother would) and shake him. Say "No." Don't let a puppy play alone with a child.

Within several days of acquiring your puppy, break him to collar and leash. Place a collar that fits around his neck and while you're supervising, let him wear it. His antics are amusing until the collar feels natural. After the initial introduction, place it on his neck only when you go outside. Teach him to get his collar. Take him to the place where you keep it, sit him down, place it around his neck, and after attaching a leash, take him outside.

Adolescence is a wonderful time for your Portuguese Water Dog puppy and you.
Stuart White

Sensible, common sense care will give you many years of joy with your dog.
A.G. Prangley, Jr., MD

208

Leash breaking is just as easy. Attach the leash to the collar. Allow the pup to drag it about—under your supervision only. Within minutes, you can pick up the other end and allow him to lead you about. When he gets to the end of the leash and it tightens, lightly zip it back, praising him as you do. The leash and collar quickly become like a "security blanket" when you walk him outside.

Socialization is the most important task you have until the pup is five months old. Socialization means taking your pup for daily rides in the car, for walks in parks, in the country or on city streets. It means holding him in your lap, allowing him to retrieve objects in fun, taking him to schools to meet and play with children if there are none in your home. It means loving him.

Meeting the world around him head-on while he is young helps him gain confidence of what life around him is like. Don't wait until he is past four months to begin socializing him. The well-adjusted dog is socialized early.

If you get your Portuguese Water Dog during the winter, you may have to wait for water introduction. But you can still give him basic water training right in your own house, using a large bucket or bathtub.

To teach him how to dive, for instance, give him a treat (a weiner works fine) right above the water bucket water line; gradually lower treats until they are given to him on the water line, and then under the water line. By the time the ice thaws outside, your diving training will have been well begun.

It is important to have professional help when your dog is ill.

Invest in a good canine medicine companion book, such as *The Dog Owner's Home Veterinary Handbook* by Delbert G. Carlson, DVM and James M. Giffin, MD (Howell Book House).

The Adolescent Portuguese Water Dog (16 Weeks to 18 Months)

This is a wonderful time of life for your puppy and you. Adolescent Portuguese Water Dogs are brimming with exuberance, curiosity and fun. Every activity you give him will enlarge his horizon and help him develop his full potential.

Start his show training. Begin his obedience and water training. Don't forget his grooming.

A male will begin lifting his leg to urinate at about eight to ten months of age. A female will come into her first heat at about eight to ten months. But both male and female are still puppies. Don't breed either at this time.

Many Portuguese Water Dogs don't begin to exercise their guard dog abilities until they are past a year of age. Most enjoy barking at passing cars, at daily visitors such as the mailman, the neighbor's dog, and at children running. Scolding may quiet your dog temporarily, but as soon as you are out of sight, he may resume barking. If he's outdoors, the best remedy for indiscriminate barking is to spray him with water from a hose or from a water pistol. If that is not available, throw a pail of water over him. Use a stern "No barking" command as you do. This temporary cure is not severe. But it may save you many distressing moments yelling at him and it will save him punishment. Throwing water on him will not make him dislike swimming or diving. Many Portuguese Water Dogs don't particularly care for baths, but love to swim.

If you don't plan to breed your dog selectively or to show him, you may want to spay your female or neuter your male. Spaying means surgical removal of ovaries. Neutering means removal of the testicles. Spaying and neutering permanently sterilize the animal. These surgical safeguards do not change the dog's basic temperament. The female remains female all of her life; spaying does reduce her chance of getting cancer of the mammary glands or of the ovaries (common diseases in unspayed bitches). Neutering does not make the male dog less of a male; it does inhibit wandering. Because the dog is not sexually inclined he doesn't display undesirable sexual behavior.

Spaying and neutering pet dogs means you may travel with your female without worrying if she will come into heat; the male will forego his sexual interest in female dogs and he'll be a lot easier to live with. However, before you spay or neuter, allow your Portuguese Water Dog to get through adolescence. When the Portuguese Water Dog is from 18 months to two years old, many owners wonder if all their training has gone out the window! It hasn't. During these months the pup may "go out," but everything should come together and you'll be glad you didn't spay or neuter.

Because of the rarity of the Portuguese Water Dog breed, be sure to check with your dog's breeder before spaying or neutering.

Older Dogs

Thanks to modern veterinary care, sensible canine diets, and better general pet care, dogs are living longer.

The Portuguese Water Dog has a life expectancy of from 12 to 14 years. Nevertheless, as he ages, you have to help him adjust to the infirmities of old age. Keep him out of drafts, don't overload him with exercise, dry him off thoroughly when he's wet, make him feel better by grooming him more frequently and update food and vitamins as prescribed by your veterinarian because of his changing metabolism.

Sensible, common sense care will give you many years of joy with your Portuguese Water Dog.

12

Basic Genetics and the Portuguese Water Dog

RECENTLY, at the airport, a young man approached Cyril Braund, who was cuddling in his arms a puppy bound for a new home.

"That's a beautiful puppy," said the young man, wagging a finger against the puppy's nose. The puppy reached out and licked the young man's finger. "How much is it worth?"

"We're insuring him for $1,000," Cyril answered.

"Halleluyah!" exclaimed the young man. "That's a lot of money. I think I'll go out and buy a male and female dog and go into the puppy business."

You know from the effort you've put into selecting a Portuguese Water Dog, one doesn't breed quality puppies simply by mating one dog to another.

The mechanism of breeding one dog to another to ensure quality puppies requires more than the basic knowledge of the sexual act in dogs. It requires methodology; it requires art in selection; it requires a sound working concept of the scientific principles involved in genetics. Good breeding is planned quality which cannot be done by amateurs. Our greatest cattle and horses came from planned breeding. Trainer LeRoy Jolley, who trained the Kentucky Derby winner, Foolish Pleasure, gave a great description of breeding: "It's a complex mixture of statistics and hunch."

If you want to become a dog breeder, it's wise to contemplate the following: Those of us in dogdom are able to detect flaws in other breeder's dogs, but when it comes to our dogs, we're blind! Here is something else to remember. If you want to become a respected dog breeder, one whose word is listened to, never discuss another person's breeding except in a positive manner.

The Mechanics of Heredity

We're not going to explore in depth the complex subject of genetics here. You may gain intelligent basic genetic knowledge by studying the many excellent books on the subject. We will, however, outline the basics of genetics for you. Here are two fundamental facts.

1) The sexual instinct prevails over all other instincts in all living things. This is nature's method of ensuring that life is never ending.

2) The genetic blueprint of each dog born in the world is different from that of any other dog.

Each species of plant and animal has a constant number of chromosomes within each cell. The cell is the building block of all plants and animals. The chromosome is the rod-shaped genetic building block within the cell. Forty-eight chromosomes are in each human cell. There are six chromosomes in the mosquito and 78 in the dog.

Half the chromosomes of each cell are contributed by the male of the species and the other half by the female.

Genes, so minute they can't be seen with present day microscopes, are lined up along the chromosome. Genes are units of heredity, mighty miracles of nature responsible for all inherited physical and mental traits. In dogs, there are over 25,000 genes on each pair of chromosomes.

There are several types of genes. A *dominant* gene bequeaths a trait which shows up immediately. A *recessive* gene will not show up unless a twin recessive gene appears through the mating procedure. This may take several generations. There are good recessive genes; there are also bad ones. An *additive* gene contributes to (forms) only part of a trait. We know the least about additive genes. A *modifying* gene alters the trait of some dominant and recessive genes. A *repressor* gene prevents a dominant gene from showing up.

Some genes, named *simple dominant* and *simple recessive,* don't require other genes to become active. But most genes must act with other genes before they are expressed.

Breeding Systems

There's always the element of chance when the genes contributed by the male link together with those contributed by the female. Yet, with experience, you can trace many combinations.

It's not very difficult to trace genes at work in *mixed breed* animals. You may see their physical effect in a Labrador-Dalmatian cross whose single coat is white with black spots (Dalmatian inheritance); the dog also sports a heavy build and "otter" tail (Labrador inheritance). It's impossible, however, to mate mixed breeds with any assurance of consistency in offspring type and temperament.

On the other hand, it's often difficult to trace genes at work in outcrossed (outbred) dogs of one breed. Outcrossing is the term used when you mate dogs of the same breed with no common ancestor in the pedigree. Good breeders outcross only when they know something about the ancestors in the pedigree. Unfortunately, outcrossing is heavily practiced by pet owners of popular breeds who haven't the slightest knowledge of genetics. A pet owner may breed his or her animal to an animal of the same breed who lives down the street. Both have "AKC papers!" Most people breed dogs this way in the belief the resulting puppies will look and act just like dear old mom or dad. Now, the puppies may be strong and healthy because they have what is called *hybrid vigor* but many of the puppies that these puppies later produce will show the recessive weaknesses hiding within the ancestry of one of the parents. A hybrid bred back to a hybrid loses the vigor and traits so desirable on the first cross. This is because there's an overabundance of unknown hereditary factors. No one can predict results when no thought is given to eliminating—by selective breeding—possible inheritable recessive traits. Luck alone begets a good dog in haphazard breeding. Many breeds have been damaged by breeding this way.

Line breeding is breeding loosely within a family strain; it concentrates on breeding a good bitch to a good dog with one or more exceptional common ancestors in the pedigree. The common ancestors—granddaughter bred to grandfather, cousin bred to cousin, niece bred to uncle, etc.—pass on identical genes to both sire and dam, making the parents positive (prepotent) for that particular genetic inheritance, good or bad. Linebreeding, of course, may expose genetic faults. These in turn may be eradicated through continued but cautious linebreeding before they take hold and are fixed within the line. Linebreeding still gives variations in type, soundness, balance and size.

Inbreeding is intense breeding; it's the deliberate mating of close relatives—for example, sister to brother, daughter to father. The dogs mated as well as the close relatives in the pedigree must be superior—not just good—animals. They must be as free of structural and temperamental faults as possible because by inbreeding you're not out to create new genes, you're fixing or preserving (intensifying) the genes already present. One price for inbreeding is reduction in fertility. Uniformity is the bonus. If you don't have outstanding animals as sire and dam, you may easily preserve bad as well as good genes. Many people believe inbreeding worsens temperament. This isn't true. If there's only good temperament in the line, it is accentuated. Yet so delicate is this method of breeding that if you have one soft, shy dog in the genetic background, the strain slowly erodes. One bad apple . . . . .!

As you can see, the last two methods of breeding described, linebreeding and inbreeding, fix ancestry in the pups because they establish a genetic pool. The dogs perpetuate identical genes. This is why many litters of linebred and inbred dogs tend to be uniform, whereas those of outcrossed litters vary in structural, temperamental and type characteristics. In outcrossed litters, several pups might resemble one parent but act like the other while the remainder, products of recessive genes, won't act like or resemble either parent. You can't tell where the influence comes from.

Successful breeders breed to create better dogs, not just more animals, breed for uniformity by breeding out (outcrossing) and then inbreeding excellent specimens for several generations. This type of breeding will never go out of style. It produces top quality animals. Any geneticist will tell you that.

Now, don't be lulled as a breeder by the above statements on line and inbreeding. You may breed two dogs together the second time around, hoping for a repeat of the first litter's consistent quality. You discover the second litter is completely different. This shows you the enormous variation possible in gene selection. Genetics is always in motion! During the course of evolution gene selection contributes to gene immortality. Gene selection is what will give you a faulty, straight coat along with curly and wavy coats after your strain has produced only proper curly and wavy coats for 30 years. This is one reason we urge you to explore the fascinating study of genetics. It will gift you with a fresh view of evolution.

Genetic influence isn't everything. When evaluating live dogs, you must consider environmental influence. Adaptation to environmental conditions plays a large part in forming the animal, particularly temperament.

The art of breeding is to know what you want and to be able to recognize good and bad genes and understand what happens to them in your breeding program. This is not an easy thing to do. Only through study and selective line and inbreeding with sensible outcrossings will you create a strain of ideal Portuguese Water Dogs.

Pedigree Study

When Deyanne Miller imported her first Portuguese Water Dog puppy, Renascenca, in 1968, followed a year later by a male puppy, Anzol, it was impossible to determine if these puppies when adults would nick (mate well) together. Given choice, she wanted linebreeding, not inbreeding. Anzol, the male pup, was a half-brother to Renascenca. But after all,

214

there were only 25 Portuguese Water Dogs left in the world. She had to take what was available!

Nevertheless, it wasn't just luck that the puppies, when grown, produced quality offspring. Forty-odd years before Renascenca was born, Vasco Bensaude began a breeding program to produce quality Portuguese Water Dogs. This is why good breeders plan their breeding program at least ten years ahead.

How can you do this? How do you learn about the individuals in back of the printed names of dogs on a pedigree? To give you an example, let's go back to 1931. That's when Leao was born on the Algarve in Portugal.

Let's go over Leao's pedigree together. Leao was sired by Lontra ex (meaning out of) Cigana. His sire and dam were working Portuguese Water Dogs. Their ancestors were unknown. Leao, therefore, was a dog born of an outcrossed breeding with a few known genes but no known "fixed" ones.

When Leao sired pups, Vasco Bensaude kept most of the pups in order to study their inheritance. He learned Leao was prepotent (dominant) for the good qualities he himself exhibited because the majority of the pups Leao sired looked and acted as he did! Vasco Bensaude's tremendous breeding integrity was based, in large part, on the intense study he made of Leao's offspring, generation through generation.

Leao sired a total of eight litters for Vasco Bensaude, beginning in 1937. The first litters were outcrossed; as time went on, they became both line and inbred. To ensure vigor of the line as well as to widen the genetic breeding pool, Vasco Bensaude made careful outcrossings periodically.

Let's examine the pedigree of the first Portuguese Water Dog imported to the United States from Portugal—Farmion's Renascenca do Al Gharb. Look at the breeding behind her: you'll then see exactly what we mean.

Renascenca do Al Gharb, bitch, born July 12, 1968, out of Liz Algarbiorum ex Enga Algarbiorum.

Liz Algarbiorum, dog, born August 25, 1966, out of Guincho Algarbiorum ex Enga Algarbiorum.

Enga Algarbiorum, bitch, born September 9, 1963, out of Tabu ex Salema Algarbiorum.

Guincho Algarbiorum, dog, born March 7, 1962, out of Silvo Algarborium ex Orca Algarbiorum.

Tabu, unknown (R.I., initial registration approved by the CPC).

Salema Algarbiorum, dog, born June 9, 1960, out of Padrao Algarbiorum ex Palma Algarbiorum.

Silvo Algarbiorum, dog, born June 9, 1960, out of Padrao Algarbiorum ex Palma Algarbiorum.

Orca Algarbiorum, bitch, born August 19, 1958, out of Pacato Algarbiorum ex Palma Algarbiorum.

Padrao Algarbiorum, dog, born December 18, 1953, out of Azinhal Algarbiorum ex Dala Algarbiorum.

Palma Algarbiorum, bitch, born December 18, 1953, out of Azinhal Algarbiorum ex Dala Algarbiorum.

Pacato Algarbiorum, dog, born December 18, 1953, out of Azinhal Algarbiorum ex Dala Algarbiorum.

Azinhal Algarbiorum, dog, born July 26, 1949, out of Hastil Algarbiorum ex Urze Algarbiorum.

Dala Algarbiorum, bitch, born October 13, 1947, out of Escol Algarbiorum ex Pata.

Hastil Algarbiorum, dog, born July 19, 1941, out of Leao ex Guia Algarbiorum.

Urze Algarbiorum, bitch, born November 5, 1945, out of Quito Algarbiorum ex Pata.

Escol Algarbiorum, dog, born October 15, 1940, out of Leao ex Murta Algarbiorum.

Pata, bitch, born April 1, 1943, out of Silves Algarbiorum ex Tavira Algarbiorum.

Leao, dog, born June 1931, out of Lontra ex Cigana.

Guia, bitch, born August 14, 1939, out of Leao ex Tavira Algarbiorum.

Quito Algarbiorum, dog, born March 27, 1942, out of Leao ex Murta Algarbiorum.

Murta Algarbiorum, bitch, birthdate unknown, out of Leao ex Venesa.

Silves Algarbiorum, dog, born November 1, 1937, out of Leao ex Dina.

Tavira Algarbiorum, bitch, born May 1, 1937, out of Leao ex Dina.

Lontra, dog, unknown.

Cigana, bitch, unknown.

Venesa, bitch, birthdate unknown, out of Landrin ex Troia.

Dina, bitch, unknown.

Chenze, whose pedigree traced back to Leao, was the foundation dam of the Algarbiorum bloodline in America. Whelped July 12, 1968, she passed away on September 1, 1983 after celebrating her fifteenth birthday.

Many Portuguese Water Dogs can be traced to Chenze. Chenze was an affectionate, intelligent, self-assured animal who will always live on because of the good qualities she threw.

Although Vasco Bensaude knew there were chances to be taken in breeding, he left little to chance. The breed's present quality is due to his foresight.

Vasco Bensaude took on the responsibility of nature, knowing that if he wanted to resurrect the Portuguese Water Dog, he had to select breeding animals with the best dominant characteristics possible. Vasco Bensaude

The breeding behind Renascenca do Al Gharb, shown here with Deyanne Miller, makes an interesting study. *Jim Kallett*

also knew that behavior was inherited as well as physical characteristics. He deemed it important to further mental characteristics as well as physical ones. So he had all his Cães de Áqua trained in that which Leao was expert. He was gratified that the dogs who outlived Leao also passed on useful mental characteristics as well as excellent physical ones.

Look at your Portuguese Water Dog's pedigree. Bloodlines are important. The two prominent bloodlines in the breed were Algarbiorum (Vasco Bensaude) and de Alvalade (Dr. Antonio Cabral). The ideal Portuguese Water Dog is a combination of the two. Some breeders are presently high on Algarbiorum stock because, by comparison, some pictures in the Alvalade's archives show short-legged and long-backed dogs. But these breeders should look at the Portuguese standard which describes the breed as rectangular. Rectangular proportions can result in a long leg and short back as well as a long back and a short leg. Short legs and long backs were common in some of the first Alvalades. But again, de Alvalade incorporates many bloodlines. Algarbiorum may have incorporated eight bloodlines at one time, but the dogs were essentially of one consistent type.

Algarbiorum dogs were taller, bigger, rangier. Some were 26 inches tall. A more compact dog fits the standard better. The heads of the Alvalades have nice, square muzzles and are in proportion to the body. Lumpi de Alvalade sired beautiful, broad heads. Algarbiorum breeding may also transmit a hair loss factor.

Taro produced a balanced body and Algarbiorum transmits a dark eye. From de Alvalade comes wavier coats, but also more browns than from Algarbiorum. Incidentally, sometimes brown dogs have blue eyes until they are five months old. Then the eyes turn brown.

The de Alvalade lines carry a genetic trait for having large litters. There has been only one Caesarian in 106 litters.

When Herb and Deyanne Miller showed Fausto a picture of two puppies, a picture taken in 1974, Fausto admonished Deyanne to watch out for too much white.

Because of the near extinction of the breed, some American breeders may wonder if there was any mixing of breeds to bring the Portuguese Water Dog back from the "brink." There wasn't any mixing. Any dog that was used for breeding was approved with the R.I. (initial registration approved by the CPC).

Let's study one more pedigree. It is that of the first Miscellaneous class winner, the first American champion and the first American Best in Show dog, Ch. Charlie de Alvalade, also a Farmion-owned dog. Among Charlie's great contributions to the breed is correct temperament, superb showmanship and excellent water ability.

Charlie de Alvalade, dog, born May 16, 1978, out of Taro (R.I.) ex C.B. Truta de Alvalade.

218

Ch. Charlie de Alvalade, owned by Deyanne F. and Herbert H. Miller, Jr. and bred by Dr. Antonio Cabral, is the bellwether for the breed in America. Initially calling attention to the Portuguese Water Dog while the breed was still in the Miscellaneous class, Charlie impressed judges and dog fanciers with his quality and charisma. He became the first champion, first BIS dog and numbers among his other achievements winning the water trials in Portugal on a return visit *after* coming to America, being BB at the first two Westminsters open to Porties and placing in the Working Group both times! This remarkable dog is shown here being awarded 4th in a top-drawer Working Group at the historic AKC Centennial show (November 1984) under Mrs. Augustus V. Riggs, IV. Charlie's handler for this and most of his other numerous triumphs is William J. Trainor. *William P. Gilbert*

Taro, unknown ex unknown.

Truta de Alvalade, bitch, born October 19, 1970, out of Lumpi de Alvalade ex Ria (R.I.).

Lumpi de Alvalade, dog, born July 25, 1965, out of Lagos de Alvalade ex Lampreia de Alvalade.

Ria, bitch, unknown ex unknown.

Lagos de Alvalade, dog, born September 23, 1958, out of Silves ex Gale.

Lampreia de Alvalade, bitch, born August 20, 1962, out of Lagos de Alvalade ex Gale.

Silves, dog, born June 1954, out of unknown.

Gale, bitch, born March 8, 1957, out of Silves ex Farrusca.

Farrusca, bitch, born August 30, 1951, out of Azinhal Algarbiorum ex Dala Algarbiorum.

Azinhal Algarbiorum, dog, born July 26, 1949, out of Hastil Algarbiorum ex Urze Algarbiorum.

Dala Algarbiorum, bitch, born October 13, 1947, out of Escol Algarbiorum ex Pata.

Escol Algarbiorum, dog, born October 15, 1940, out of Leao ex Murta Algarbiorum.

Pata, bitch, born April 1, 1943, out of Silves Algarbiorum ex Tavira Algarbiorum.

Leao, dog, born June 1931, out of Lontra ex Cigna.

Murta Algarbiorum, bitch, unknown, out of Leao ex Vanesa.

Silves Algarbiorum, dog, born November 1, 1937, out of Leao ex Dina.

Tavira Algarbiorum, bitch, born May 1, 1937, out of Leao ex Dina.

Venesa, bitch, unknown, out of Landrim ex Troia.

Dina, bitch, unknown.

In comparing the two pedigrees, note that although Vasco Bensaude inbred his animals, he also outcrossed every few generations.

This pattern for breeding, incidentally, has been followed by European and British breeders for hundreds of years. Many breeds have been established in this manner with breeding a methodical, conscientious, and often painstaking process. It sometimes had tragic results. Selective breeding isn't always successful, even for the veteran breeder.

Chenze and Charlie have been found to be prepotent for the excellent attributes of the breed, much like their famous ancestor, Leao.

Farmion's owner, Deyanne Miller's yearly trips to Portugal have resulted in selective gene banks with an ever-widening gene pool. Trovoada de Alvalade was the de Alvalade foundation bitch in the United States. She too traces back to Leao. She was the dam of 50 puppies. As such, she figures in more pedigrees than does Chenze. On the AKC stud book cut-off date of June 30, 1983, Deyanne Miller had bred 21 litters and assisted at 29

ALVALADE

Import from Portugal
Alvorada de Alvalade
1976-
Dame of several litters
1st brown import
to U.S.A.

Dauphin do Mar
1984-

Ch. Nativo
do Mar
1979-
Bis Specialty
1984

Alma do Mar
1978-

DO MAR

Trezena Monte
Clerico
1976-1980
Winner (Bis) of
3 Specialty

Ch. Natale
do Mar 1979-
Best in Winners
Specialty
1984

Adonis
do
Mar
1978-

Ch. Isadora
do Mar
1982-

Booyista
do Mar
1983-
Several points

Isabella
do Mar
1982-
Several pts

Real do Mar
1977-
Best in Show
Puppy (4 months)
1977 Specialty
Brookhaven 2nd
Rarebreed
March 1977
Sire of 2 American
Champions

Import from Portugal
Anzol do Al-Gharb
1969-1978
BIS
Moodus Rare
Breed Match

Ch. Bandido
do Mar
1983-
(11 months old)

Morena
do Mar
1979-
Dam of American
Champion

Rainha do Mar
1977-
Best puppy (3 months)
1977 Specialty
Bos (15 months)
Specialty 1978
Dam of 1 American
Champion, 1 PWD
with 9 points

Import from Portugal
Zingara de Alvalade
1975-1981
Bos (17 months)
Brookhaven First
Rare Breed Hatch

do MAR LINE

Beaulieu
do Mar
1983-
Several points

Ch. Firmamente
Kalakua
1981-

Rosmaninhal
do Mar
1977-
Dam of several
American
Champions

Ch. Firmamente
1983-

Firmamente Zingara
do Mar 1983-
Best puppy
Sweepstake
Specialty 1984

Import from Portugal
Portuguese Champion
Baluarte de Alvalade
1978-
Sire of several American
champions and P.W.D's
with 1-9 points
Sire of Specialty 1984
Puppy Sweepstake
Winner

ALVALADE

Dona do Mar
1984-

My Last Litter and 100% ALVALADE

whelpings. She raised four litters other than those she bred and furnished 29 breeders with their foundation bitches. Carrying the Farmion prefix or imported by Deanne Miller were 45 sires.

Let's look also at the accompanying chart, showing how the do Mar strain has come into being and the careful breeding done at the Santos' kennels.

Not all genes carried down through generations of dogs on any pedigree are good genes. While careful breeding often removes bad genes, sometimes genes act randomly and may devitalize—through the work of one lethal physical or mental trait—an entire strain or even breed of dogs.

Close to 200 canine genetic defects have already been discovered and identified. Some of these have plagued the Portuguese Water Dog revitalization breeding. Some are already being eliminated.

It used to be thought that breeding was a gambling endeavor. We know that the science of genetic breeding is just beginning to unfold. Although at present there's enough magic and uncertainty in breeding to keep breeders constantly on their toes, there is also certainty in breeding. By careful breeding of good qualities to other good qualities, we are assured of seeing those good qualities transmitted to most offspring. Those that carry genetic defects are culled (sold as unbreedable pets).

Let's examine some genetic defects that may be found in the Portuguese Water Dog. The best way breeders can eliminate problems is to locate and face up to them. While we can seldom modify diseases once they show up, we can try to breed them away.

Hip Dysplasia

Hip dysplasia (HD) is a developmental malformation of the hips. The disease has been recognized in humans since 370 B.C. (Hippocrates). It's been recognized in canines since 1933. Until the late 1970s, many dogs in Europe were never x-rayed for dysplasia. Many still aren't in America.

When an outbreak of HD in Portuguese Water Dog stock was found in the mid-1970s, a concerted effort was immediately begun to eliminate HD from all breedable stock. All PWDCA-member breeders are urged to have two-year-old dogs x-rayed by their veterinarian for Orthopedic Foundation of Animals (OFA) evaluation.

Juvenile Cataracts

Not found in the Portuguese Water Dog, cataracts, at whatever age they occur, are lens opacities which cloud vision by covering part or all of the lens of the eye. This is a fairly common canine disease; when genetic in origin, it will appear before the dog is three years of age.

222

Certainty in careful breeding: Farmion Cabo de Sta Maria; Cabo's dam, Trovoada de Alvalade; sitting on Deyanne Miller's lap, Farmion Esperanca, Cenze's daughter from the fifth litter; Renascenca; and Mrs. Judith Bartsch holding Farmion Areira, Cenze's daughter from the first litter.   *Wes Albright*

Puppies exhibiting hair loss around eyes.   *Kathryn Braund*

Epilepsy

This is another common canine disease, not yet found in the Portuguese Water Dog, but a disease which has been found in related breeds. Epilepsy is a nervous system disorder which attacks the muscles. The dog affected exhibits seizures with a temporary loss of motor control. Epilepsy usually makes its first appearance before the dog reaches one year of age.

Cirrhosis of the Liver

This disease is progressive, resulting in excessive formation of connective tissue within the liver. Not always genetic in origin, it may also result from nutritional deficiency, parasites or toxemia.

Hair Loss Around Eyes

Hair loss (alopecia) around the eyes has been found in the breed.

Here's a story about one owner's experience with hair loss around the eyes. The dog who had the problem is named Onix Tafia (Fia) and belongs to author, Kathryn Braund.

Fia, like several of her litter mates, first exhibited hair loss around the eyes at eight weeks of age. The breeder's veterinarian tested the pups for mange. The culture was negative. However, the pups still exhibited this hair loss at 16 weeks, the age at which my husband and I acquired Fia when visiting Deyanne Miller in Connecticut.

When we reached home, we took Fia to our veterinarian. He tested the area of hair loss for both mange and ringworm. Both tests were negative. Like the breeder's veterinarian, he could find no immediate cause for the hair loss.

We treated Fia with a remedy found effective for this type of hair loss found in the breed—we fed Fia a bottle of clam juice daily for two weeks. It did not help. Next, we placed her on a high protein diet and gave her heavy doses of vitamin B, a natural skin and coat conditioner. We also treated her eyes daily with an eye ointment. At the end of 60 days, Fia still had hair loss.

When Fia was about 10 months old, the condition began to correct itself. Almost overnight, the streaks of bare skin around her eyes filled in with hair. Then as suddenly as the hair filled in, the hair disappeared. This pattern continued.

Our veterinarian sent cultures of sections of the affected skin to two pathologist-veterinarians, one in- and one out-of-state. They reported the dog appeared to have a mild dermatitis and agreed that this could be due to an allergic condition.

We changed foods. First, we eliminated soy bean oil from her diet. After 60 days, we eliminated wheat. After another 60 days, we eliminated all manufactured dog food from her diet. The hair loss continued.

When Fia was 1-1/2 years of age and seven weeks in whelp, I nonetheless took her to a fourth veterinarian for one more opinion! He read the reports from the other veterinarians and said he didn't believe he could add to them. However, on the outside chance that the condition could be caused by a fungus type infection, he took a culture from a hairless area. If it was positive, he told me, the culture would show results in about nine days.

His office called me on a Friday afternoon a week and a half later to tell me the culture was positive. "What for?" I asked. "Ringworm." "My gosh!" I exclaimed. I immediately drove to his office to pick up medication for Fia. By the time I arrived, the veterinarian had left for the day. However, his technical assistant confirmed my opinion that ringworm was contagious, particularly for young animals who had not built up an immunity.

Fia was due to have puppies within a few days! My Dalmatian bitch had given birth to eight Dalmatian puppies just eight days previous!

Rushing home, I applied the medication to the affected area beneath Fia's eyes. I then checked each Dalmatian pup thoroughly. Their tails looked splotchy. I tried hard not to panic. Most veterinarians in the area had already closed shop for the weekend. Unless I wanted to treat this as an emergency I had to wait until the next morning—Saturday—to have an "on-call" veterinarian check my Dalmatian puppies.

The veterinarians who saw the Dalmatian puppies that Saturday morning listened to my story. They took cultures of the hair from several of the pups' tails and agreed it was likely that the hair loss on their tails could be caused by ringworm. They could not be sure until the cultures were returned. They agreed it would do no harm to give them preventative treatment, using the same medication I had obtained for Fia.

That night Fia gave birth to four puppies. The veterinarian who came to aid a weak puppy the next morning examined all our dogs for ringworm. All our adult dogs except Fia appeared clear. He suggested the Dalmatian puppies have treatment until they could build up their own natural immunity. He also thought the newly born Portuguese Water Dog puppies could get ringworm from their mother. He suggested we disinfect the two litter rooms and everything in them as well as treat the 12 puppies and Fia.

My husband removed the two whelping boxes, scrubbed them, painted them, and then sterilized them. I scrubbed and disinfected walls, ceiling and floors. I sterilized all bedding used by the dogs. Clorox was the disinfectant used (one part Clorox to eight parts cold water). We also called in house cleaners. They scrubbed and fumigated the carpeting in the entire house.

Every other day for the next four weeks, we gave each of the eight

Dalmatian puppies and the four Portuguese Water Dog puppies baths. We used a prescribed antiseptic shampoo. We applied ringworm salve on each of the fourteen puppies daily, running through 14 expensive tubes of salve in four weeks. We had the veterinarian take several cultures of both Dalmatians and Portuguese Water Dog puppies. Both tests taken for the Dalmatians came back negative. The first culture for ringworm taken from the Portuguese Water Dog puppies (at eight days) came back positive. We were glad we had already started treatment on them! The second and third cultures taken from the Portuguese Water Dog puppies at five and seven weeks of age came back negative.

With daily ringworm treatment (using salve prescribed by the veterinarian), the hair below Fia's eyes began growing. Since Fia's problem was presumably a long-standing one, from puppyhood, she was also treated for one month *after her puppies left home* with 500 mg. Fulvicin, one tablet taken daily following two tablespoonsful of corn oil. (She loved lapping up the corn oil from a dish.) Fulvicin treated the ringworm beneath the skin. Our battle was won in a month; the cause of Fia's hair loss was evidently due entirely to ringworm. Only one of the Dalmatian puppies was infected by ringworm later in life, at five months of age. She had left the nest at nine weeks of age; it is believed she was susceptible to ringworm spores found in her new environment.

There are at least 1,000 different forms of ringworm, yet just three fungi cause 99 percent of all canine ringworm. Some Portuguese Water Dogs, as Fia, may be susceptible to ringworm. Each breed—and each dog—has its own genetic weaknesses! Spores are found everywhere—even on you and me. It is transmitted to dogs from other animals, from man, or from the soil. While most cases of ringworm show up under ultra-violet light, some Portuguese Water Dogs may be afflicted with a mild, non-itching variety which causes hair loss or *dry seborrhea*. This is usually found around the eyes beginning when a pup is about eight weeks of age. It may appear (with streaks of hair loss) and disappear (hair filling in) throughout the dog's life unless treated. The only positive way to trace all forms of ringworm is by having a skin scraping taken and cultured. If one culture turns up negative and the problem doesn't correct, have the veterinarian take a second culture. The fungi live on the nonviable keratin of the skin, hair and nails. They don't dig under and invade layers under the skin.

This is certainly not the end of the hair loss story in the breed. Research is going on into other possible causes. For instance, a thyroid imbalance helps produce amino deficiency which allows fungus, such as ringworm, to take hold. However, one can get an amino deficiency without thyroid deficiency.

The Portuguese Water Dog fancy is grateful to Bruce G. MacDonald, DVM for agreeing to place all findings on hair-loss in the breed under scientific analysis at his clinic. Every Portuguese Water Dog breeder and pet owner who has information on hair loss in the breed should contact Dr. MacDonald at Rocky Mountain Animal Medical Center, 1401 Northwest Bypass, Great Falls, Montana 59404.

Hypothyroidism

This metabolic disease, a deficiency of hormones secreted from the thyroid gland, seen in several other breeds, may be a cause of hair thinning, dryness of hair or other similar condition. Again, this is a common disorder in dogs. In some breeds, daily dosage of thyroxine taken in tablet form is normal treatment. Thyroid deficiency is determined by the veterinarian taking a skin biopsy and checking both T3 and T4 levels. The thyroid produces four hormones, T1, T2, T3, and T4. T1 and T2 may be low. When these reach a cell site, they turn into T3 and T4.

The Genetic Feedback Program

To lead the way in helping genetic defects disappear, the PWDCA approved a *Genetic Feedback Program* in May 1978. Questionnaires were sent to a control group. The control group determined the validity of questions asked as well as the ability of owners to complete the questionnaire. An approved questionnaire was then sent to all owners of Portuguese Water Dogs over one year of age. The statistics were compiled, evaluated and given to all breeders for their use in future breedings. Confidential evaluations were made of the dogs for owners who requested them and "were interested in eliminating or increasing certain recessive traits in the offspring."

In that year, from the answers received, it was found that 37 percent of the dogs were curly-coated and 50 percent wavy-coated with 13 percent showing straight or wiry hair (improperly coated). Twenty-nine percent were found dysplastic yet more than fifty percent had never been x-rayed. While more than 60 percent were able to be bred from, only 10 percent of these were used for breeding. The average litter size was 7.4 pups. This figure is still being quoted as of this writing as viable.

On the Plus Side—Allergy Tolerance

We can't close this chapter without detailing a genetic plus for the breed. It is allergy tolerance.

Although no formal study has been done, as early as 1974 allergic owners were reporting to Deyanne Miller that they were able to tolerate Portuguese Water Dogs. Interestingly enough, these allergic people were not able to tolerate other breeds, including Poodles. Deyanne Miller, having allergies herself, became intrigued in this aspect of the breed. One

227

owner, Mrs. John S. Hilson of Greenwich, Connecticut wrote to Deyanne Miller:

> I was interested in the report about Portuguese Water Dogs and asthmatics. I am a very bad asthmatic; both dogs (our Portuguese Water Dog and our Newfoundland) are not permitted in the house—only in the kitchen and a back room which they enter via a door cut out where their sleeping cots are. I have *never* had an attack after petting Juan (the Portuguese Water Dog) or from scratching him behind the ears. When I groom him, I don't ask for trouble. I wear a mask over mouth and nose. This is done from long habit more than anything. In truth, I sincerely doubt that I'd have an adverse reaction, but we asthmatics are taught to be over-cautious and even a bit neurotic about our condition, if we're smart! Juan likes to be clean—a good factor for asthmatics—if it's a general characteristic of the Portuguese Water Dog. This is not to say he doesn't get marvelously muddy at times or smell of methane du swamp!

It's good advice to follow this suggestion in applying basic genetics to breeding: Avoid inbreeding as much as possible. Choose matings with dogs that will widen the gene pool, instead of tightening it. Use dogs with the fewest problems to breed from and concentrate on upgrading breed type, structure, and intelligence.

13

Selective Breeding of the Portuguese Water Dog

BE AN EXCEPTIONALLY SELECTIVE puppy buyer if you even guess you might some day want to breed Portuguese Water Dogs.

Your purchase of a potential brood bitch should be done carefully. The bitch, more often than the stud dog, determines the quality of her pups. So be sure you choose her from good ancestry with as few faults as possible.

The brood bitch's care begins when she's lifted out of the litter box by her new owner. That is also the ideal time to commence the total care of a future stud dog.

Estrus

Most healthy Portuguese Water Dog bitches come into their first estrus, or heat cycle, at about nine months of age. A few come into season at six months of age; another few wait until after a year of age.

There are several signs which alert you to the impending estrus cycle. The first sign is a slight swelling of the vulva. This is not always observed because the Portuguese Water Dog grows hair on and around the vulva and not all owners clip this hair regularly. The second sign is that the bitch licks her vulva frequently. She's cleaning away the slight pre-heat discharge.

There's another way to tell when estrus may be approaching. Climatic changes definitely stimulate the onset of estrus. In the wild, nature protects most new life by scheduling birth during the least stressful season: springtime. Domestication has altered this phenomenon in dogs. They may bear young anytime; bitches come into estrus at any definite climatic change.

On the first day of estrus, blood begins to discharge from the swelling vulva. The discharge may be slight or profuse.

During the next five to six days, as the bitch bleeds (due to the enlarging and softening vulva), males aren't overly excited. Isolation is not yet necessary.

However, every bitch must be confined, at the latest, on the seventh day of estrus. She must remain confined until the standing heat phase of estrus is over—at the end of, not the beginning of, the 21st day. By this time, her vulva has shrunk back to normal size. The discharge or bleeding has disappeared.

Before being allowed to be with other dogs she should be given a bath. Without being bathed, the heavy scent of estrus remains with her and males may still deem her sexually attractive. Nature encourages males to mate by scent alone.

During estrus, the bitch will not normally accept male advances until she is in standing heat (ovulating). However, inexperienced males, if allowed, continually test her willingness.

Some females will accept a male from the ninth through the sixteenth day, though they may not be fertile the entire period. An example of this occurred with one of Kathryn Braund's dogs. A maiden bitch was contracted to be bred to a dog living 2,000 miles away. Arrival was planned to coincide with her tenth day of heat. She stood for the stud dog as soon as they were introduced. They were bred on the tenth day and again on the 12th day. After two apparently successful services, the bitch was returned home. However, when she was taken to the veterinarian on the 25th day after the first service to be palpated, the veterinarian couldn't locate any puppies.

She grew heavy in the following weeks. But her nipples did not turn pink or enlarge and her weight gain was on the top of her back, not along her ribs or abdomen. Neither did her vulva stay soft and somewhat flaccid, normal after heat when the bitch is pregnant. On the 50th morning, an average time for a false pregnancy to prove itself, she appeared thinner. She had lost her water weight. It was obvious she carried no puppies.

This bitch was bred successfully eight months later at her next standing heat. The days the breeding took hold were the 16th and 18th days of estrus, even though she began accepting the male on the tenth day. No bitch should be bred during her first estrus. Although she may be sexually active, she isn't structurally or mentally mature enough to bear and rear a litter successfully.

What does one do with a bitch in estrus? One choice is to place her in a kennel for the entire period. This may be hard on both you and the bitch. Another choice is to confine her to one room in your house and take her outside only on lead. Deyanne Miller takes her bitches to one spot only outside. She carries a bottle containing a 1/4 cup clorox and 3/4 cup water, pouring it on the spot after the bitch has urinated. Never allow a bitch in estrus to go outside off leash. Some highly motivated bitches might dash off and jump or climb a fence to find a male. Others might rush to a male, who has come into the yard attracted by her scent.

You may breed the bitch on her second estrus. Many breeders prefer to wait until the bitch is two years old. By waiting, they assure themselves she is fully developed physically. Also, at age two, she may have her hips x-rayed and certified by the Orthopedic Foundation for Animals (OFA). See the OFA section below. There's no harm in waiting until she's three years old before breeding her for the first time. After a bitch reaches three years of age, pelvic bones tend to set themselves tightly if she has not been bred. Breeding bitches for the first time at ages four and five may increase whelping difficulties. Still, there are instances where bitches bred for the first time at five years of age whelped good-sized litters with no problems.

Once bred and with a litter behind her, it's wise to skip a season before rebreeding her. This gives her time to rebuild strength, regain muscle tone, replace calcium reserves, and to return to normal.

Most Portuguese Water Dog bitches have two estrus cycles a year, six to eight months apart.

It's normal and natural for some bitches to develop a false pregnancy (pseudocysis) 60 days after estrus, if not bred. She may eat and gain weight; her teats and abdomen may enlarge; she may even drip milk, nest, and fill her nest with toys she can cuddle. If she takes toys with her, remove them. Often the false pregnancy stops if she has nothing to cuddle.

Care of the Stud Dog

The potential stud dog requires the same kind of diet and exercise program the brood bitch does.

Several days before each use at stud, increase his vitamin and protein allotment. Beef liver, beef heart, ocean fish, and raw ground beef are all excellent sperm builders.

The male is attracted to the bitch in estrus by scent alone. When the dog smells a bitch in standing heat he becomes sexually stirred, he mounts, mates and hopefully impregnates her.

Most bitches will repulse the male by growling, snapping, or running away if they're not ovulating. If a bitch is accustomed to playing with other dogs in the household—bitches or males—her scent will get on them. The stud dog will then try to mount these animals. He's fooled.

Health Checkups for Bitch and Stud Dog

A Portuguese Water Dog should have a complete health checkup at least three weeks before mating. Health checkups should include checking the dog's stool for worms and worming it, if necessary. Worming should be done early, since two treatments, done at three week intervals, are required. You must never worm a bitch in estrus.

And, even though the bitch and stud dog have had regular checkups and all inoculations are up to date, it doesn't do any harm to give each a parvo, distemper, hepatitis, leptospirosis and rabies booster approximately a month before the bitch is due to come into estrus. Never give a parvo booster just before breeding. If a parvo booster is not given well in advance of estrus it should be skipped. It might prove injurious to the unborn puppies. The bitch's pre-estrus examination should include a dental check. Both dog and bitch should also have a brucellosis test performed. Brucellosis is a bacterial disease transmitted to dogs, usually through sexual contact, which produces sterility. It is highly infectious and can sterilize a whole kennel of dogs.

Orthopedic Foundation for Animals

When your bitch or stud dog is two years of age, have his or her hips x-rayed so they can be certified clear of hip dysplasia by the Orthopedic Foundation for Animals (OFA). It's best to do this before you decide to use this dog for breeding. Here are the procedures. Advise your veterinarian that you want hip x-rays done on your dog, and that the pelvic x-rays are to be sent to the OFA for certification. This alerts him to use OFA kits. These have to be processed at the same time he takes the x-rays of your dog's hips. If he doesn't use an OFA kit, OFA will refuse to evaluate the x-ray. The OFA returns the evaluation to you and to your veterinarian with the following grades; 1) excellent hips; 2) good hips; 3) fair hips; 4) mild dysplasia; 5) medium dysplasia or 6) severe dysplasia. Dogs with grades 4, 5, or 6 should be eliminated from the genetic pool. Only by strict adherence to these guidelines has dysplasia been reduced in many breeds.

If you want to breed your Portuguese Water Dog earlier than two years of age, your veterinarian can x-ray and evaluate the dog's hips for you. The OFA, however, will not certify hips unless the dog is two years of age.

Please don't have hips x-rayed just before breeding. Both authors believe x-rays may hit the area of reproductive organs (hip and pelvis) and thus alter body chemistry and hormones needed for maximum cell reproduction.

Breeding Procedure

Once the bitch is in estrus, you may wish to give her a "diabetic test paper" *every* a.m. and p.m. starting from day one of estrus. When the bitch is in standing heat, the color of the test paper changes to green. Diabetic test papers may be obtained at any drug store. Giving only two or three test papers on the approximate days you believe the bitch is ready for mating may result in inaccurate information.

If the stud dog lives at a distance, it's customary for the bitch to be sent to the male to be bred. In theory, the bitch is calmer than the male under stress of travel; nature guarantees that the bitch ovulates when in standing heat; nature does not guarantee that the stud dog will deliver sperm when he's under stress.

When the bitch meets the male, if she is receptive to his mounting, she "flags" her tail by raising it slightly and drawing it to one side, leaving her vulva exposed.

Before she allows him to get too close to her, however, she usually wants to play. This pre-mating play is stylistic. The dogs turn, romp and leap. Finally, the bitch stops, stands still, and with front legs braced, she invitingly flags her tail and exposes her hind parts.

Both dogs should be under control in a small area for both the pre-mating play and mating. It's not a good idea to allow the dogs to run together in a large yard or to place them in a garage, close the door and go away, allowing them to mate by themselves. Bitches will frequently turn on males in confusion or anger, discouraging an inexperienced stud. Or the dogs tie, and the bitch struggles to get away, injuring both of them.

So, put both male and female on collar and leash. Allow them to play. After he has excited her by licking her vulva and ears, he'll prepare to mount her. At this point, take the bitch by the collar and calm her. An assistant helps the male mount her. His thrusting is done haphazardly and if there is a size variance, it is sometimes necessary to guide the dog's penis to the vulva. Virgin bitches often cry out in pain as they experience initial penetration.

Sometimes, virgin bitches have obstructions within the vulva. Veterinarian assistance may be required to remove them before she can be bred.

Once the penis is inside the vulva, the dog's penis engorges; the female's muscles contract. The dogs are tied in mating. They cannot come apart until the dog's erection subsides and the penis returns to normal. Let them stay in this position for several minutes. Never try to pull dogs apart that are tied. You may damage either or both internally. After the dogs are tied for several minutes, you may turn the dog so his hindquarters face the female's hindquarters. The dogs are now comfortable until the tie is complete. It may last from five minutes to an hour. When the penis disgorges, it slips out of the vulva. The mating is complete. During the tie the sperm cells travel to the uterus where a tiny fraction fertilize the ripe eggs.

Once the mating is over, both dogs should be allowed to rest quietly.

Several hours later, give both dog and bitch a meal of raw meat. Raw meat is slow to digest and while it is being digested, the dogs rest quietly.

Artificial Insemination

Artificial insemination (A.I.) is used if the sire is too tall for the bitch or if it is too difficult to get the bitch to stand for the particular male. In this procedure, semen is withdrawn from the male and inserted into the female's vulva. If you feel there is a possibility that you'll have to breed via A.I., alert your veterinarian. The AKC considers applications to register litters "resulting from artificial insemination provided both the sire and dam are present during the artificial mating, and provided that both the extraction and insemination are done by the same licensed veterinarian." Your veterinarian certifies on the AKC form that he has effected the artificial breeding.

Artificial insemination has a 70 percent success ratio, only ten percent less than impregnation by natural breeding.

The number of the A.I. AKC form is R94-2. Its title is *Artificial Insemination Using Fresh Semen.* You may obtain these forms by writing to AKC and requesting them.

Frozen Semen

A whole new world has opened up with the collection and use of frozen semen. Quality litters sired by renowned studs may be created years after these excellent dogs have died. The AKC describes this process on their form R198-1, entitled *Artificial Insemination Using Frozen Semen.* Again, copies may be obtained by writing AKC requesting them.

Care of the Brood Bitch

Once bred, the bitch may resume her normal activities. Nutritionists advise not to give the pregnant bitch an immediate increase in food. The bitch should have an increase in protein and vitamins. For instance, instead of adding 15 percent meat or fish protein, as when she's on a normal maintenance diet, increase protein to 25 percent. Instead of giving her two multi-purpose vitamins daily, give her three.

When the bitch is 24-25 days pregnant, take her to your veterinarian for palpation. At that time, he will suggest when and how to increase her total food intake and when to begin limiting her exercise.

It's vitally important not to overfeed the bitch. You want the food to go under her back, not on it. If unborn pups get too fat, delivery may be difficult.

It's equally important that the bitch get plenty of exercise. She needs well-toned muscles to help her expel her pups without difficulty. Swimming is wonderful exercise for a pregnant Portuguese Water Dog. She may swim until she is at least five weeks into whelp.

Nevertheless, be careful not to expose the bitch to too many different experiences during her initial three week period of pregnancy. It is now believed by many veterinarians that viruses may cause some of the conditions heretofore thought to be hereditary, such as cleft palate. Particularly guard your bitch against being exposed to viruses during the third week of pregnancy. A mild virus then could cause defects in the pups.

At five weeks increase her food consumption. Offer three or four feedings daily rather than her normal two. The pups are pressing against her stomach. She needs more food but in smaller quantities.

A bitch will limit her activity the last several weeks; however, she needs help from you. After the sixth week, don't allow her to play with other dogs; don't allow her to roughhouse with small children. You don't want a puppy to twist inside her uterine horns, thereby making for a difficult labor.

The pressures on her abdomen and bladder increase as the puppies grow. They push against her internal organs. She needs plenty of opportunity to empty her bladder. She also requires frequent filling of her water dish.

Preparations for Whelping

Whelping Box: A good size whelping box for the Portuguese Water Dog is 3 × 5 feet. This amount of space allows the bitch to lie stretched out to feed her pups. Later, when the pups sleep alone, it gives ample room for a blanket or sheet to be spread across half of the box with papers spread along the remaining half. Broom handles or poles cut to fit should be anchored four and five inches above the floor along each wall. Keep them in place for the first week of the pups' lives. They prevent the bitch from accidentally crushing her pups against a side wall if she lies against it as she's sleeping. Sometimes a pup climbs over the bitch's back and falls against the side. She may inadvertently crush it if there's no railing. It's also nice to have one side of the whelping box hinged half way up and keep the top half folded down so the dam can step over it and not injure her teats by jumping over a high side. When the pups are big enough to crawl over the lowered side put it up and fasten it. By this time the dam's teats have returned to a more normal size. Also install a door in one wall of the whelping box so the dam and puppies may walk in and out. Then pups won't be programmed to climb over walls.

The floor of the box should be raised off the floor. Trapped air is warm. Line the floor under the whelping box with either a blanket or rug to prevent cold air from leaking in.

During whelping cover the floor of the box with newspapers. The bitch may want to shred them or mix them up. Newspapers assist in easy cleanup after the litter is whelped.

When all the pups have arrived, place them in a box lined with a heating pad and covered with a blanket and towel, and clean the whelping box. You may wish to line the floor with a foam rubber mattress and cover it with a whelping mat case made of canvas, sailcloth or denim and edged with velcro. This may then easily be removed for washing. Or you may line the floor of the box with newspapers and cover these with a blanket. As the pups grow, the blanket is folded and so reduced in size. The papers allow the pups to eliminate a distance away from their bed.

Place an electric heater close to the litter box. The ideal model has thermostat control and disengages itself if it is knocked over. We suggest setting the thermostat at 94 degrees for the first day. Set it at 90 degrees the second day through the end of the first week, to 85 the second week.

The Whelping Day

Canine whelping charts establish whelping dates as occurring from 59 to 63 days after the first mating. Puppies born before day 59 are called premature and have a low survival rate. Bitches who deliver pups after 63 days may have run into some kind of internal problem. As with all statistics, there are exceptions. Some bitches begin delivery on day 58, end it on day 59 and all pups are okay. Others don't present pups until day 67. Many whelpings take place on the 60th day.

The Portuguese Water Dog is still a primitive breed. One of the ways they exhibit this is in reproduction. They are easy whelpers.

If you worry that the bitch may be going to present pups before day 59, get in touch with your veterinarian. And if you feel the days have slipped by and she isn't showing signs of whelping and you've done everything possible to make her comfortable, take her for a long walk. Often, this physical exercise relaxes her so she can return to her whelping box and present puppies.

Sometimes, psychological stress takes a hand in delaying whelping. Once, one of Kathryn Braund's bitches' normal 48 hour approach to labor had begun:

> The first sign was a drop in her temperature from 101.5 down to 100. A temperature drop from the norm of about 101.5 to below 100 is a proven sign that whelping is near. The second sign, a mucous-like discharge from the vulva, appeared when I was walking her that same morning. The third sign, swelling of the vulva lips, was noted.
>
> I took my bitch to the whelping room. She lay quietly most of that day and night; the next morning she began shivering. Her temperature had dropped to 90 degrees F. This was extremely low; consequently her whole system was extremely depressed. The veterinarian was advised. He stood by the telephone, ready to give assistance, if necessary.

Although lethargic, she refused to remain in the whelping box to which I had accustomed her during the last week of her pregnancy. Instead, obviously in the second stage of labor—panting, restless—she kept running to the master bedroom and into its dark closet. It finally dawned on me that she wanted a den in which to whelp her pups.

I quickly placed the grooming table inside the whelping box and covered it with a dark blanket. The moment she saw the dark opening, she went inside and without as much as tearing up one piece of paper, deposited a pup. She was so exhausted her instinct to care for the pup had to be aided. We removed the sac from the pup, we rubbed the puppy, cut the cord and placed the puppy on a teat. Stimulated by the pup's suckling, her maternal instincts took over. We only needed to stand by and watch as she whelped the remainder of her eight puppies.

So much for psychological stress!

If everything checks out okay and your bitch still exhibits distress, get in touch with your veterinarian.

It happens that some unborn puppies are malformed or malpositioned or dead. If the second stage of labor—dilation of the cervix and contractions—occurs without a puppy appearing within an hour, it's possible a Caesarian section might have to be performed. Don't hesitate to get in touch with your veterinarian.

Here's a summary of signs that show whelping is close:

a) Her temperature drops from 101.5 to below 100.
b) She has a mucous discharge from her vulva.
c) She refuses food.
d) She lays quietly for from 24 to 48 hours.
e) She pants briefly, shakes and shivers, may cry out, and may vomit.
f) She turns and looks at or licks her hind parts.
g) Her water bag breaks or she urinates in her whelping box.
h) She pants again and makes straining actions.

The last sign tells you that a puppy's birth is imminent. If the labor for this particular puppy is difficult, it might be an hour before the puppy is born. If two hours have passed, contact your vet immediately.

Tale of a Whelping Marathon

Deyanne Miller's record of a litter whelped by Trovoada de Alvalade (Truvie) on June 22, 1976 follows. The litter Truvie was about to whelp would be the largest litter of Portuguese Water Dogs whelped in the United States.

Truvie was born October 19, 1970. C.B. Lumpi de Alvalade was her sire and Ria was her dam. Deyanne Miller imported Truvie in May, 1972. She was already the dam of PWDCA litters No. 3 and No. 4. This was to be PWDCA litter No. 14. Truvie would, in the future, be the dam of litter No. 26.

On June 22, 1976, Truvie was four and 3/4 years of age.

Here's the story.

"Truvie's temperature began going down on June 17th, signaling culmination of pregnancy. At about noon that day, she recorded a temperature of 100. The next day, Friday, June 18th, there was no specific change; on Saturday, the 19th, her temperature went up to 100.2 and then to 100.4. Sunday, the 20th, it fell back to 100.2. On Monday, the 21st—at 9:15 a.m., it held steady at 100.2. But at 10 p.m. Monday night, it had fallen to 99.8.

"The weather was very hot, very muggy. Truvie was panting quite a bit. She spent some part of Sunday night and Monday afternoon lying in the litter box.

"This morning, Tuesday, June 22, her temperature was still below 100.

"Truvie, I asked her, when will you whelp?

"Truvie didn't answer, but went to her dish. So I fed her.

"Truvie, being Truvie, contrary to what it says in the books, ate everything up. She kept asking for snacks until about 5 p.m.

"Our veterinarian stopped by on his way home because we were anxious about her and wondered if something could be wrong.

"When he arrived, we were out by the pool. He checked her over but found nothing amiss. He commented that she looked fairly draggy and uncomfortable. He shook his head in amazement as he watched her eat some hors d'oeuvres. He left.

"Helen Roosevelt, the owner of the stud, came by. Truvie was glad to see her and Helen exclaimed over her condition. Truvie watched people swim and wagged her tail happily when Father came home from the office. That was that up through 8 p.m.

"She went into her whelping box shortly after that. I think she had waited for the weather to cool down.

"Naturally, I went to sit by her.

"At the stroke of 9 p.m., she gave effortless birth to a boy. He was curly. There was an afterbirth.

"Since it's important to keep track of all afterbirths in whelping, I charted the appearance of each. For those of you who haven't yet had a bitch in whelp, there's one afterbirth (placenta) for each puppy. Sometimes, the bitch doesn't expel one. This may cause trouble for the bitch.

"At 10:05 p.m., I noticed a bubble already halfway out of Truvie's vulva. It was cloudy and milky-appearing. I couldn't see any puppy inside. Fifty-five minutes later, at exactly 11 p.m., the puppy arrived with an afterbirth. He too was curly.

"At 11:15 the next boy was presented head first, dangling a leg in front and one leg in back of him.

"Truvie, I should mention at this point, is perhaps the heaviest I've ever seen her; in fact, she's absolutely the heaviest bitch that I've ever seen

he litter Truvie whelped on June 22, 1976 would be the largest litter of Portuguese Water Dogs
whelped in the United States.

with any litter. Her first litter totaled nine pups and the second litter 14. We're sort of geared to figure that she must have at least 14 puppies inside her this go-round. We could, of course, be wrong.

"At 11:41 p.m., she presented another curly boy. We checked off the afterbirth. All so far, okay!

"Truvie has eaten two afterbirths. It's my custom to allow a bitch to do this because it helps the uterus to contract; also afterbirths contain nourishment. We believe it keeps the instinct of the bitch in whelping going so she completes her assignment without help. After she's allowed to eat two, we dispose of the rest.

"At midnight, Cinderella arrived. The first girl of the litter was curly. We were so excited, we questioned the arrival of the afterbirth. Sometimes, you know, the afterbirth will come when the next puppy arrives. We have had only three so far out of five pups.

"All these puppies are good-sized and vigorous, but two we had a little trouble getting started to nurse. I'll go into that detail in a few minutes.

"At 12:20 a.m., there's another boy. The afterbirth is accounted for. He too looks curly.

"We'll have to wait on these coats until they dry out a bit more, then we can indeed tell if they're curly or wavy. At birth, curly coats resemble a Persian lamb coat; very very tight curls. The wavy coats appear sleek.

"What we have now at 12:30 a.m. are five boys and one girl. Truvie began her delivery at the stroke of 9 p.m. She's been whelping for 3½ hours and has delivered six pups.

"She's resting.

"At 2 a.m. I notice a bit of green water. At 2:10 a.m. a boy is born. He has white on a paw—a gauntlet. I don't see an afterbirth.

"Now it's 2:28 a.m., right on the dot—here comes more discharge. Truvie is licking herself. She presents a pup at 2:40. Number eight is a boy with a half gauntlet (half-white paw).

"At 3:50 a.m. there's a greenish discharge and Truvie is contracting. Incidentally, in most of the literature you've read about whelping, it's stated that green or green-tinted discharge is a big alert signal that something is wrong. Well, I've seen that most bitches have some sort of greenish-tinged discharge. Actually, the afterbirth itself and some of the bags of water carry some green, so don't be terribly alarmed if you see green. Simply bide your time. Depending upon the wait between births— there should be no more than two hours between pups—if the bitch is contracting, it's not the hours that count so much but the fact that the bitch is contracting during this time. That's the why of my note at 3:50 a.m.; 'With a green discharge and contracting. . . .' Everything is okay.

"At 4 a.m. another boy is presented.

"At 4:35 still another boy!

"At 5:05—what! Another boy. That's six boys since midnight. That's a total of 11 boys and 1 girl.

"Well, hooray—Truvie—at 6:25 a.m. you present us with a girl. We now have two girls and 11 boys.

"It's been a sort of long and lonely night in a sense, and for any of you who have been to visit Farmion, you know that our house was built in the year 1725 and downstairs there's a room called the *borning room*, which is indeed our whelping room. So, where the women used to have their babies to be close to the big hearth in the hearth room and the big fireplace, our bitches now whelp Portuguese Water Dog puppies.

"I had some help here. Herb, because he has to work today, went to sleep early on. Linda, who stayed with me, finally stretched out on the hearth room hide-a-bed, while I grabbed about an hour and a half's sleep on a chair.

"Right now, I'm going to take a couple of pillows—I mention this because you may get into a long whelping—put them in the bathtub in the downstairs bathroom, where we whelp, and take a few magazines—and lie down in the tub to rest. I'm going to pull the whelping box close to me so that I can pat Trovoada, and also so that I can see what's going on. If you're going to be in for a long whelping or a big litter, you might as well get yourself comfortable with the supplies handy. Do keep a clock close by; one that has a minute hand (I'm thinking of one you can use for temperature taking as well as for timing arrivals.

"Anyway, let's get back to schedule.

"At 8:35 a.m., I took Truvie outside. Sometimes you have to put the leash and collar on and really drag the dam out. She relieved herself and came back.

"At 9:30 a.m. she gave birth to another girl—the third girl. Whoopee. At 9:45 a.m. the afterbirth finally came along. Truvie ate it.

"All throughout her whelping she has been offered different broths, like Bovril and chicken neck broths, and she was not at all interested in yogurt, thank you. She was interested in some hamburger. So much for the light diet rule during whelping.

"Now at 10 a.m. there are more contractions; at 10:55 a.m. another boy appears.

"That's 12 boys and 3 girls. I'm really beginning to wonder at this point, you know—how many more?

"At 8:35 when I took her out, the vet stopped by. He felt her. She seems fine. He checked all the puppies. They seemed fine. They all appear to be of a fairly good size, although we have not weighed them as yet and will not do that until later. At this point—it's been possible since the 9th puppy—to see Truvie contracting. Before that, she was so heavy, she was a balloon. It seemed as though there was almost not enough space for her to draw in a breath, let alone make any contractions. So we've been able to see contractions from the 9th puppy on.

"Now, because she may have another puppy or so, we haven't given the shot of oxytocin which is customarily given at the end of whelping. It makes the uterus contract and get rid of any retained birthing matter.

"The reason we don't want to give it yet is that it is sometimes given too early on. I know once we had—I think it was in 1958—when we gave a Standard Poodle a pituitrin shot; obviously we didn't know it was too early to give it to her because 24 hours later we had a dismembered puppy born. So I think although oxytocin is necessary at times, sometimes you'd better make sure that the bitch has indeed finished whelping.

"All right now, this is Wednesday, at 11 a.m. I can see a contraction. We can really see it now.

"At 11:15 a.m. a boy is born; he can't seem to suckle too well; along with him arrived two greenish-black furry sort of bags which are a little separated; I assume they're afterbirths. I wonder if this greenish furry substance might have been a reabsorbed foetus. I would like to question this later with a veterinarian.

"At 5:30 this afternoon another afterbirth arrived. Truvie seems quite normal throughout all of this.

"The vet has stopped by again; he's given her a shot of vitamin B because certainly she is tuckered out, although she seems normal. She's just awfully tired.

"At 7 or so this evening she saunters into the kitchen. There's a roast turkey being carved and she is sort of standing there, as much as if to say, 'Now listen here, you know, I want some of this.'

"And right at that precise moment, another afterbirth comes along.

"So I've lost count of afterbirths, after all. I think this is pretty understandable, because our total count now is a dozen boys and three girls. Fifteen puppies. All are well; again, I've not weighed them but will do so; we're all a little tuckered out at this point.

"Thursday, June 24th at 4 p.m. Truvie registers a temperature of 104.8.

"Obviously, this is cause for alarm. She has a discharge which is gummy and mucousy-looking.

"The vet returns. By 5:30 she is quiet; she's had a bufferin tablet. Her temperature was 105 when he gave it to her. The temperature came down; she's now been given another bufferin. She's had her shot of oxytocin.

"We're watching her carefully. We're taking her temperature every six to eight hours. Right now, her stool was jet black. She ate placentas, that's why.

"She dripped blood for two weeks; passed blood in her urine for about three weeks. All of this is normal after whelping.

"Many bitches shed hair after whelping.

"Truvie didn't.

"Ah, Truvie. You're a marvel."

242

14

Feeding the Portuguese
Water Dog

THE WORKING Portuguese Water Dog ate well. He ate from a quarter to a half a man's daily ration of fish.

Vasco Bensaude continued the tradition of feeding fish to his Albarbiorum Water Dogs. Ocean fish is rich in nutrients and vitamin B.

After the Portuguese Water Dog came to America he was introduced to and fed, in large part, a variety of processed dog foods—many guaranteed by manufacturers to be all the food the dog needs to eat—the foods are "complete and balanced."

We suggest that although you find it convenient to feed the highly convenient, palatable and complete and balanced processed food you might wish to supplement the Portuguese Water Dog's diet with natural foods.

When you do so, please add the amounts in a 15 to 25 percent ratio to the processed food. Otherwise, so nutritional experts tell us, it will unbalance the "complete and balanced" processed food.

Deyanne Miller suggests feeding two cooked eggs a week, one cod liver oil perle and two garlic perles a day (available in health food stores). You may also want to add grated carrots and dried carrot tops to food and increase the protein consumption with the addition of boiled fish and its juices, or beef or lamb.

Following are the diets which both authors use. We believe Portuguese Water Dogs should have extra nourishment during stress periods—

that is, during pregnancy, lactation, show and obedience exhibition, water work or whenever your dog needs more than a maintenance diet.

Prorate all diets on the dog's weight. Be sure to measure all food given. By doing this, you'll find it's easy to adjust for weight gain or loss.

Here is a diet for a brood bitch from her fifth through ninth weeks of pregnancy.

Sample Pregnancy Diet—Fifth Through Ninth Weeks

Breakfast: One large, hard dog biscuit (cleans teeth); premium quality high-protein meal; milk; raw egg yolk, or scrambled whole egg, or hard-boiled egg (raw egg whites, if given more than twice weekly, eliminate avidin, a vitamin of the B family, from the dog's stomach); one teaspoonful wheat germ (flakes or oil); one multi-purpose vitamin.

Lunch: Complete and balanced high-protein meal; choice of cottage cheese, boiled ocean fish or clam juice.

Dinner: High-protein meal; choice of beef heart, beef kidney, chopped lean ground beef (plain hamburger contains too much fat—use ground beef with 18 percent or lower fat content); teaspoonful wheat germ, multi-purpose vitamin.

Snacks: Fresh fruit, fresh vegetables.

For extra nutrition, simmer beef liver for fifteen minutes in enough water to cover it. To the water add osterized garlic cloves and egg shells. Refrigerate and use sparingly.

Note: Don't allow a pregnant bitch to get fat. Give her ample exercise. Exercise translates into good blood circulation and muscle tone; therefore, she'll develop better pups. Exercise also translates into easy whelping.

Dam's Diet During Nursing

Birth Until Four Days of Age
Breakfast: Choice of cream of wheat or oatmeal. While the cereal is cooking, mix in a raw egg. It will cook in the cereal. Add a handful of raisins or dates. When cooked, thin with milk. If using canned milk, dilute with water in 1/2 ratio. Do not dilute fresh milk.

Mid-Morning: Glass of milk laced with tablespoonful of wheat germ.

Lunch: High protein meal with cottage cheese.

Dinner: Choice of high protein dog meal or cooked cereal with milk, honey and egg.

Bedtime Snack: 1/2 cup milk.

Note: It is important to keep the bitch's diet light, milky and highly fluid the first four days after puppies are born. Don't give her all the food she wants. Mastitis (breast caking) may stem from overfeeding the bitch during this period. Remember, milk has already developed in her mammary glands in the latter days of pregnancy. She has also eaten some high-protein afterbirth. It's best not to give kibble to the bitch the first four days. It lies too heavy in the stomach.

Pups are tiny. Their sucking power is not well developed. By not overloading her teats with milk until pups have gained ample sucking power to drain them, you reduce the chance of breast problems.

This highly fluid but rich diet may make your bitch's stools loose. This is not diarrhea but you might want to reduce the diet's richness.

Fifth Day to Fifth Week

As soon as the puppies learn to suckle lustily—about the fifth day of life—add quality protein to the bitch's diet. Add it gradually until the bitch is eating about three times as much as when she is on normal maintenance. Start cutting back during the fourth week of the puppies' lives to help her wean her pups gradually.

Breakfast: High protein dog meal with milk.

Mid-Morning (10 a.m.): Cooked cereal with egg. Add raisins or dates. Thin with milk before serving.

Lunch: High-protein dog meal with sardines. One teaspoonful wheat germ.

Mid-Afternoon Snack (2 p.m.): Drink of milk.

Dinner (6 p.m.): Rice and meat or fish mixture. Here is the recipe.

Boil two cups natural brown rice in 4-1/2 cups water for about 50 minutes or until done. Add 1/2 teaspoonful salt, two teaspoonsful Mazola oil. In another pan, simmer 1/2 beef heart, 1 whole beef kidney or 1 small boned ocean fish in 4 cups water for 1/2 hour. To the water add several cloves garlic, 1 diced carrot, several minced egg shells, sprig of celery, parsley and 1/4 cup beef liver. When cooked, combine in a blender. Combine with cooked rice. Into this mix 4 teaspoonsful bone meal. This recipe, adapted from Dr. Kronfeld's column in *Pure-Bred Dogs— American Kennel Gazette,* should make enough food for several days. Store in refrigerator.

Bedtime Snack (10 p.m.): Drink of milk with several bits of dog meal or kibble.

Note: Don't forget to add garlic perles to your bitch's food during mosquito season.

Fifth to Seventh Week

At the beginning of the fifth week you may choose to wean the pups completely from the bitch's milk (we recommend doing this during the sixth week), decrease the bitch's food by 1/8 cup increments at each meal. Gradually eliminate the morning, afternoon and bedtime snacks.

On the day she (or you) decide pups should be fully weaned, you may want to aid the process by fasting her the entire day and keeping her *away from the pups.* This is difficult for many to do. The next day, return her to two regular daily meals. Keep her away from the pups this day also. If, after several more days have passed, the bitch still wants to nurse her pups as well as play with them, allow her to do so. She will be weaning them as long as you keep her on the maintenance diet. Since her milk has lost its rich quality, the puppies will undoubtedly prefer eating the food you serve.

Weaning

Puppies thrive on their dam's milk. Her milk is a complete food, reaching maximum quality during the third week of the puppies lives. It then gradually decreases in richness. It is, therefore, better not to supplement the mother's milk diet before the beginning of the puppies' third week. If you must do so, give the puppies small amounts only. Their digestive systems should be allowed to develop without undue stress. Remember, among other benefits, puppies develop facial muscles while they suck. Most breeders are in too much of a hurry to wean puppies from the bitch's milk.

At about 21 days of age, puppy teeth begin to emerge. The teeth are needle-sharp. Also, toenails grow thicker, stronger and sharper. The pups bite the dam's teats with their milk teeth and irritate her breasts with their toenails. The combined bites and scratches irritate her. The bitch begins to find motherhood quite wearying. Do make it a practice to wash her teats with warm water, soothing them as well as cleaning them. Puppies' nails should be kept short for their sake and the dam's.

After the pups are 21 days old, just *after* the mother feeds the puppies, prepare the following snack for them. Use half canned milk and half warm water, make the mixture lukewarm, neither hot nor cold, pour some into a saucer. Remove the bitch from the whelping box. Put her outside. She shouldn't be in either eye contact or earshot.

In a separate area, away from the other pups, place a puppy on your lap. Dip a finger into the milk and let the puppy smell and then lick your finger. Then place the saucer on the floor. Hold it steady. Allow the puppy to walk into the saucer. When he does, he smells the milk, he sniffs it and tries to suck it. Eventually, he'll lap a little.

Do this with each puppy. Several will choke and cough and sputter. This is okay. You're only giving each puppy a taste. When all have tasted, place them around the saucer and add more milk. They'll be making all kinds of noises—singing, squealing and sputtering—trying to get a drink. After a few minutes, allow the bitch to come in to finish drinking the milk. The pups will watch her, learning by her example. She'll also lick the spilled milk off her puppies' bodies. They'll then nurse again eagerly.

Repeat the procedure each morning. As the week progresses, the puppies learn to lap.

Supplemental Feeding of Puppies Until Fully Weaned

First Three Days of Fourth Week (21 to 28 days of life)
Offer one milk drink daily. Example: 1/2 canned milk to 1/2 water, lukewarm. If bitch's milk is completely satisfying, some pups refuse this milk drink. Remember, this is the week the bitch's milk is at its richest quality.

Last Four Days of Fourth Week
Trade the saucer for a large, glass pie pan. Glass is heavy and not prone to upsets when pups walk into the pan. Add a small amount of baby cereal, such as oatmeal or rice, to the milk drink. Try to divide between the litter equally. Feed once daily.

Fifth Week (29 to 35 days of life)
According to size of litter, use one or two glass pans or choose a low double-sized dog dish.
Breakfast: Milk and cereal. Add one raw egg yolk for each three pups.
Lunch: Offer a thumbnail size ball of raw ground beef to each puppy. Use ground round or finely chopped lean roundsteak. Don't use ground meat with more than 15 percent fat content. Meat fat may harm immature digestive systems. If you live in an area where raw beef is suspect, simmer the beef and offer a tablespoon of cooked beef and its liquid. Present the taste of meat to each pup from the end of your finger. As you offer it, whistle softly. Within days, whenever a pup hears your soft whistle, he'll come running to you. This low whistle is also a hearing test.
Dinner: Simmer lean beef for fifteen minutes in enough water to cover. Chop fine and offer a small amount of both beef and broth to pups from their large pans. Twice a week, simmer ocean fish for fifteen minutes in enough water to cover and offer the broth and deboned fish to the pups.

Sixth Week (36 to 42 days)
Feed each puppy from his own dish. Supervise all feedings so puppies who gulp their food don't push the slower eaters away from their dishes. Most Portuguese Water Dogs are slow, delicate eaters, taking their time and enjoying each bite.
Breakfast: To milk, cereal and egg breakfast add a small amount of *complete and balanced* dry puppy food. Offer the puppy food with the intention of eliminating milk, cereal and egg by the end of this week.
Lunch: Raw chopped meat mixed with a sprinkling of wheat germ.
Dinner: Finely chopped, simmered beef mixed with dry puppy food. As alternatives, substitute cooked beef heart, kidney or ocean fish. Finely chopped lean lamb, turkey, chicken or venison is also good. Some puppies later develop skin allergies from horse meat and venison. Never feed pork, seasoned meats or fat.

From weaning on, Water Dog puppies should have some ocean fish two to three times weekly. Don't use river or lake fish. These do not contain ocean nutrients. If fresh or frozen ocean fish is not available, use canned ocean fish products.

Note: Don't forget to whistle softly each and every time you place food down for the puppies. You are instilling response to the whistle come command.

Seventh Week (43 to 49 days)

As the puppies become completely weaned from the bitch's milk, you may gradually wean them from natural foods. Do this to prepare them to leave for homes which will only feed a processed dog food.

Wise breeders give diet sheets to each puppy buyer to help them decide how best to feed their puppies. Diet sheets should contain this or a similar statement: *When changing your Water Dog's diet, do so gradually—at the ratio of 1/4 cup per day. To change food more abruptly may upset your puppy's delicate digestive system.*

As stated earlier, some bitches enjoy nursing their puppies until they leave the nest. Don't discourage this if your Portuguese Water Dog bitch offers her puppies milk. If you have followed instructions and have fasted her for one day before full weaning and then returned her to her normal maintenance diet, all she'll be giving them will be milk "treats." Most bitches are glad to get puppies off their teats. The teats then dry up easily.

After Weaning

At the end of the seventh week, all puppies should be on established puppy diets.

Feeding Puppies, Eight to Twelve Weeks

Until puppies are 12 weeks of age, a four- or five-meal-a-day regimen should be maintained. Their stomachs are small and they absorb nutrients better if they are fed frequently.

Owners who work and cannot give their puppies a midday meal require "help with lunch" until the puppy is 12 weeks old.

Feeding Puppies, Twelve Weeks to Six Months

Puppies should be fed three meals a day. If you work, the third meal may be a snack in the evening an hour before bedtime. This allows for some elimination before bedtime. Don't feed the puppy at bedtime unless you're willing to get up during the night to take him outside to eliminate.

Feeding Older Puppies and Adults

After five or six months, depending on the growth, health and appetite pattern of your puppy, you may omit the third meal. If so, feed the smaller amount in the morning and the larger amount in the evening. When the puppy fails to eat his puppy meal readily, you may transfer to a *complete and balanced* adult dog meal. Add supplements sensibly.

You may prefer, as many breeders do, to keep your puppy on a puppy meal diet until he is a year old. Remember, if your Portuguese Water Dog is a slow eater, it's better to keep him on three meals a day until he's a year old. He must have maximum absorption from his food.

Leaving food available on a 24-hour-a-day basis is not a good practice in average situations. Many adult eating problems begin in the litter box when food is constantly available for puppies. Many become picky eaters and consequently problem eaters in new owners' homes. Serving the dog his food on a strict two- or three-meal-a-day basis is easier on his stomach. If you want him to rest most of the day, feed the heaviest meal in the morning, if you want him to be quiet during the night, feed the heaviest meal in the evening.

Some people prefer to feed their adult dog only one meal a day. This is okay. But pet dogs feel better when fed twice daily.

When travelling, do give him raw ground round as part of his natural food supplement. You'll find he rests well during long hours on the road.

By using common sense in adding supplements to your Portuguese Water Dog's diet, you'll have a healthy and happy dog, his life long.

We suggest adding warm liquid to processed food and let it soak for a few minutes before giving it to the dog. Otherwise, processed food may "blowup" in his stomach.

Store dry food in a cool and dry place. Never purchase more than you can use in a month. Dry food may mold or become rancid if kept too long. Manufacturers say dog food spoils in nine months. It's a good idea to check manufactured date when purchasing food.

Deyanne Miller recommends a dog food product which is frozen meat, without preservatives. It comes in one or three pound packages and is easy to store in a freezer, "on land or sea."

Cottage cheese, buttermilk and yogurt are all excellent foods for dogs. The whey content helps keep stomachs healthy. After an illness, offer any of these to your dog; they restore normal intestinal bacteria. If a dog can't eat anything else, he will eat dairy foods.

Older dogs need protein, contrary to popular belief, and fresh meat added in 15 percent increments to dog meal is an excellent supplement.

Be careful about giving dogs bones. Bones are good for dogs when given in limited quantities. Pups need bones to chew to exercise gums. But some dogs have difficulty digesting bone. To be on the safe side, never give your dog a bone or, if you feel you must, make it a policy *never* to give your dog small bones. Bone splinters may get caught in his windpipe or intestines and remain there for years or perforate the walls. Good bones to give dogs are roundbones or large knuckle bones. Roundbones contain marrow, excellent food for dogs but it may get stuck around a dog's lower jaw. To pry it off you have to use oil on his lower muzzle with vaseline. Never give your dog chop bones, steak or poultry bones. Too many bones may cause compaction in the stomach. This in turn may cause a dog to have a seizure. Don't offer your dog a bone when he finishes eating a meal. The dog may think he should swallow it. If he does he may have to pass it or have diarrhea for weeks until the bone dissolves in his stomach.

When a dog eats grass, don't be alarmed that his digestive system is upset. All dogs eat grass for roughage. The problem with dogs eating grass from cultivated lawns is that they often eat insecticides and fertilizer. Their stomachs become upset. Couch grass, field grasses of all kinds are eliminated through the feces, not through vomiting.

Don't feed your dog overdoses of vitamins. Too much vitamin B may cause the dog to grow taller than he would normally and too much vitamin C may irritate his urinary tract. Too much vitamin E may cause hair loss. Overdoses of vitamin A and D are extremely toxic.

When your dog is sick or convalescing, place him on a bland diet of rice with protein in the form of lamb, chicken or beef (in that order). Never feed him pork. Pork or commercial dog food may irritate his already irritated intestines. Give him buttermilk, yogurt or yogurt tablets to bring back normal intestinal bacteria. Have him drink lots of water. Bland diets for humans work well for sick or convalescent dogs.

15

Showing Your Portuguese Water Dog

ONE OF THE GREATEST JOYS of having a dog is showing him and, hopefully, winning with him. A Portuguese Water Dog has the potential to take many wins in the Working group, as well as Best in Show awards, because he is much-admired by both judges and spectators.

While showing dogs is a sport, judging them is an art. Judges are knowledgeable of the breeds they judge, yet they vary in their opinion of what is best. They interpret the breed standard differently.

This is why your dog may win one show and lose another. Good dogs may win 50 percent of the time while outstanding dogs win 75 percent of the time. Poor dogs may win also on occasion. Seldom does any dog win 100 percent of the time.

Showing your dog may become more than a hobby; it may become a way of life. Exhibitors often become breeders; breeders often become judges.

The rules for training dogs for showing in the conformation ring sound easy; but as in all sporting endeavors, learning to execute the rules is not as easy as it appears. Just learning to handle skillfully requires time and patience.

Ring Procedures

When handlers and their dogs enter the show ring, the judge usually has the handlers gait their dogs counterclockwise around the ring at a trot so he can watch the dogs move in unison. Many judges, adept at observing conformation faults, mentally eliminate some at the first gaiting.

Next, the judge has the handlers pose their dogs in a standing (stacked) position so he can examine each dog.

After the examination, the judge has each handler trot his dog around the ring. As the dog moves, the judge studies the dog's side, front and rear movement.

The judge may then again ask several handlers to repose or regait their dogs. He is comparing the dogs, one against the others.

He may have all handlers gait their dogs around the ring again. He wants to be sure he has not overlooked the good qualities of any dog before him.

Finally, the judge awards up to four place ribbons—blue for first, red for second, yellow for third, and white for fourth.

There are six possible regular classes at all-breed shows: Puppy (6 to 9 months), Puppy (9 to 12 months), Novice, Bred by Exhibitor, American-bred, and Open. Dogs and bitches in these *regular classes* are vying for championship points. The sexes are judged separately, with dogs judged first.

The first place winners from each class are compared with each other. The judge awards Winners Dog (WD) and Winners Bitch (WB) to what he considers the best of each sex. Each receives a purple ribbon and one or more championship points if competition is present. He also awards Reserve Winners Dog (RWD) and Reserve Winners Bitch (RWB). These two dogs get purple and white ribbons. Only the Winners Dog and Winners Bitch receive championship points. These two are next compared with any champions of record entered in a Best of Breed/Variety class. One of these dogs will receive the Best of Breed (BOB) purple and gold ribbon and one will receive the Best of Opposite Sex (BOS) red and white ribbon. The Winners Dog or Winners Bitch is chosen Best of Winners (BOW) and given a blue and white ribbon. If Winners Dog or Winners Bitch also goes Best of Breed, Best of Winners is automatic.

Becoming a Champion

It takes 15 points for a dog or bitch to become a champion. At least six of these points must be won with two "majors." Major points consist of 3, 4, or 5 points won at one show. Points given at a show are predetermined by the AKC yearly by the average number of dogs shown in different areas of the country. For instance, in 1984, the first year Portuguese Water Dogs were shown as a recognized breed, two dogs of one sex had to compete to win 1 point; three dogs gave the winner 2 points; four dogs gave the winner

Here is a group of Portuguese Water Dogs at the CPC Lisboa dog show, June 1984. Deyanne Miller, front, judged.   *Real*

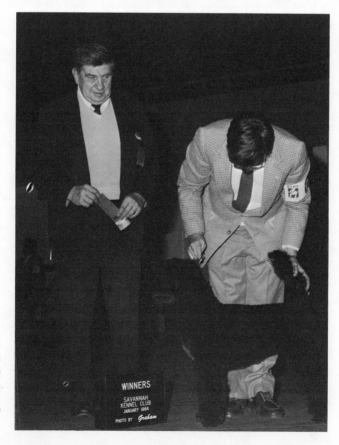

t AKC points in America
ere awarded to Farmion
preira by Judge John M.
ssevoy, January 6, 1984.
Graham

a 3-point major, five dogs gave the winner a 4-point major, and six dogs gave the winner a 5-point major.

The complete *Rules Applying to Registration and Dog Shows* is obtainable free of charge from the American Kennel Club (51 Madison Avenue, New York, NY 10010). The regulations describe everything you need to know about dog shows and how to enter them.

Show Training

In the show ring, the dog is actually under the judge's scrutiny for less than three minutes. With so little time in which to show him, it's important to learn to present him well.

This is why it's wise to begin your Portuguese Water Dog's show ring education as soon as he is settled at your house. Show training is really only an extension of house training.

Here's how to do it so you and your dog enjoy learning.

Each day, after you have groomed your dog, stand him on the grooming table, giving him the command "stand" as you get him on his feet. Use the grooming post and "loop" or steady his head with your hand under his muzzle. Remember this rule: Control of the dog's head means control of the whole dog.

Several times a day at different places both inside and outside the house, place a show collar and lead on him. As you stand him, offer him treats from your hand. Don't give him a treat if he jumps up on you or sits down. Reward him only when he stands for it. Use the command "stack" or "stand" as you stand him.

When he understands what you want, encourage him to look at you by holding the treat close to your mouth and then lowering it. Move backwards; this helps him move forward naturally into a better stance. If he doesn't, help him stand up as described earlier; then give him the treat.

Practice until he learns to stand watching you without moving his feet. You may want to slide your foot in front of his front paws to prevent him from getting out of position. If it's easier for you, move a knee instead of a foot forward to hold him back. Talk to him. Have fun.

Now pose him on the grooming table. The words in the breed standard tell you how.

> The Portuguese Water Dog . . . is shown in its natural stance, which is for the front legs to be positioned so that the feet are slightly forward of the shoulders and the hind legs are positioned approximately under the rump.

To help your dog learn to stand alertly, his tail wagging, you'll have to practice posing him many, many times. Stand on his right side, so that his "show" side—his left side—faces away from you. Place the show lead on his neck close behind his ears. Hold the lead in your right hand, tighten it in order to hold his head high and fold the remainder of the lead in your right hand.

Now reach over his shoulders with your left hand. Take hold of his left elbow and place his left front leg in the proper position. As you do, shift his front weight to the left paw. There are two ways to do this: the first is by turning his head slightly to the right; this forces him to lean to the left; the other way is by removing weight from his right front leg by lifting it. He'll transfer his weight to his left paw.

Next, transfer your hold on the show lead from your right to left hand. Keep a taut hold of it. Then with your right hand, grasp his right elbow and place his right paw on the ground so he is standing in the correct position.

Practice again by placing the left front paw correctly and then placing the right front paw correctly. Now, practice placing both front legs correctly without allowing him to shift his position. Give him a treat while he holds this position.

When this procedure becomes familiar and he learns to keep his front legs in place, begin posing his back legs. With the slack from the show lead folded in your right hand—the lead held high behind his ears to hold his neck high without choking him, position his front paws. Without releasing tension on the show lead and keeping the dog in the four-square heads up position, slide your left hand smoothly along his back. Praise him for remaining steady. Set his left back leg. Take hold of his left hock, close to the stifle joint from between his legs, not to the outside. Lift and replace his hock so that it is perpendicular to the ground. Do the same with the other rear leg. Watch the other three legs to be sure they stay in position.

Praise your puppy with a treat. Place your left arm in front of his chest; hold the treat several inches out and up from his mouth. Steady him with your arm holding him still. You want him to reach forward for the treat without breaking position. For him to grab the treat without moving, he has to stretch his neck and shoulders forward and up. If he moves a rear leg, remind him to "Stay." Repose his legs if necessary.

Practice. Pose him on the grooming table. Pose him on the floor. Work several times a day. As you practice, compliment him.

Now teach him to walk into a show pose. This is easier said than done; however, your preliminary training has given him a good idea of what you want. If, in walking him into a show pose, he continually moves forward when you want him to stand four-square, he's confused. Retrace your training steps until he understands.

To complete the show pose training, your dog must allow you to lift his tail upright so that the tuft on his tail falls gracefully over his back, yet never beyond the kidneys. Lift the tail slowly, sliding your hand from under his hindquarters to tail tip. Praise him. Relax.

The final step in teaching your dog to pose quietly is to teach him to stand quietly while he is being examined. Stand at his left side. Grasp his upper muzzle with your right hand, his lower muzzle with your left. With your fingers, raise and lower his lips so you can examine his bite. Slide your hands over his muzzle, skull and ears. Then slide them over his shoulders, front legs, back, tuck-up, hindquarters, and back legs. Praise him as you work. Practice. Have members of your family and friends examine him in this manner.

Teaching these standing and examination procedures takes lots of practice. Some days your dog forgets what is expected of him. Be patient. Be sure to stop when each session ceases being fun. Remember, there's not a dog alive who won't please for petting and food. But dogs, like humans, have good and bad days.

The next step in show training is to teach your dog to move with you as a polished unit.

Place the show lead high on his neck, close to his ears. Hold it in your left hand, close to your left hip, with barely any slack in it. Keep your elbows against your body. Keeping the dog at least a foot distant from your left side, his chest even with your left leg, start walking with him in a large left-hand circle. By walking in a left-hand circle, he cannot lag or get too far behind you as you turn; therefore, it's easier to teach him the habit of moving in place beside you. All the while you walk, watch him. You cannot train unless you keep your eye on your dog.

Zip him lightly when he gets out of position. By zipping, we mean to make sharp jerks on the show lead. As you zip, chatter to him exuberantly, "Gee, we're taking a show walk," "This is fun," or words to that effect. Be sure to walk briskly. When he learns to move beside you in a large, counterclockwise circle and stays in position on a loose lead, begin making turns. Make right, left, and right- and left-about turns. Try not to change your step when making these turns. As you turn, give him a turning signal. When teaching him to turn to the left, move your right arm across your body so your hand leads into the turn. When teaching him to turn to the right, zip lightly on the lead and move your left hand across your body. These hand-and-lead directions will help him learn to move cooperatively with you. In the ring, the judge will check his agility in turning, so important in a Portuguese Water Dog's function.

After you practice turning, practice walking slowly. Then practice gaiting at the trot. As you practice, talk to your dog. You want him to wag his tail and present a picture of happiness. The dog gets his spirit from you.

Keep practicing the above procedures until your Portuguese Water Dog learns to move with you on a loose lead at whatever gait you use and whatever direction you turn.

Finally, test him. Ask members of your family and friends to watch the two of you perform your show exercises. If you have worked consistently, your dog becomes conditioned to the show routine. He won't be distracted.

As you progress, expose him to different distractions. Pose and gait

256

him among crowds at shopping centers and at parks. Many people will come up to admire your Portuguese Water Dog; their attention contributes to his composure.

When you feel he is thoroughly acclimated to show procedures, loosen the lead so he moves beside you at an arm's distance. He should be able to stretch out because in the show ring the judge will be able to observe him better.

Conditioning

The final step in the making of a winning show dog is physical conditioning. Commence light roadwork with him when he's about nine months of age. Before that time, muscles are loose and legs often unsteady. This is because bones and muscles need time to set. However, when Portuguese Water Dogs reach nine months of age, if they are not swimming daily, roadwork should commence. An excellent alternative is to turn them out in fields where they can run up and down hills. Remember that a Portuguese Water Dog is still a puppy at nine months so don't overdo. Don't put your puppy through strenuous exercise until he's at least 15 months. Allow the muscles to develop naturally.

Entering Competition

You may wish to enter your Portuguese Water Dog in a puppy class at a regular dog show. Early showing exposes him to the exciting yet distracting ring atmosphere. He'll delight in meeting other Portuguese Water Dogs.

However, when showing a puppy, he is being exposed to a multitude of bacteria, fungi and parasites. Protect him with the timely vaccinations your veterinarian prescribes. Never risk unnecessary infections. Keep his vaccinations current all his life.

Before exhibiting your dog in a regular dog show, try to exhibit him in local "fun" matches or "sanction matches." These are informal dog shows held to acclimate dogs to the environments and procedures of championship dog shows. Locate your local kennel clubs through your chamber of commerce or telephone or city directory. The secretary will tell you about the club's activities. The corresponding secretary of the PWDCA may be able to supply you with the addresses of several kennel clubs near you.

Another source is the AKC's official magazine, *Pure-Bred Dogs— American Kennel Gazette*. Once each year this monthly magazine lists every dog club in the United States eligible to hold dog shows and obedience trials. The magazine is not sold on newsstands. Write to the AKC, 51 Madison Avenue, New York, NY 10010, for subscription information.

Don't give up if you aren't confident over several months of training.

Promise yourself to exhibit your dog at several shows. Each time you enter the ring you will gain experience and technique.

If you still feel uncomfortable handling your own dog, hire a professional handler, or agent.

The cost of hiring a professional handler is often less than you would have to pay for traveling to shows. Dog showing costs money and you don't want to risk failure because of inept handling.

You may hire a professional to take your dog from you at ringside or have him keep your dog until he becomes a champion.

In the first instance, you travel to the shows with your dog and present him, groomed, to the handler an hour or two before the scheduled start of breed judging so your dog and handler can become acquainted. If you do this, you'll probably have to watch the ring activity from a discreet distance, so the dog doesn't pick up your scent and look for you. After he is shown, the handler returns the dog to you.

In the second instance, you take or send your dog to the handler. The handler assumes complete responsibility for your dog—he boards, grooms, and shows him. The fee is higher, but it includes all the extras, including travel expenses.

A professional, even though he may win only 50 percent of the time with your dog, will undoubtedly win far more than a novice handler would.

You may wish to write to the Professional Handlers' Association (PHA) or the Dog Handlers' Guild (DHG). Either association will send you a list giving names of member handlers all across the United States. Call or write AKC for the name and address of the current secretary.

You may also hire a handler at a dog show. When observing handlers at a show, take notes. You'll learn a great deal watching and recording the techniques handlers use in presenting dogs to judges. You'll be impressed by the handlers' total commitment to the dogs in their charge. Many work together, contributing to each other's success. The dogs are usually stimulated beyond belief by the bustle, excitement and constant attention they receive from professionals.

Whatever method you use in selecting a handler, be sure to make full inquiries on how your Portuguese Water Dog will be cared for when away from you. You want him in the best hands possible.

You should subscribe to *Pure-Bred Dogs—American Kennel Gazette*. This official magazine is written expressly for the dog fancier, for the novice as well as for the veteran. Its articles will help introduce you to the world of dogs. Since it's an official magazine, it contains the names of current dog show superintendents (organizations licensed to stage dog shows). Superintendents supply the entry forms for shows over which they preside. The *Gazette* publishes complete lists of upcoming shows, judging panels at these shows, current show and obedience trial rules as well as breed standard changes.

Dog World is another popular and valuable canine publication carrying informative and educational articles on the care, health and training of dogs. It also lists dog show superintendents and the shows. Actually, there is a great variety of magazines and other periodicals devoted to dogs. As an active fancier you'll come across many of them.

In showing your dog, remember that dog showing is both sport and art. Like all sporting and art forms, there's no guarantee of perfection or success each time you exhibit.

When showing your dog, display good manners. Thank the judge for any award you receive. When another dog bests yours, congratulate the owner.

Dress tastefully when showing your dog. You're exhibiting the dog, not yourself or your clothes.

Above all, have fun and be a good sport.

Champions of the First Year

Here is the list and photo gallery of Portuguese Water Dogs who won their championships the first year they were exhibited in the Working Group—1984. To aid you in your study of pedigrees, we have included, along with the name of the champion, his or her sex, sire and dam, breeder, and owner.

Ch. Charlie De Alvalade (D)
   Taro × Truta De Alvalade
   Breeder: Canil De Alvalade
   Owner: Deyanne F. Miller and Herbert H. Miller, Jr.
Ch. Keel Beleza, CD (B)
   Trezena Monte Clerico × Keel Torreira
   Breeder: Joanne Cakoyanis
   Owner: Pamela and Jon Schneller
Ch. Spindrift Galley, CD (D)
   Ancora Do Al Gharb × Spindrift Kedge, CDX
   Breeder/Owner: H. Edward and Barbara A. Whitney
Ch. Spindrift Genoa, CDX (B)
   Ancora Do Al Gharb × Spindrift Kedge, CDX
   Breeder/Owner: H. Edward and Barbara A. Whitney
Ch. Alfama Uberrimo of Regala (D)
   Ch. Spindrift Galley, CDX × Avalon Yvivo
   Breeder: Sharon A. Broadhead
   Owner: Eleanor Pierce

Ch. Bittersweet Zizi (B)
    Victor's Vencedor × Zinia De Alvalade
    Breeder: Helen Roosevelt
    Owner: William D. Shew
Ch. Trezena Konstelada (B)
    Ancora Do Al Gharb × Trezena Meia Praia
    Breeder: Mrs. E. Niles Kenyon
    Owner: Maryanne B. Murray and Linwood A. Kulp, Jr.
Ch. Firmamento Kalakua (D)
    Adonis Do Mar × Rosmaninhal Do Mar
    Breeder: Kathryn B. Hovey
    Owner: Karen A. Miller and Jerome Yavarkovsky
        and Bertram M. Tormey
Ch. Farmion Geo, CDX (D)
    Farmion V De Gama × Farmion Nazare
    Breeder: Deyanne F. Miller
    Owner: Cyril J. and Kathryn Braund
Ch. Isodora Do Mar (B)
    Baluarte De Alvalade × Rainha Do Mar
    Breeder: James Edward & Sonja Santos
    Owner: Bill F. Flohr and Sonja Santos
Ch. Nativo Do Mar (D)
    Real Do Mar × Alma Do Mar
    Breeder: J. E. Santos and Mrs. Salome Kaehny
    Owner: Joseph and Jeralyn Goodman
Ch. Bandido Do Mar (D)
    Baluarte De Alvalade × Morena Do Mar
    Breeder: Mr. and Mrs. James Edward Santos
    Owner: Dr. Richard T. and Mrs. Dawn Woods
Ch. Farmion Zimbreira (B)
    Ch. Charlie De Alvalade × Farmion Nazare
    Breeder: Deyanne F. Miller
    Owner: Clara Corcoran Doyle
Ch. White Cap Bianca of Brinmar (B)
    Ch. Nativo Do Mar × Ch. Keel Beleza, CD
    Breeder: Pamela and Jon Schneller
    Owner: Maryanne B. Murray and Linwood A. Kulp, Jr.
Ch. Canopus Galacia, CD (B)
    Duke Do Jamor × Alianca Do Vale Negro
    Breeder: Grace M. Meisel
    Owner: Eleanor Dee and Rudy C. Pierce

Ch. Keel Beleza, CD, Ch. White Cap Capitao do Monab and Ch. White Cap Chloee.

John L. Ashbey

Ch. Alfama Uberrimo of Regala, the first of the breed to win a Group 1. Handler is Michael A. Pawasarat. Judge is Antonio N. Quiroga.

Ch. Trezena Konstelada was selected BOS at the AKC Centennial Show, November 17, 1984.

Graham

Ch. Firmamento Kalakua completed his championship at the Trenton KC May 5, 1984.

John L. Ashbey

Ch. White Cap Bianca of Brinmar. Judge is Mrs Eileen Pimlott. Owner Maryanne Murray is handling.

William P. Gilber

Ch. Farmion Geo, CDX, owned by Kathryn Braund, was the second of the breed to win a Group 1. Diver is owner-handled here to a Group 3 under Judge Joe C. Tacker.

Missy Yuhl

Ch. Shanesca Pico Alto, CD, shown with owner, Dawn Woods. *Ludwig*

Ch. Umbrion Kerry, owned by Marjorie and Richard J. Hopkins and bred by Una Barrett O'Neill, was the first brown female champion in the United States. *Klein*

Ch. White Cap Craca, owned by Jane Harding.

Ch. Bandido do Mar, owned by Dr. Richard T. and Dawn G. Woods and bred by James and Sonja Santos. The first California champion, this brown curly was owner-handled to his title at 10 months. *Rich Bergman*

Ch. Canopus Galacia, CD, owned by Eleanor Dee and Rudy C. Pierce. *Cirincione*

Ch. Isodora do Mar shown completing her championship at the San Gabriel Valley KC, May 1984.

Ch. Natale do Mar.

Ch. Natale Do Mar (B)
  Real Do Mar × Alma Do Mar
  Breeder: Mrs. James E. Santos and Mrs. Salome Kaehny
  Owner: Catherine M. Kalb
Ch. White Cap Capitao Do Monab (D)
  Keel Lobo × Ch Keel Beleza, CD
  Breeder: Pamela and Jon Schneller
  Owner: Sue Ann Pietros and Pamela Schneller
Ch. Firmamento's Zirconia (B)
  Baluarte De Alvalade × Rosmaninhal Do Mar
  Breeder: Kathryn Bowling Hovey
  Owner: Mark and Deborah Gressie
Ch. White Cap Chloee (B)
  Keel Lobo × Ch. Keel Beleza, CD
  Breeder: Pamela and John Schneller
  Owner: Walter L. Ward
Ch. White Cap Chamejar of Regala (D)
  Keel Lobo × Ch Keel Beleza, CD
  Breeder: Pamela and Jon Schneller
  Owner: Eleanor Dee and Rudy C. Pierce

Ch. White Cap Chamejar of Regala.   *Cirincione*

To teach the dog to down, place left hand on his collar in back of his neck. The left arm must lie straight down along the dog's back. Right arm lifts the dog's front legs and places them on the ground. "Down."

Wayne Arnst

16

Obedience Training, Tracking and an Introduction to Agility Work

DOG OBEDIENCE TRAINING had its formal beginning in Europe in the early 1900s. Colonel Konrad Most, a German dog trainer, a pioneer in the study of dog psychology, wrote about training dogs in his book, *Training Dogs* (1910). This book is still recognized throughout the world as a training classic.

A second dog trainer who contributed to popularizing pet dog training was Lt. Col. E. H. Richardson, British Commandant of the British War Dog School in World War I.

In the 1930s, an American Poodle breeder, Helene Whitehouse Walker, and her kennel assistant, Blanche Saunders (later called America's first lady of obedience), introduced "dog obedience" to America as it was taught in England. In 1933, Mrs. Walker proposed to the AKC that obedience tests similar to those held in England be held in the United States. Due to the efforts of these two ladies, the AKC adapted obedience regulations from their guidelines. The first AKC sponsored obedience trial was held in March 1936.

The Scope of Obedience Training

AKC's *Obedience Regulations* state that: "The purpose of obedience trials is to demonstrate the usefulness of the pure-bred dog as a companion of man . . . it is essential that the dog demonstrate willingness and enjoyment of its work . . ."

Training a dog in the stylistic obedience exercises detailed in the AKC *Obedience Regulations* will help your dog achieve his full potential. The exercises are designed to teach a dog to respond immediately to commands.

The basic (Novice class) exercises teach the dog to heel (walk nicely at your side), to sit, to stand, to lie down, and to come when called. Advanced exercises (Open and Utility classes) teach him to retrieve, to jump over obstacles, to scent discriminate, and to respond to signals as well as voice commands.

In formal obedience trials, dogs are tested and scored in the exercises. When a dog has performed the exercises with his handler at his class level—Novice, Open, or Utility—at three different obedience trials and scored a passing grade or better, he earns a title. He becomes a Companion Dog (CD) after he has completed the requirements for the Novice class; a Companion Dog Excellent (CDX) title after he has completed the requirements for the Open class; and a Utility Dog (UD) title after he has completed the requirements for the Utility class. The titles are progressive. It may take four to five years for some dogs to advance from a CD title to a UD title. Some never make the grade; the exercises become more difficult in each succeeding class.

Obedience training teaches the dog's owner as well as the dog. The most valuable lessons are learning to communicate with the dog on the dog's level of understanding, and how to help the dog adapt and live in harmony in man's environment.

A trained dog is a confident dog. He is in control of himself. When taught positively, most Portuguese Water Dogs love obedience work.

First Obedience Titles

As stated earlier, the first two Portuguese Water Dogs to win AKC obedience titles were Spindrift Kedge and Spindrift Genoa. The dogs qualified for their CD titles just five days after the breed had been accepted into the Miscellaneous class (June 3, 1981). Their work was exemplary.

Kedge went on to become the breed's first CDX as well as the first to win the coveted UD title. She won her first UD leg on May 16, 1982. Barbara Whitney, who trained Kedge in obedience, then "had a very frustrating spring and summer." Kedge had problems completing correctly first one exercise, then another. Finally, on September 6, 1982, at Schooley's Mountain KC, Kedge received her second UD leg. On September 12, 1982 at Port Chester OTC, she won the title.

The stand is taught using gentle pressures.   *Wayne Arnst*

The dog learns to heel in synchronization with his owner in a figure 8 skill exercise.
Wayne Arnst

Kedge was not quite seven years old when she won this honor. Her name is a nautical term meaning an anchor used for getting a boat free when it has run aground. In obedience work, Spindrift Kedge has certainly been the anchor of the breed.

The Portuguese Water Dog has the potential to be an excellent obedience dog. He's attentive, adaptable and intelligent.

Usually, after several lessons, he understands what you are teaching him. To gain accuracy and proficiency in the exercises, of course, he must be worked on a regular basis.

Diver (Ch. Farmion Geo, CDX) competed successfully in the AKC Novice Class after only six weeks of five-minute daily training sessions. He won his CDX title after only eight weeks of 10-minute daily training periods. Diver became the first Portuguese Water Dog to win the CDX title after the breed became fully recognized. He earned the three necessary "legs" on October 12, 13, and 14, 1984 on the fall Montana circuit.

In obedience heeling the dog must walk close to his handler no more than a half-foot away. In conformation gaiting the handler is at least several feet away from the dog so that the judge may clearly observe the dog's movement. And when teaching a dog to stand for obedience examination, no baiting is allowed. Neither may a dog move his feet. For the conformation ring, baiting is allowed and movement is tolerated.

In obedience, consistent practice and patience in training is all-important. It takes time for dogs to assimilate what we want them to learn.

Tracking

Tracking is an extension of obedience work. There are two titles dogs can earn in tracking, Tracking Dog (TD) and Tracking Dog Excellent (TDX). Some owners like to start their dogs in tracking before entering them in obedience. AKC's *Obedience Regulations* list the rules. Two good books on tracking training published by Howell Book House are *Go Find!* by L. Wilson Davis and *Training Tracking Dogs* by William R. Koehler.

The breed's first tracking title was earned by Trezena Meia Bela, TD on September 23, 1984. Bela was not quite eight months old when she won this title. Bela's owner, Virginia Dorsman, an obedience instructor from West Grove, Pennsylvania, began tracking Bela when the pup was eight weeks old!

Virginia says: "I began Bela's lessons in the basement—she found things I hid in a fun-and-games manner. At 12 weeks I started teaching her tracking in the yard, using tracking flags.

"Tracking titles should be easy for Portuguese Water Dogs to earn. It's a working dog just as much in a hayfield as in water."

Many Portuguese Water Dog owners enjoy teaching their dogs command words in Portuguese as well as in English. Here are some

Leaving the dog on a sit-stay for the recall exercise. *Wayne Arnst*

The dog sits in front. *Wayne Arnst*

The dog jumps over the broad jump. *Wayne Arnst*

Throwing the dumbbell for the retrieve over the high jump.

Wayne Arnst

The dog clears the jump.

Wayne Arnst

Portuguese commands you may enjoy teaching your dog. (Of course, you'll have to learn how pronounce them!)

Assentas	Sit
Vem ca	Come here
Dar a Maozinhd	Give a paw
Fa Naninhas	Go to sleep
Esperas	Wait
Dar	Give
Dar Beijinhos	Give kisses
Querida	Loved one
Fo-fo	Cute
Olhinhos	Eyes
Malinha	Bad
Tao Linda	So lovely
Tao Bonita	So pretty

One last bit of advice—in the show ring you work with your dog. In the obedience ring, the dog works with you. And in obedience, you must be smarter than your dog.

Agility Tests

We can't leave the subject of obedience without acquainting you with *Agility,* a dog jumping competition which has been enjoying official Kennel Club status in England since 1980. Agility tests were originally designed to provide the Crufts dog show audience with a truly spectator-oriented event.

Let's have Bud Kramer, a well-known American obedience trainer and hunting enthusiast, tell you about *Agility.* His Portuguese Water Dog is a United States Agility team member.

"Great ideas most often occur as a result of a need. To fill a void in the main arena between the finish of the dog obedience championships and the start of Group judging at the English Crufts Dog Shows, John Varley conceived the idea of a dog jumping competition. John Varley was quite familiar with horse jumping events, but had little expertise in training dogs to do similar exercises. So he contacted dog trainer Peter Meanwell of Lincoln, England to develop a test based largely on the desire and ability of dogs to jump. During the planning stages, Peter Meanwell considered each aspect of the test in reference to three important requirements: 1) the test should be fun for both dog and handler; 2) it should be free of any dangerous aspects; and 3) it should provide spectator appeal.

"The first demonstration of Meanwell's efforts was held at Crufts in February 1978. The crowd loved it. The Kennel Club granted official status to Agility by introducing *Regulations for Agility Tests* and giving Crufts

The dog returns the dumbbell smartly to his handler. *Wayne Arnst*

After a training session, the dog needs some fun and games played his way. *Wayne Arnst*

Obedience training helps the dog adapt and live in harmony in man's environment. Shown here is a Portuguese Water Dog Club of Fairfield County (regional club) obedience class. *Lisa Norgard Miller*

274

permission to hold the first official test under the Regulations at the Crufts dog show in 1980.

"Agility is a speed-oriented event resembling an obstacle course in which most of the obstacles are some form of hurdle that the dog must jump. Standard Course Times (SCT) are determined for each course to ensure that dogs are not taken slowly through the course in an attempt to prevent faulting. Calculation of the SCT is based on the length of the course and a yards per second time factor. Depending on the class, time factors of 2 to 3.5 yards per second may be used for courses that usually vary from 100 to 180 yards. This provides a range in the standard course times of approximately 29 to 51 seconds. The design of the course takes much thought and has to provide a balance between speed and skill requirements with a SCT appropriate for the particular class.

"One or more of the various jumping hurdles—high jumps, broad jumps or hoops—are interspersed among the other types of obstacles. The broad jumps may be over boards or water. This could be a real test for water-loving dogs such as the Portuguese Water Dog. An 'A-frame' consisting of two sides at 45-degree angles joined to form a peak six feet high, tests the agility of dogs in climbing and descending steep slopes.

"Another obstacle is the 'dog walk' formed from a 12-foot plank raised 4-1/2 feet above ground with inclined ramps at both ends. The objective of this obstacle is to test the sure-footedness of the dog while walking on a narrow board at a height well above ground. Testing this same agility factor even further is the teeter-totter or see-saw. The dog must be able to balance itself as it walks on a moving 9-inch wide plank.

"Agility in crawling is tested by two types of tunnels through which the dog must move. One tunnel is rigid while the other is a collapsed canvas tunnel that the dog must force its way through.

"Finally, in the midst of all the excitement of racing through the course, the dog must jump up onto a platform and show its self-control by remaining there for five seconds.

"Dogs are allowed only one run-through the course. Since there is no required pattern or sequence in the arrangement of the obstacles, the unfamiliarity with a given course adds to the excitement.

"In scoring, deductions are made for both slow times and general faults incurred by either handler or dog while running the course. For example, a one-point deduction is made for each second beyond the SCT required to complete the course. A non-qualifying score is given when a run exceeds a maximum course time (MCT), generally calculated at 1-1/2 to 2 times the SCT.

"Precision is not important in the execution of the obstacles. In fact, second attempts at traversing obstacles are allowed with 5-point deductions. Each of the various obstacles have specific requirements which, unless met, require a deduction. A refusal to complete an obstacle requires a 10-point deduction but it does not impose a non-qualifying score. Although some subjectivity enters into the scoring, there is far less than in either breed or obedience judging. The simplicity of the objectives of the competition and the more straight-forward scoring makes the entire event more easily understood by spectators. This, of course, greatly increases its appeal to the audience.

"In order to allow each dog to participate more than once on a given day and to allow dogs with less experience or ability to share in the winning, a system of several Novice, Open and Novelty classes were introduced in the English trials. The Novice and Open classes utilize the standard equipment and scoring as specified in the Regulations. One of the Novelty classes, called Gamblers Stake, allows a dog to traverse any obstacle from any direction a maximum of two times and continue until a signal indicates the end of a standard period of time. Each obstacle has a point value and the dog with the most accumulated points becomes the winner.

"Another Novelty class is the *Snooker Agility Stake* in which a total of nine hurdles, three red and six variously colored, are used in an analogous way to that in which the balls are played in the game of snooker. A red hurdle must be alternated with each colored hurdle. However, the colored hurdles must be jumped in a predetermined sequence with each subsequent colored hurdle bearing an increased point value. The course must be completed within a standard time limit in order to obtain the maximum points with point ties decided on the basis of the actual time taken through the course. Team tag and team relay competitions also may provide great fun and excitement. Novelty classes such as these, are limited only by one's own imagination.

"In the United Kingdom, only one course using standardized equipment is set and all breeds must compete using the same obstacle set in the same way. This, of course, makes it difficult for some breeds, especially the Toys, giants and some others such as the Basset Hound and the Pekingese. The Portuguese Water Dog is an excellent size for the standardized equipment and the great jumping ability and enthusiasm for having fun make the Portuguese Water Dog an excellent candidate for Agility.

"Although Agility has enjoyed great success in a short period of time in England, it is very new to this country and only now has some scattered interest begun to appear.

"In my opinion, the gap between Novice and Open obedience has always seemed too great for many new to the sport. Perhaps Agility could serve as another outlet and help maintain interest in the sport until those individuals are able to overcome that first-time step into the Open obedience class.

"My hope is that this new form of dog training will become officially

276

Trezena Meia Bela, TD, tracking with her owner, Virginia Dosman. Bela is the first dog in the breed to earn a Tracking title.

Bud Kramer and his ten-week-old Roughrider Diver's Cascade.

recognized as an obedience class by the American Kennel Club and thus become something more than just an interesting demonstration used at special dog events.

"As I write this, my new Portuguese Water Dog puppy, Cassie (Roughrider Diver's Cascade), is asleep under my chair. Wouldn't it be great if this little gal could help establish this new aspect of dog training as an important part of dog competition in this country!"

First Titles After Recognition

Before we leave this chapter on Obedience, here are the names of the Portuguese Water Dogs earning titles in 1984, the first year the breed was fully recognized as a member of the Working Group. We list them as we did the champion titled dogs: name, dog or bitch, sire and dam, breeder, and owner.

Companion Dog (CD) Titles

White Cap Briny of Actondale, CD (B)
      Ch. Nativo Do Mar × Ch. Keel Beleza, CD
      Breeder: Pamela and Jon Schneller
      Owner: Jane G. Hoops and William A. Hoops, Jr.
Arrowhead Daroeira, CD (B)
      Trezena Marmelite × Felizardo Odeimira
      Breeder: Dr. Virginia Glover
      Owner: Ellen S. Allen
Birchbrooks Mariner Miguel, CD (D)
      Mareke V. Kelsey × Farmion Flagday
      Breeder: Mary Ellen Vernon
      Owner: Karen Taylor

Companion Dog Excellent (CDX) Titles

Farmion Geo, CDX (D)
      Farmion V De Gama × Farmion Nazare
      Breeder: Deyanne F. Miller
      Owner: Cyril J. and Kathryn Braund

Tracking Dog (TD) Titles

Trezena Meia Bela, TD
      Coracao Navio × Trezena Meia Praia
      Breeder: Mrs. E. Niles Kenyon
      Owner: Virginia M. Dorsman

17

Water Work and
Water Trials

ONE OF THE REASONS you wanted a Portuguese Water Dog is that the breed is renowned for swimming and diving.

Getting a Portuguese Water Dog pup into the water is usually no problem. Portuguese Water Dogs have been bred for water work for centuries. Some Portuguese Water Dogs, of course, like the water better than others. Also, owners of puppies born during winter months aren't always able to acquaint them with water until the next summer. This does not mean you should wait until summer to acquire a Portuguese Water Dog pup. You can successfully introduce Portuguese Water Dogs to water at any age.

First Hand Experiences

Ch. Farmion Geo, CDX (Diver) was not introduced to the water until winter. He was six months of age in January of 1983. There was a reason he was "water tested" in the middle of winter instead of waiting until spring. "I needed a picture of a Portuguese Water Dog coming out of the water for a story for the *AK Gazette* (published, Sept. 1983). Luckily, Great Falls, Montana was enjoying a 'January thaw.' The ice was out of the Missouri River. Because Diver loved retrieving a field dummy, I thought he would be an excellent model for the picture I wanted.

"Stuart White, the photographer, and I drove Diver to the river. We

279

had to trudge through snow, ice, and mud to get to the bank. Ice and mud caked our boots and Diver's legs.

"Stuart White set up his camera. I threw Diver's dummy into the water. Diver dashed into the cold water and retrieved his dummy. He had never been in the water before, except in the bathtub. I threw the dummy for him several more times, throwing it farther out each time. Diver never hesitated. He enjoyed the experience. His heavy coat kept him warm. When we were ready to go home, his hair was thoroughly caked with mud and ice, yet his tail wagged happily.

"It was slightly more difficult introducing our bitch, Onix Tafia (Fia), to the water. She was born in January and came to us in late April. We didn't have time to introduce her to the water until late that summer. I did not know if she would learn to swim, since I had not "force broken" her to retrieving and she wouldn't retrieve anything in fun. Therefore, the procedure I used to introduce Fia to both water and water retrieving was different. This technique may be used with other Portuguese Water Dogs who don't appear to enjoy retrieving.

"I waited for a warm day. I took her from the car to the water on leash and collar. I walked into the water keeping her next to the shore until she gained confidence. I encouraged her to get her feet wet. I then splashed water about her—not on her—all the while talking to her softly and telling her what fun we were having. I then walked her onto land for a few minutes before repeating the lesson. Within five minutes Fia was splashing about in the water, enjoying it.

"I knew I might not get her to learn to swim, however, unless I gave her an incentive to do so. Leaving the collar on her but taking off the leash, I brought Diver down from the car. (He gets so excited about water retrieving that he finds it difficult to remain on a sit-stay near the water unless I am there to steady him.) I threw his dummy into the water. To my amazement, Fia joined Diver in going after it. Her introduction released an instinctive desire to retrieve from water.

"To test her new-found desire to retrieve, I threw the dummy on land for Diver. She retained her enthusiasm. Soon she retrieved on land as quickly as he did.

"Next, I threw two dummies into the water simultaneously—the standard-size dummy for Diver and a puppy-size dummy for Fia. Fia swam to the first one she saw splash. It was Diver's dummy. While she had a difficult time getting her small mouth around it, she did and proudly brought it to hand.

"At our next water training session, I took both dogs to a boat dock. Fia leaped off the dock as eagerly as she had dashed into the water from the beach. She was eager to retrieve any thrown dummy.

"I added a whistle command to the retrieve. An effective whistle command is a steady, full-sound 'toot-toot-toot-toot.' Fia, like Diver, was

280

Diver dashed into the cold water and retrieved the dummy.   *Stuart White*

I walked her into the water, keeping her next to the shore until she gained confidence.
Wayne Arnst

To test her desire to retrieve, I threw the dummy on land.

Wayne Arnst

Next, I threw two dummies into the water, one for Diver and one for Fia.

Wayne Arnst

She was eager to retrieve any article.

Wayne Arnst

I added a whistle command to the retrieving exercise.   *Wayne Arnst*

Fia, like Diver, was soon swimming in rough water as well as in calm.   *Wayne Arnst*

soon swimming half way across the Missouri (as far as I could throw her dummy) to retrieve. She would do this in rough water as well as calm."

Portuguese Water Dogs are capable of much more than retrieving dummies from the water. They can be taught to help pull boats along by tugging on ropes; they can be taught to dive to retrieve objects on the bottom. They can be taught to retrieve birds. The possibilities are unlimited.

Deyanne Miller's pups get a boating ring in the whelping box to teeth on. Pups also get metal shoe horns and boat bumpers. She likes to see pups follow or paw the objects. Once she gets the pups out of the whelping box, weather permitting, she attaches a shoehorn to a boating line and dangles it through a plastic pool encouraging the pups to put their muzzles under water. As the pups get bigger, she takes them to the Millers' large pool and dangles a weighted rubber ring attached to a clothesline.

Development of Water Trials in America

Several fun water trials have been held in the United States for Portuguese Water Dogs by the Fairfield County Portuguese Water Dog Club (FCPWDC), a regional club. At each trial, Portuguese Water Dogs have been tested in simple water exercises and awarded certificates. The FCPWDC has adopted the CPC and Newfoundland Club of America (NCA) water trial tests. They plan to revise these as members' dogs gain practical experience. This regional club emphasizes family dogs, water safety with children with a Portuguese Water Dog aboard family boats and keeping alive the water working ability of the breed.

In 1982, the PWDCA set up a Working Water Trial Committee to formulate trial guidelines. William Hopps, who owns White Cap Briny of Actondale, was appointed chairman. Although guidelines for formal water trials have not (at our publication date) been presented to the PWDCA membership for approval, many interesting ideas have been expressed. Members may choose to pattern their water trial tests on those now given by the Newfoundland Club of America (NCA). The NCA presently grants two titles to their dogs, the novice Water Dog title and the advanced Water Rescue title.

Water trials will preserve the function of the breed.

Water Trials in Portugal

There were several water trials held for the Cão de Água in Portugal in the 1930s. The Clube Portuguese de Canicultura (CPC) sponsored them. Leao, however, performed at many exhibitions held at the zoo in Lisbon. Crowds flocked to see him perform in the hippopotamus tank there.

In 1981, urged to do so by Herb and Deyanne Miller, who wanted to

284

Deyanne Miller dangles a weighted rubber ring attached to a clothesline.

Steve Krongard

see how the trials were conducted in the homeland before introducing them to the U.S., the CPC reinstated Portuguese Water Dog water trials. In fact, Herb Miller joined the Directors of the CPC in judging the trial held at Praia da Falesia, in the Algarve, October 11, 1981.

The second CPC sponsored trial was held in the Algarve, October 10, 1982 at the Algarve International Show. Ch. Charlie de Alvalade took part. Both Herb and Deyanne Miller handled him and Charlie won the trial!

We have translated the CPC rules for the Portuguese Water Dog trials. Ch. Charlie de Alvalade, in the accompanying pictures, describes the tests.

Special Rules/Regulations for Portuguese Water Trials

ART. 1—These tests should take place in the proper "ambient" surroundings in which this breed works—in the sea. The natural prey of these dogs are fish; but, given the difficulty of the tests taking place with this prey, use objects that satisfy "the end"; and when a Director of the Canil Clube Portuguese finds it convenient, these tests can also be realized with aquatic fowl to determine winners.

ART. 2—All the model contestants which are not being tested should be tied on a lead at a place determined beforehand by the Organization Commission.

ART. 3—Five (5) minutes before the test starts, the owner or handler has the right to give a little exercise in the water. These five (5) minutes are announced by the Test Commissioner.

ART. 4—The tests for this breed are dispositioned individually, and the order of entry of the contestants in the various tests is determined by lots, starting the work with the contender who has the lowest number; the exception is the order in ARTICLE 11.

ART. 5—Wherever possible, the tests should be realized in equal circumstances for all the contestants.

ART. 6—No contender can be submitted to two (2) consecutive tests except in the case of there being disputed tests.

ART. 7—The order of tests should be observed conforming to the arrangement that follows, which can be altered only by the judges, in compliance with the owners of the contestants, and with the knowledge of the Delegates/Commissioners of S.C. of C.C.P.

ART. 8—First Turn/Test: Swim.

Second Turn/Test: Bring back to hand an object thrown into the water.

Third Turn/Test: Dive, and bring to hand an object thrown to the bottom.

The first and second tests can be combined into one (1) only if the Judges and Commissioners of the S.C. of C.C.P. find it convenient.

286

The ultimate measure of a fine dog is a proven ability to do the breed's work. In the case of the Portuguese Water Dog, that means being physically able to function on a boat and in the water itself; he should also have the unflinching courage to meet the sea on its own terms. These pictures demonstrate that today's Portie is equal to its time-honored heritage. The model, Ch. Charlie de Alvalade, also mirrors the breed's fun-loving side as he enjoys his frisbee on the beach. *E. Trainor and D.F. Miller, Jr.*

ART. 9—The maximum duration of the tests stay at the discretion of the Judges, who should observe equal time for all the contestants.

ART. 10—In the first test, the Judges appraise the qualities of swimming of the contestants, paying special attention to the following points:

a) The form in which the animal throws himself into the water.
b) The speed obtained during the course, which should be clocked, using a chronometer.
c) Style of the swim.

ART. 11—If the judges find it advantageous and the owners of the contestants/competitors and Delegates/Commissioners of S.C. of C.C.P. are in accord, this test/trial can be held together.

ART. 12—In the second test, the essential points to be observed are:

a) The manner in which the animal marks the point where the object fell afloat.
b) The form in which the animal fetches the object in which it should show rapid decision and courage.
c) The manner in which the object is given to hand—it should be given to the handler quickly and promptly.

ART. 13—In the third test, the Judges should observe:

a) The manner in which the animal marks the point where the object sank.
b) The energy of the animal.
c) The form in which the animal dives; the depth reached and the result of the search under the water.

ART. 14—The Judges should pay even more particular attention to the qualities of intelligence and obedience demonstrated during the test.

ART. 15—In case of a doubt, the Judges can submit the contestants to supplemental tests; that is, they can order a repeat of one or all of the tests that constitute the test.

ART. 16—Eliminating faults consist of slow, "morose" swimming, not bringing to "hand," complete loss of instinct or of obedience, and "formal" refusal of diving.

ART. 17—The Judges offer Working Certificates for those dogs who can't be rewarded but, nevertheless, did not commit any of the eliminating faults mentioned in the ARTICLE 16.